Dr. Green,
Enjoy!

Mother's

Mother's

**A novel of hoarding,
friending and mischief**

Linda Salisbury

Tabby House

ISBN: 978-1-881539-61-2

ISBN: 978-1-881539-62-9 (e)

Library of Congress Control Number: 2011929900

Cover design and illustrations: James Balkovek

Tabby House
P.O. Box 544
Mineral, VA 23117
www.tabbyhouse.com
www.lindasalisburyauthor.com

"A man who is not born with the novel-writing gift has a troublesome time of it when he tries to build a novel. I know this from experience. He has no clear idea of his story; in fact he has no story. He merely has some people in his mind, and an incident or two, also a locality, and he trusts he can plunge those people into those incidents with interesting results. So he goes to work. To write a novel? No—that is a thought which comes later; in the beginning he is only proposing to tell a little tale, a very little tale, a six-page tale. But as it is a tale which he is not acquainted with, and can only find out what it is by listening as it goes along telling itself, it is more than apt to go on and on and on till it spreads itself into a book. I know about this, because it has happened to me so many times."

Mark Twain, author's note to
The Tragedy of Pudd'nhead Wilson

"Maybe hoarding is creativity run amok."

Randy Frost, PhD, and Gail Steketee, PhD
Stuff: Compulsive Hoarding and the Meaning of Things

Contents

Lunie

One

LUNIE SNAPPED HER LAPTOP closed and yanked the plug out of the porch wall socket. She leaned back in her porch rocker and closed her eyes.

It just wasn't working—the novel she planned to write in thirty days as part of a contest offered by the new bookstore in town. She had started the first chapter six times, each with a different main character. Her characters were all alike—boring—no matter what she named them. And they packed no plot with them. Lunie had assumed that once they had made their initial appearance, she would know exactly where the story was headed. But no. The characters were churlish, silent, and unimaginative, like a crowd of Florida tourists on a bus in Puerto Rico, surprised that it was pouring in the rain forest and complaining that no one told them to carry umbrellas.

Lunie squinted at the battery-operated wall clock with birds that chirped each hour; a present from her mother. She gritted her teeth. It was almost four PM, when the crow's raucous call would sound the time, as if there weren't enough crows on her block as it was. If she were still working at the Mosby Gap Building Department, about now she would stretch and walk around the cramped cubicles to let Evelyn take one final afternoon smoking break from greeting the public, contractors, and answering the phone. It annoyed her that Evelyn, a slacker, had been kept on during the department's temporary layoff,

11

while Lunie, a highly responsible employee who verified permits, and two other co-workers, had been sent home. Lunie had decided that bitterness wasn't her style, and she would make the most of her time. She'd get her house cleaner, write the novel she had always dreamed of, and work on family problems, most notably her mother Dolce's estate. The most difficult project would be dealing with Mother's house, possessed by possessions, as Lunie liked to put it. Her layoff would be time well spent. She'd return to the office when the economy improved, refreshed, with life under control and a novel ready for publication.

Lunie uncrumpled the lined notepaper on which she had jotted down names of potential new characters—Twila Morningstar. Herbert Coomers. Nancie Withers. Ira Ruddell. Peleg Sweet. Peleg was an old family name that cropped up in Virginia genealogy charts, where Lunie sometimes received inspiration when the phone book, obits, or names on Internet spam yielded nothing of note. Family lore—Dolce's, actually—hinted that Peleg was one of the Confederate Captain Mosby's locally popular Raiders. Lunie had never seen proof, but who knew what she and her brother would find when they cleaned Mother's. Lunie recrumpled the paper, and aimed at a basket. To her relief, the clock cawed feebly, a sign of a weak battery.

She discarded titles as equally unworkable: *Sweet Home Road. Marina Fever. Marina Fear. Dogface Pufferfish.* The last had potential, but more as the nickname for an unsavory character. Someone in the Mafia, perhaps.

How do famous authors do it? Lunie wondered. I mean, sit at their computer and have words just flow brilliantly? Authors such as Stephen King or those romance writers who keep coming up with new ways to tell the same story. They're like people who can sit down and play anything on the piano without reading music or practicing. Not fair.

Her skinny yellow cat, Phil, with crossed gold eyes, padded furtively up the porch steps and ducked under a comfortable wicker chair. She could tell by Phil's speed and the shape of his face that he was carrying something. The squeaking was confirmation, but before she could yell at the rangy cat, the chipmunk raced across her foot and dove off the porch into the ivy. Phil squeezed out from under the chair and looked around in feline bewilderment, his long tail thrashing in exasperation.

"C'mon, Philly boy, let's go in before dark. Neither of us is getting anything accomplished here," Lunie said, tucking her laptop under her arm. She turned and put her hand on the latch, then *it* hit her. She dropped the computer on Phil's tail as she slid to the floor. She clutched her head where the object had struck above her right ear before bouncing off the aluminum door frame and rolling behind her rocker.

It took Lunie a moment to recover enough to say, "Shit!" Still hunched over on the floor, she looked for what had attacked her. "Shit," she said again, reaching for the golf ball. It was not an expletive she normally used.

She stuffed the ball in her pocket, and examined her laptop. It still worked. Phil was nursing his tail and pride somewhere in the rhododendrons.

Lunie struggled to her feet, placed the computer on a small wooden table, and looked around for the source of the propulsion. It had to have come from the yard across the street where a guy had moved in a few months ago and cut down ten mature oak trees. His wife had told neighbor Cara Newton that they were afraid the acorns would harm their teacup greyhounds so the trees had to go.

If the ball had come from that yard (Lunie couldn't remember the new neighbors' names), then where were they? She hadn't seen anyone at 4030 Bilgewater in days.

Perhaps Dayton would have an idea. She pulled open the door and nearly stepped on Phil, an orange blur dashing past her on his way to the laundry room with something again dangling from his mouth.

Dayton, almost three years her junior, had been living with their mother before she had died tragically six months earlier. Her death came shortly after he had reached Bryce Canyon where he would spend part of his summer. He tearfully told Lunie that he wouldn't be able to return in time for the services in Mosby Gap—that he would have a memorial of his own in the wilderness, taking solace among the hoodoos. Then he would head for the national parks in California or Wyoming. His job kept him on the move.

Dolce had proudly displayed a picture of Dayton wearing a yellow uniform and standing near a WELCOME TO YOSEMITE sign. Although he might not have agreed, Dayton was Dolce's favorite child, and he returned the kindness by favoring her looks. Soft and round without triggering a diet warning from the family doctor. For much of her childhood, Lunie resembled the stick figures she sketched in the margins of her notebooks. The one she drew of herself had no mouth. The one of her mother looked cross, and Dayton's showed a wide smile. As an adult, Lunie had fleshed out, but was still slender and solemn. She would not describe herself as unhappy, just quiet, efficient, and proud of creating order.

Each fall since high school, after his summer responsibilities concluded, Dayton returned to their mother's house when the western mountain roads were about to become impassable with snow. He spent the winter in Virginia sorting through all his pictures of moose, elk, prairie dogs, Stellar's jays, and tourists, and worked at various odd jobs, including preparing income tax returns for the neighbors. He regaled Mother with his summer adventures in the West. Lunie declined their invitation to join them for Storytime, as they termed it.

Dayton had boxes and boxes of photos from his trips. He said one day he would create picture albums. His boxes had filled the guest bedroom at his mother's house, and her attic—what space there was available. Lunie, who prided herself on minimal clutter (just enough to make a house homey), was horrified when she realized the extent to which her mother, and perhaps even her brother, were hoarders. She had been awaiting his return before starting the cleanup of Mother's.

Before he made this last cross-country drive home, Lunie emphatically told Dayton that he could not, under any circumstances, bring junk with him if he was going to stay with her even for one night. He mumbled that he understood, but before he took his last look at the Rockies, he packed one bulging box after another into his 1968 VW camper.

"We'll call a trash hauler and have a yard sale to sell her good things, if there are any. We can't put Mother's house on the market like it is," Lunie told him the night he arrived.

Dayton looked terrified. "We have to go through her things carefully," he said. "Mother had great stuff."

"Who would know!" said Lunie, with undisguised sarcasm. "You still can't sit down in her kitchen. It's a pigpen. You can't sit down anywhere." She shuddered as she thought about the sink festooned with Christmas decorations, and the long-unseen oval table heaped with pizza cartons and plastic jugs that their mother had been saving for a craft project four years earlier. Two year's worth of laundry was on top of them.

"Don't talk about our mother that way," said Dayton. "She was the best. She probably has all the birthday cards you drew for her since you were four."

"Yeah, shoved in the oven, or maybe in the medicine cabinet," said Lunie.

"That's not funny. She had issues," said Dayton.

"I have issues. You have issues. Everybody has issues," said Lunie impatiently. "If we don't get going on cleaning out her mess it will be summer again and you'll be off among the big sequels," knowing that would annoy him.

"*Sequoias*, Lunie. I've got some really nice pictures of them," said Dayton. "They're huge. You should drive west with me sometime." He buttoned his red-checked wool overshirt.

"I don't really want to," said Lunie. She turned her back so she couldn't see the hurt look in her brother's light blue eyes, set in his round face fringed with a curly brown beard. In fact, she would love to see the sequoias and everything Dayton told them about from his travels, but not with him, and not in that gawd-awful VW camper bus. He had left Wyoming at the end of September, but due to frequent tire and engine problems, had arrived three weeks later. It should have taken him four days at most.

Her head throbbed where the golf ball had found its target. "Who do you know that plays golf on our block?" Lunie asked. She pulled the ball out of her pocket.

"No one," said her brother.

"I just got clunked in the head with this," said Lunie. She ran her fingers through her short brown hair with natural highlights and touched the lump.

"Let me see," said Dayton.

"Absolutely not. I'm afraid you'll start a collection." She dropped the ball into the kitchen trash basket. Dayton waited until she had disappeared into the laundry room to look for Phil before slipping on rubber gloves. When she returned, Lunie caught him sliding the ball into a freezer bag.

"I told you no!" she scolded like their mother had done when they were children.

"But, Lunie," he said, "it might be evidence. We should keep it." He peeled off his gloves after sealing the bag.

"Evidence of what?" she asked, hands on her hips.

"Murder," he said. "Someone might be trying to murder you."

Lunie leaned forward and shook her head. "The only murder in this house is the chipmunk that Phil decapitated in the clean laundry. Take care of it, Dayton. My head hurts."

Dayton nodded and slid the zippered plastic bag in his pocket.

Lunie wrapped a dish towel around a handful of ice cubes and held it against the throbbing knot above her ear. Golf ball murder. That could be a story line. It was too preposterous and probably someone had already used it. Lunie, however, mulled the idea.

She heard Dayton start the washing machine. "Don't forget the laundry powder—fill it to the line," she called. He didn't answer. "And, Dayton, you can't keep the chipmunk."

THE TENDER LUMP WAS STILL there the next morning. Lunie was careful not to brush her hair above her ear. She studied her chin in the mirror. It amazed her that she could still boast of a zit after her fortieth birthday.

If Dayton had any, they were well hidden by the beard that he cultivated for the rugged look of someone who works in a national park. He covered his balding head with a cap that read: DON'T APPROACH THE BEARS. He said everyone else wore apparel that cautioned people not to *feed* the bears, but he thought the hat's phrase might convey a safer message.

Lunie had heard him telling their mother about the animals he had seen and photographed. That was after the first summer that he had gone out West to work, when there was still a small path from Dolce's front door down the hall to the living room couch. The couch was now covered with orange and brown flowers—ten baskets of them.

Hoarding abhors a vacuum. Before Christmas two years earlier, the path had narrowed, and was carpeted with layers of rugs that her mother had purchased on sale at the Dollar and Dim. (It was the Dollar and Dime until the Class of 1999 had stolen the "e.") She also had acquired six vacuum cleaners, seven electric brooms and three rug washers since 1996, mostly at yard sales. None worked.

By the time Dayton returned the following fall, he had to stoop over to follow the same route and the couch was snowed in with sheets, blankets, and comforters from a motel that was going out of business. Lunie had refused to enter Mother's; she couldn't even see in the first floor windows and so she occasionally used a webcam to visit with her mother when there was a need to talk face to face. Dolce didn't sit still in the chair by her computer where Lunie could view her unkempt, thin, naturally dark hair, and her sullen brown eyes. Instead, her mother bobbed about during these Skype sessions, moving boxes and searching through their contents. Her voice was granulated, like new sandpaper making the acquaintance of a rough board.

Dayton was never bothered about their mother's house. He had an upstairs bedroom that their mother had planned to make into a guest room after he had graduated from Mosby Gap Community College in the Blue Ridge Piedmont and moved out. But Dayton had been the only guest, never leaving home. Once, when the stairs became impassible and threatened an avalanche, he took one of the three extension ladders leaning against the garage, and climbed up and through the window.

"You should see me in the mountains," he said with a laugh. Somehow Lunie couldn't. Dayton did not appear to be in the sort of physical shape that was required to leap like bighorn sheep around Zion Canyon's walls.

A soft *thud* caught Lunie's attention. "C'mon, Phil. Off the table." The thump of the cat hitting the carpet was louder than the hardback mystery that he had deliberately pushed off a moment earlier.

Lunie picked it up, blew imperceptible dust off the table and placed the book square with the edges of her grandmother's tatted doily. Her house gave her deep satisfaction. Rather than return to her mother's home after attending college in Richmond, Lunie had rented the small house at the top of the hill with an option to buy. Her landlord encouraged her to paint it in her own colors (she picked hues of beige as her basic scheme) and he was good about making repairs. He appreciated her neatness and promptness in paying. Doubling up payments, Lunie had only two years to go before the house would be titled in her name.

Touching the book reminded her of her own project. *I've got to write at least three chapters today,* she thought, *or I might as well give up.* Fresh air. A brisk walk around the block might help. Lunie slid into her cross-training shoes and a light-green sweatshirt jacket.

Phil scratched at the front door, stretching his lanky body to almost two feet. He brushed past Lunie and she followed him down the steps, but not into the bushes where only his long tail was visible. *Where do cats go all day, and why?* Lunie wondered. Phil probably could tell a story or two; probably a better story than she was coming up with so far.

When she reached the pavement she hesitated for a moment, then turned to the left, walking briskly, arms swinging.

There was still no sign of life at the house across the street. A small white van sped past her, ignoring the posted speed regulations of 30 MPH CHILDREN AT PLAY. It pulled into the driveway three houses down. The magnetic sign on the side proclaimed Lucky Maids, a cleaning service that worked for several people on the block. A large cloverleaf and a pot of gold decorated the cheerful signs. *I wonder if they'd be willing to tackle Mother's? Could you pay anyone enough?* Lunie shuddered again.

She recognized Agnes, one of the company's more popular employees, sorting through her stock of fluids, mops, brushes, and cloths—the perfect assortment of materials to use in the widower's house. Agnes removed a large leather-bound book from the front seat, wrapped it in a beach towel and hurried up the walk, her dyed-bronze curls bobbing.

Lunie assumed that the ever-helpful Agnes had run an errand for Hobart Finbarr, the reserved community college professor who lived there. He was pleasant, but rarely home. Like Lunie, he apparently preferred order to chaos. *Maybe he'll come to the neighborhood potluck again this year,* she thought. For the last gathering he had purchased a lovely broccoli-salmon-and-noodle casserole from the hot foods deli at a new gourmet supermarket in Outer Mosby. It was much better than Cara Newton's predictable homemade macaroni-and-beets horror. Lunie had taken only a dab just to be polite, but quickly covered it with her napkin. Even Cara hadn't touched it.

Lunie waved to Agnes, who had returned to gather her supplies, then continued down the hill. She was pleased that she was keeping up a brisk pace despite turning her ankle two weeks ago when she had climbed off a step ladder after washing her bedroom windows, a weekly chore.

Lunie thought she saw Phil sharpening his claws on a hickory in a tree-filled lot between Professor Finbarr's house and Wilma Wolenski's. "If that's you in there, Phil, go home," she called. She didn't look back to see if the cat had paid attention. Likely not.

Wilma had been her mother's most longtime friend in the neighborhood. For years, Dolce had gone over to Wilma's for morning coffee and they went to yard sales together. Wilma never had to take a broken coffee cup or torn jacket to the curb in front of her house. She just walked them across the street to Dolce's. If her friend couldn't push through the piles in her kitchen in time to answer the doorbell, Wilma simply left them on the porch.

Lunie had been in Wilma's white Cape Cod many times. It was filled with family antiques, including an uncomfortable horsehair sofa that was valuable, according to what Wilma could gather from watching the *Antiques Roadshow*. Lunie suspected Wilma kept it not for its value—it was unlikely that her children with classic pseudo Swedish tastes would want it—but because its prickly surface kept visitors from staying too long. No matter how long their legs or torsos, they squirmed and shifted positions while balancing delicate teacups and saucers, then found a reason to continue their day somewhere else. Not so Dolce. She turned sideways and put her feet up on the worn crimson velvet, and balanced her floral teacup filled with instant coffee on her ample bosom.

Most of the neighbors and a few of her mother's former co-workers at the bank had come to Dolce's calling hours and memorial service. Wilma, a self-published poet with four slim volumes produced under the Crumpet & Blackberry Jam Press imprint, read a piece she had written for the occasion.

Unlike most of her poems that had strict rhyming schemes—sonnets, triolets and villanelles—Wilma's tribute titled "A Friend is a State of Mind" had been composed in free verse. "It fits the spirit of the woman, bless her heart," said Wilma unapologetically, knowing that her poetry group would find fault.

At the reception, catered by Raiders Dixie Bistro, Wilma confessed privately that although the initial words flowed, she wasn't happy with their focus on the hoarding. So she concentrated on the months soon after Dolce had moved into her two-story light gray house, a divorced single mother with two young children. She remembered that they had fun decorating and furnishing it with what they found at the recycle center, secondhand stores and from what had been placed at the curb on neighborhood cleanup day.

"I didn't want to write about how all of that evolved into the current—" Wilma did not want to use the H-word. She was afraid she was saying too much at an inappropriate time, when happier days should be recalled.

Lunie had simply lightly embraced her mother's last best friend, and surprised herself by saying she would like a copy of the poem.

The shades were still down at Wilma's. Lunie wondered if she was up, working at her kitchen table on another poem. Did Wilma ever write prose? Did she ever suffer from writer's block?

Lunie barely glanced at her mother's house, about 300 feet down the hill on the left, with the same orientation toward the sunrise as her own. Lunie's little house was at the top of the street, where, on a clear winter day from her favorite room on the second floor, Lunie could almost make out the Blue Ridge Mountains.

For the last decade or so, Mother's siding had displayed a splotchy pond-scum green patina, mercifully covered over in places by ivy and weedy vines. The scummy green seemed to seep through the windows into Dolce's house, applying itself to objects, piles, and appliances. Lunie suspected that soaking the entire house in bleach wouldn't make a difference.

Mother's lawn badly needed raking. Maybe Dayton would work on that today while she started chapter 1 again. *What if I don't begin at the beginning? Maybe that's the problem—coming up with the first line. It's supposed to suck readers into the story, the way fresh-baked bread or cookies make prospective buyers place an offer on a house. I'll start with chapter 3. Plunge into the middle of my characters' lives. Maybe they'll be at a party. If they wander around with* HELLO MY NAME IS *badges, I'll know who they are, especially if they talk about their background.* Lunie smiled. She felt more hopeful. Her fingers itched to touch the keys of her laptop and get started again.

She turned around, walked quickly back up the hill. There was no sign of Phil in the wooded lot. Lunie heard a door close at the professor's house. Agnes looked up and down the street before carrying a small wooden box to the front seat of her van. *Another helpful errand,* Lunie mused. *I'll ask her about cleaning Mother's.*

Two

DAYTON STILL WASN'T UP WHEN Lunie returned. Phil was nowhere to be seen either. Lunie filled her Grand Canyon
North Rim mug, which Dayton had given her for Christmas
two years ago, with black coffee. While waiting for the single
slice of rye toast to pop up, she set her laptop on the kitchen
table where, if her eyes needed a break from the screen, she
could look out the window at the trees and bird feeders alive
with feathery activity.

Chapter 3. Yes, she'd start with the party. But what kind of
a party? A newcomers' party at a church? No, there might not
be drinking. Not that Lunie drank, but she thought that having lips loosened over a couple of glasses of wine or shots of
bourbon might make the characters more talkative. What about
a singles group on a cruise ship? Now, there was a possibility!
The book could then have a lot of adventure as the characters
explored exotic Caribbean islands. Snorkeled. Stroked giant
rays. Swam with sharks. Sunbathed on a secluded beach.

Lunie thought of the excitement she felt when she booked
a cruise three years earlier. She flew to Miami where she was
to meet Mags, her second cousin once removed who lived in
Fort Lauderdale, and would share a porthole cabin on the
fourth level with her. Mags, who was between husbands, and
Lunie, who had never married, wore floppy hats and big
sunglasses, which they refused to remove when the ship's

photographer bid them to stand next to a pirate to have their going-aboard photo taken.

As amplified steel drums played "Hot Hot Hot," Lunie and Mags joined their fellow passengers dancing at the sail-away party on the deck, imbibing tall rum drinks with little paper umbrellas perched on the top. By the time the sun set, theirs, along with two other grand white cruise ships draped with strands of lights, had cleared the long channel and were at sea. Lunie had figured that she and Mags would change out-fits for dinner if their suitcases were delivered to the state-room. However, the bags didn't show up until 10:00 PM, so the cousins went in casual outfits to the buffet line and discov-ered an overwhelming array of food.

After her long flight (north to Chicago, then a layover in Newark, before it turned south) to Miami, Lunie was ready for an early evening, but Mags had just begun. And that was the way the trip would be. Mags met a succession of single men, or so they said, late night in the bar and signed up for shore ex-cursions with them.

Lunie was glad she had brought several long books to read—books she didn't have much time for when she was working for the county. Her life was busy. She studied yoga on DVDs one night a week. Another night she took a self-guided Span-ish course with twenty-seven tapes and a thick workbook. Her chat-room book club, with readings selected by members was on a third night. She devoted the remaining nights to an online course in creative writing offered by Professor Finbarr as part of the community college's outreach curriculum.

"You need to go out where you can meet people," her mother complained on more than one occasion. The last time Dolce had mentioned it, her mother was unpacking boxes that a Habi-tat rummage sale hadn't been able to sell. She had offered to take them off their hands for $5.

"Where? Like you do rummaging for junk at the flea mar-ket?" Lunie retorted crossly, immediately regretting her tone.

She was in no mood to discuss her life with her mother, of all people.

Lunie returned to the blank screen and glanced at the clock on the stove: nine. She knew it was only 8:55, but she had set it ahead so that Dayton would get places on time, such as for interviews for temporary positions during the months he was at home. His casual approach to work disturbed her, especially when it seemed that people like him were the ones rewarded by management—not the responsible people like herself.

After her layoff, due to the downturn in the housing market, Lunie scanned the classifieds, both in the paper and online. She wasn't too worried about employment at the moment, but would have to actively look in about a month—if she didn't get called back. She just needed time to get projects done, such as cleaning her mother's house and, now, her book. She had seen an ad for the novel-writing contest in the morning paper. Although most of her writing as an adult had involved filling in forms on building permits and writing denials to contractors, she had always dreamed of being a writer. She had worked on the school newspaper in elementary school and won a prize in an essay contest in her sophomore year. She was sure her mother still had it somewhere.

Had she gone with Mags to shows, games, pool parties, hairy-leg contests, and bars, Lunie might have come home exhausted and with a well-deserved hangover, but she also would have known what the nightlife was like on the ship and whether people wore HELLO MY NAME IS badges at such events. Now she would just have to imagine it for her characters.

"Morning, Lunie-toons," said Dayton rubbing her shoulders. "This cold dry toast something you fixed for me?"

"Have it," she said, wishing her mother had named her something other than Lunette. She never liked it or the inevitable nickname Lunie, or the jokes Dayton and the kids at school made about her name. Maybe if she moved to another community she could reinvent herself and start over with a new name, such as Fran or Carol. *There's a thought. One of my characters, Sue, could be doing just that.*

> Sue starts to write the name she's weary of on her adhesive badge, then scribbles out the letters and gives herself a brand-new life.

That will be the first sentence of chapter 3, Lunie thought. *At last, a start.*

Lunie heard Dayton warm his coffee in the microwave. Hers also needed reheating.

She typed "Chapter 3."

Do writers still use the word chapter, or just the number? How about chapter names? Should you put a name on the chapter if you haven't written it yet?

She typed, tentatively at first, then faster:

> Sue wasn't sure if she would find Mr. Right at the sail-away party on the top deck. But there was no point in wasting time on the seven-day cruise. Sue had brought a new package of HELLO MY NAME IS badges that she had purchased in an office supply store at a mall just before entering the city of Miami. She uncapped her black marker and wrote "Sue" on the badge. So dull. So boring. So kindergarten-teacher-Sue. Sue scratched out her name, which fortunately she had printed fairly small, thought for a moment, and wrote "Vivian," with a grand flourish. If last names were needed, she'd come up with a new one, too.

"Whatcha, doing, Lunie-goonie," said Dayton. He spilled milk on the table when he whitened his coffee. Lunie handed him a napkin to wipe it up. Dayton merely put the napkin on top of the puddle and placed his chipped HUG A SEQUOIA mug on top of it.

"Something new," said Lunie, immediately wishing she hadn't said that. "Sleep okay?"

"Except for your cat. He has no sense of time or people's needs."

"Close your door then."

"I did. Phil scratches and yowls."

"If we can clear out Mother's place, you can move back there until we can get it sold," suggested Lunie. "Meanwhile, her yard needs raking. If you could get that done this morning we could go through boxes later—the two of us."

Dayton's brown eyes looked pained. "Selling it so soon would be disrespectful of the dead. I'm not sure that's what Mother would want. There's no rush. All we're paying is utilities."

"And taxes, and insurance, and who knows what needs to be fixed in there. We can't make it into a National Hoarding Shrine in her memory," Lunie said. "I've waited long enough for you to take the first step, and you keep finding excuses. We're moving things to the curb today."

"Please don't. I've only been back four days," wheedled Dayton. "What would the neighbor's say if they saw her stuff by the edge of the road?"

"You don't think they know how bad it is inside?"

"Not as long as we keep up appearances. Curb appeal. I'll go rake."

"That would be a start, but we've got to work on the inside, even if it's one carload at a time." Lunie couldn't tell if Dayton was listening. He had a preoccupied look on his face as he swirled cream cheese on his bagel with his finger.

WITH DAYTON FINALLY OFF TO MOTHER'S with a leaf rake, wheelbarrow and work gloves, Lunie washed the cup that he had left on the table, and threw away the milk-and-coffee-drenched napkin.

Her fingers were less itchy; creative juices were only at a trickle, but she decided to work on the book for at least another hour. Several speakers at a writers workshop that she had attended two summers earlier had urged participants to set aside a specific time every day and to write whatever came into your mind. Eventually, there would be a worthwhile thought and the rest could be deleted. Another speaker said it was important to make an outline. Someone else said you couldn't go forward with a story unless the characters had been fleshed out in descriptive paragraphs. Their ages, looks, characteristics, pets.

That was all well and good, but Lunie wasn't there yet. She decided on the drivel option. After all, the contest didn't say that the book had to be ready for publication nor did the authors have to have their Pulitzer acceptance speech drafted. Just get that 50,000-word book written in a month. That was the challenge. Because of her layoff, Lunie had looked forward to clearing the clutter of the workday out of her life and having uncluttered time for just herself. That had lasted only three days, which she had frittered away happily with fall cleaning, and then Dayton had showed up.

Lunie sipped on her tepid coffee, her lips touching the chipped rim on the Grand Canyon mug. It was chipped when she opened the awkwardly wrapped box.

She placed her fingers on the keyboard, glad she had learned to touch-type in high school. At the time her mother wanted her to go to secretarial school. Big shots always need secretaries, her mother said. Just be your best, dress nicely and maybe you'll hook a big shot, Dolce had counseled. Lunie cringed and applied to college. Her fingers responded.

> Sue crumpled the first name tag. She didn't want to waste them, but she still had twenty-four more. If she ran out from wearing them at all the activities on the ship, she was sure she could buy more in Puerto Rico or the Bahamas. She wrote in her most sweeping, but still readable, script, *Vivian Valencia*. Below it, she added "ViVi" as a nickname. She put the stateroom card in her pocket, slipped into her purple flip-flops and opened the door of stateroom 8079. But instead of going up to the party deck, Sue saw her fellow passengers wearing orange life vests. Oh no, the boat's sinking and we haven't left the dock, she worried. Sue was almost in tears.

Lunie paused. Writing coaches always told you to write about what you know. She knew that anyone who boarded a cruise ship would have to go to their muster station for a drill before the festivities could begin. But would readers be interested in that? *I can delete that part later. Just keep writing.* This would be tricky because her own experience on the cruise with Mags was to avoid all social interactions, other than the sail-away party, to which Sue/Vivian was now headed wearing her name badge—the only person on the ship to be sporting one. Lunie would have to either wing it, or do a lot of online research to find out what Sue/Vivian would encounter as the brightly lit ship sailed into the night and on its first day at sea.

Okay, so Sue would go back into the cabin, get her life jacket, go to the muster drill. There, just as she was taking off the jacket, without being tempted to blow the little attached emergency whistle, a portly man, seemingly alone, would say:

"Ah, Vivian, or is it ViVi? What a good idea to wear a name badge. I'm Bob from Piketon. Care to join me for a rum drink on the pool deck, ViVi?"

She paused again. That sounded very artificial. Dialogue was hard to write—at least convincing dialogue. And was this Bob from Ohio a cad with a seasick missus stowed away in an inside cabin? Or was he part of group of tourists from perhaps the grange—their harvest in, ready to relax and celebrate a bumper crop of corn or soy, or whatever they grow in Ohio?

Lunie was perplexed. She already felt protective of Sue, whom she envisioned looking a bit like herself. No, that would be transparent. She would have to make her older, or younger, and perhaps heavier. At home in Minnesota she'd wear sturdy shoes with supports and she knew how to decorate colorful bulletin boards with construction paper. Sue wanted to have a good time on the cruise, but she should beware of Bob, the creep, already on his third marriage. Lunie didn't care for the leer in Bob's eyes. Sue hadn't noticed, however. She was still trying to tuck her orange plastic whistle into the life jacket straps.

The grandfather clock chimed eleven. It was earlier than that but the clock could not be trusted even when it had been adjusted at great expense by a clock maker in town.

She had made a good start. Four hundred and ninety-two words. She had a main character and a possible setting. The book could turn into a romance novel. Lunie would check on-line later to see what the formula was for them. She knew from her writing course that certain elements had to be observed. Woman meets man and then has strong feelings. The couple would act on them (steamy sex), then break up. Steamy sex with someone else. Get back together. Happy ending.

Lunie scooped what was left of Phil's recently opened cat food can. It was something that he had liked yesterday but hated this morning. She opened the cat door so that he could come and go when he pleased. She decided to help Dayton with the raking.

When she came around the side of the house from the shed, she saw that the UPS truck was leaving after depositing three cardboard cartons addressed to Dayton on her front porch. Funny, he hadn't mentioned anything about a delivery.

Her brother wasn't in Mother's yard, nor were the leaves disturbed. Lunie went around to the back. The rake and wheelbarrow were next to a large maple, as if the tree was expected to just aim its colorful discards toward the barrow on its own.

Lunie leaned her rake against the tree and walked up the steps to her mother's back porch. It was piled to the ceiling with plastic bins and black trash bags with yellow ties. She tried the doorknob. It turned. Lunie pushed hard. Of course, something was blocking it. What did she expect with all that stuff piled everywhere!

"Dayton? You in here?"

Lunie heard a muffled voice.

"Open the door?" she called, louder.

It sounded like he said, "Can't."

Lunie went back to the tree, picked up her rake, and handle-first, like a battering ram, charged at the door, shoving the handle through a four-inch crack.

"Ha wee!" she grunted, shoving again and again, with little success as she tried to pry the door open.

"Ouch. That hurts!" yelped Dayton.

"What's blocking the door?" she asked.

"Me."

Lunie withdrew part of the handle and wiggled it back and forth trying to make the door opening wide enough so she could look in and see the problem. Indeed, Dayton was sideways on the floor, covered with what appeared to be a heap of kitchenware, plus cases of canned food, bird seed bags, opened and spilling, and a toy owl.

"It's not funny," Dayton said.

"Did you hear me laughing?"

"Don't call 911," begged her brother. "I'm not severely injured. More trapped than anything."

Lunie decided to hold the lectures for later. She peered in again. "Can you move your left hand? Lift it in the air?"

Dayton carefully extracted his arm, sending a small cascade of generic-brand canned beets near his unseen chin.

"Here's the plan. I'm going to reach in and you hand me one item at a time."

"That will take hours," said Dayton.

"Got any other ideas?"

Six dented cans of pickled beets went from his hand to hers. Then ten Spams, a teakettle, a cleaver, treated very gently once Dayton figured out what it was. By eleven o'clock, Dayton's face was visible. "Did you bring lunch?" he asked.

"Keep going, if you want dinner tonight," said Lunie in a voice she knew wasn't sympathetic. Maybe now Dayton would understand what they were up against; they needed to empty Mother's house, room by room. When his torso was visible, Lunie told him to carefully, very carefully, try to sit up. She pushed the rake handle through the door again to give him something to grab onto. It reminded her of a scene from a TV police show where an innocent man had come too close to a suitcase bomb and he had to be cautioned how to get away from it without blowing up New York City.

Dayton frequently looked up and around to make sure he wouldn't inadvertently bump into unstable piles surrounding him. Lunie was silent until he finally was able to get his feet under him. "Now step closer to the door and open it very slowly."

"What if—"

"Just do what I say."

She heard pans and cans clattering inside as Dayton pushed them with his feet. He gently pulled the door and Lunie stepped inside—the first time since the week after her mother's memorial service. She flipped on the bug-filled overhead light. "Can you back up at all?" she asked.

Dayton took a few steps. "Something stinks in here," Lunie said, squeezing in after him.

"Nothing new," said her brother.

Lunie surveyed the collection of junk. It wasn't even organized by room function, otherwise, records and stuffed toys wouldn't be on the kitchen counters.

"We're starting in here," she said. "Today."

She expected an argument, but Dayton wasn't offering one. In fact he said, "I'll go back and get trash bags. I'm sure Mother has some, but I'm not sure where."

That in itself is an admission, thought Lunie. What would she tackle in his absence? Clearing a path through the room was a worthy objective. Within an hour she had made a large heap of odds and ends on the lawn near the back steps, including stained place mats, partial skeins of yarn, pieces of soap, and even a bowling pin.

Dayton had not returned. He'd been like that since he was a child. Dishes to wash, dry and put away, and Dayton was in the bathroom, a situational need that could not be easily challenged. Their mother had attributed his post-dinner problems to a delicate digestive system. Lunie, who ended up both washing and drying, knew that Dayton had a secret stash of comics and at least one *Playboy* magazine. The reading materials were under the raggy towels in the cabinet beneath the sink. *Playboy* was tucked inside an old Superman comic, the one with the most worn cover.

Lunie sighed, tossed her work gloves into the wheelbarrow, and wandered toward the street. She didn't bother to close the back door. Who could get in? And if they did, she hoped they'd steal something—no, everything.

Cara Newton lurched down the hill propelled by her German shepherds. Not that she was an expert in breeds, but Lunie knew that despite Cara's assertions, the dogs had a little poodle in them.

She didn't want to be snared into a long conversation with her recently retired neighbor. Cara had taken a buyout from the insurance company where she had worked for thirty-five years, not missing a day, and thereby earning the company's coveted Cal Ripkin Jr. award from upper management. Her co-workers, however, were delighted to see her go, because they wanted to give her an award for being single-handedly responsible for infecting them with every cold or flu that made the rounds. "Typhoid Cara," they dubbed her. She pretended she wasn't aware of their mean-spirited name-calling. They were only jealous that she was so close to winning the trophy with a gold calendar on top. In the final months, she went to work with a broken shoulder, swine flu, impetigo from her niece's day care, and cold sores that looked contagious. Nevertheless, she answered the phone as she had done for decades. By the time she had packed her personal items in three small boxes and dabbed her eyes, tearing-up that someone new would welcome the public to term insurance, the janitorial staff was already in the room with disinfectant.

Now Cara was home, and uncertain with what to do with her days. She had told Lunie at least three times that she was thinking of volunteer work—but not answering the phone for anyone ever again.

Cara picked up her pace and was crossing to Lunie's side of the street. Her dogs, Harvard and Yale, strained in opposite directions, threatening to dislocate the shoulder that wasn't in a cast.

"Whoa! Slow down, boys," Cara said, jerking their choke collars. "Hold out your hand so they can see you are friendly," she told Lunie, as she did every time they met on the road. Lunie wondered how those curly white ears felt, but was warned off from petting them when Harvard snarled through exposed fangs.

"What are you up to these days?" asked Cara. Her pale blue eyes were dwarfed by the large, rose-colored glasses. Without her frosted blond hair poofed for the office, she had a strange resemblance to . . .? Lunie realized that Cara looked like muster-drill Bob's seasick wife, Deloris. Deloris wouldn't be as old as Cara, but she would have that look, at least when she felt well.

Cara was still gabbing without waiting for Lunie to answer. Something about a volunteer job with the schools or visiting the homebound through the Sunshine Ladies.

Fortunately, Harvard and Yale took a momentary dislike to each other and exchanged nips. Lunie waved good day and hurried on up the street, leaving Cara to untangle the leashes that had wrapped around her like a coiled-basket project.

When Lunie reached the front porch, the boxes were gone and there was no sign of Dayton.

Three

PHIL, WHO HAD BEEN UNSEEN MOMENTS EARLIER, beat Lunie to the front door. "Why don't you use the cat door?" she asked. Phil crouched like an Olympic sprinter waiting for the starting gun, and shot past her at the first small opening. Lunie followed, wondering what had happened to her brother. When he didn't answer her shouts, Lunie decided to fix a small healthy salad—tuna, grapes, and pine nuts over a bed of baby field greens—before returning to Mother's with the leaf bags.

The tuna can was missing from the pantry and the grapes Dayton bought during his drive home were wizened to raisin wannabes. She decided to leave them in their little woven plastic bag from the supermarket. Dayton was likely to snack on them regardless of condition.

Lunie felt a dull ache across her forehead. Perhaps she should have another conversation with the Internet counselor, who seemed to specialize in everything. It was at Wilma's strong urging that Lunie had sought help. "You need to deal with your grief, dear" said Wilma. "You can't turn back the clock and bring your mother back. Stop bottling things up. All my poet friends have counselors. Well, actually most talk with a Dr. Jonathan Manko. We find we are better writers when we understand our issues. Promise me?"

Lunie hadn't answered Wilma at the time, mostly because she was only half listening. She was reluctant to make an appointment at the locally well-regarded counselor, whose office was across the street from the building department. Someone might see her. Instead, a few weeks later, when she was overwhelmed by the stress of cleaning Mother's and what she might find in there, Lunie searched online for someone to confide in. The most reasonably priced Web site was Dr. Z. E. V. Manngo's—a name that sounded familiar; the one recommended by Wilma's poet friends. His picture showed a man with a friendly face, a big smile, white teeth, wavy brown hair, and green fashion frames. Even though he said he had just opened his online practice, he promised success in "Dealing with Life's Challenges." Dr. Manngo said he would post testimonials from satisfied clients within days, and said he would soon have special deals for "dealing."

Dr. Manngo's site indicated that he would keep consultation costs down through multi-tasking. Lunie wasn't sure what that meant, but decided to take advantage of his free introductory session.

Although she was nervous about sharing details of her life, even with an unseen stranger, Dr. Manngo immediately put her at ease; he seemed to understand her. Lunie realized after just a single counseling session that her mother's refrigerator was, indeed, an indicator of larger issues. Lunie wished, however, that she hadn't wasted that free session by unburdening herself about the fluorescent unknown items her mother harbored at forty-one degrees.

"I know there are peas in there," her mother told Lunie just before dinner one evening. Lunie opened several burp-top containers, until her mother said, "There, that's the one."

"You can't be serious," Lunie objected. If there had been peas in there at one time, they had morphed into gelantinous fuzz. "Just rinse them off, sweetie," her mother said when she heard Lunie gasp with dismay. "Penicillin is good for you."

Later, when her mother ate out during her lunch hour at the bank, she carefully divided her meal into two portions, and brought one half home to have for dinner. Her refrigerator was filled with large unmarked foam containers; she preferred to call out for pizza. No one had opened the refrigerator at 4073 Bilgewater since Dolce had "crossed the river," as Wilma put it. *Perhaps I can donate the contents to science,* Lunie thought.

Dr. Manngo's final words to her were, after he told her what she would owe to continue the conversation: "Deal with the refrigerator, deal with anything."

Lunie hunted for his site several weeks later, but the search engines couldn't locate anyone with that name and multiple degrees from Hofenstraw State.

Lunie looked for her new jar of peanut butter. It was almost empty. She sighed and spread what was left on three healthy-grain oat-flavored, saltless crackers. She wandered into the living room, trying to swallow a double wad of peanut butter on the dry cracker, when she noticed a car coming up the driveway. It was *her* car. *Her* car stopped near the front walk, and her brother got out, and looked around furtively before opening the trunk.

She watched, unable to utter a word, while he lifted four plastic tubs and several small containers out of the trunk, then three more from the back seat.

When he reached the front door, she opened it. Dayton looked as shocked as if he had been caught shoplifting a parakeet in a pet store.

"What are you doing home, Lunie?" Dayton stammered.

"I live here, remember?"

"I thought you were at Mother's. You, know, cleaning."

"You were supposed to come back with the plastic trash bags, but instead you went off with *my* car, when you have a perfectly good vehicle of your own parked right over there."

Dayton was silent for a moment. "You have peanut butter on your lip, Lunie," he said, pointing to a spot on his beard for reference.

Lunie made no move to lick it off. "*My* car," she repeated.

He handed her the spare keys, with an oval tag picturing Crater Lake, his birthday gift for her.

"My van is still full from this summer," Dayton offered, as if that would be a sufficient explanation. It wasn't.

Lunie waited. He stared, she thought a bit hungrily, at the peanut butter.

"Okay. So, I went to the Dollar and Dim. We were out of plastic leaf bags and things."

"And what are you planning to do with the bins?" she asked.

"They're for stuff," he answered.

"Not in my house," she said.

"Oh, don't worry," he said. "After I get things sorted out, they'll go in the shed."

"What shed? We don't have a shed," she asked suspiciously.

"The one I've ordered for Mother's backyard. It's arriving tomorrow."

Lunie slammed the door in his face and leaned against it until she could turn the bolt. Tapping started. "Lunie. Open up. I can explain. It all makes sense. Just let me tell you my plan. . . . All right then. I'm going back to Mother's. I'll just have to work on everything by myself."

Dayton's pear-shaped body was distorted by the beveled glass in the panes alongside the door. Lunie watched his head and body detach and reattach as he piled his plastic containers on the sidewalk, closed her car's doors and walked toward the street without looking back.

A shed. The last thing they needed at 4073 Bilgewater was another place to store things. It's supposed to be cleanup time.

Lunie flopped on the sofa, careful not to let her feet rest on fabric. *I shouldn't have sat here,* she thought. *Not in these dirty clothes that have touched ripened trash.*

She toyed with the idea of taking a total break from the cleaning project. Let Dayton handle it for a few hours. She could spend the afternoon working on her book. Kindergarten Sue must be wondering where Lunie had gone. Sue might even have advice. Perhaps she'd been to a counselor—one with a couch—and would have suggestions for Lunie from her own experience. Sue's counselor had probably recommended the cruise and adopting a temporary new identity while she traveled. Lunie wondered if Sue had decided to meet up with Bob at the deck party. Maybe he wasn't such a bad guy—just lonely with a nagging hypochondriac for a wife. Maybe Deloris wasn't seasick but having a reaction from her most recent Botox treatment. Were Sue and Bob tipsy and doing the limbo, or had he, the roué, already met someone else before Sue had had time to toss her life jacket in her stateroom?

Lunie rubbed her temples. No, now that she had gotten things started at Mother's, she'd better see them through. Dayton would need focus and she was the only one who could provide it.

She would pack some snacks and bottles of water and meet Dayton there.

I'll only stay an hour, she figured without moving off the sofa. *Then, I've got to spend time on my novel. I've got to get words down or I might as well give up.*

She tried to remember what Professor Finbarr had told her in lesson four about getting over writer's block: Go do something else, and while you're at it, "prewrite." He went on to explain that prewriting was another term for thinking about your book—planning it out before starting the process. That's something she could do while they were cleaning.

Excited by the possibility of multi-tasking, that is, prewriting while loading trash bags, Lunie filled a backpack with bottled water, snack crackers—charitably, the salty kind Dayton liked—and two apples. She would apologize for slamming the door, and ask where he planned to have the shed located, making him understand that if they put the house on the market, he would have to decide if his shed would convey.

She slipped the backpack strap over one arm and cut across the lawn to the street.

A white appliance repair truck passed her, going a little too fast, she thought, and turned at the end of the block without stopping sufficiently.

The drawing of a refrigerator on the side reminded her of her free session with Dr. Manngo. Why had she wasted it on her mother's fuzzy peas? There was so much else that was more important, like the hoarding, that she should have discussed. Dr. Manngo's question had caught her off-guard:

What is your earliest bad memory?

Instead of giving her answer careful thought, Lunie had responded impulsively.

A refrigerator. Mother's refrigerator,

and hit the SEND button. Within seconds, Dr. Manngo typed back:

So, what was the problem? No warranty?

Lunie had flushed with unexpected excitement. Someone cared.

Mother saved leftovers for years. They were—

How candid should she really be with a total stranger?

—they were green and fuzzy. Yellow and mushy.

She hit SEND. And waited. The marvelous Dr. Manngo's next question made her really think:

How did this make you feel?

Like puking. SEND

Puking?

You, know, throw up. Vomit. SEND

I can prescribe a medicine for that.

No, it was a long time ago. SEND

How do you feel about your mother now?

She's dead. SEND

Of puking?

No. SEND

Lunie wanted to tell him about Mother's house, but by the time she got up her courage, the session abruptly ended with his counsel about dealing with the refrigerator. Had she wanted to continue confiding in him, all she had to do was enter her credit card number and agree to pay $19.95 for five additional minutes. It might have been worth it, but she had been distracted by Phil's efforts to rid his throat of a hairball in the front hall.

The appliance truck, apparently lost, came back up the hill and slowed near Lunie. The driver rolled down the window and said, "Excuse me, where's 4073 Bilgewater?"

Lunie said with a bit of alarm, "I'm headed there now, but we didn't order anything."

The driver lifted up his metal clipboard and said, "It says here, one chest freezer. It's already paid for by—" he squinted at the handwriting: Dalton somebody."

"No Dalton in this family," said Lunie. She walked faster. *I'll kill him.* She heard the truck turn around and creep after her down the hill. *I'm being stalked by an appliance truck.*

When she neared Mother's driveway, Lunie stopped, pointed and waved to the driver to keep going, as if the delivery should go to Wilma's instead, but he tapped his horn and waited until she walked up the driveway. She wondered where Dayton was.

Her brother appeared seemingly from thin air and signed the bill of lading before Lunie could question him. He rubbed his hands, tried to ignore her, and helped the driver roll the eight-foot-long chest freezer down the ramp. Together they pushed the dolly toward the back of the house and Dayton pointed to an area, next to the pile of trash that Lunie had created in the morning.

Lunie didn't like the smug smile on the driver's face as he strode past her.

"What are you going to do with the freezer? Put a whole cow in it?" she finally asked, gritting her teeth.

"I got it cheap because it doesn't work," said her brother. "It keeps things at room temperature."

Lunie's eyes opened wide. "Have you lost your mind?"

Dayton didn't answer. He pushed his way into the kitchen and came out with an armful of handbags, sweaters with tags on them, and balled-up black socks. He lifted the freezer top and carefully placed them inside.

"Dayton, we've got to talk. Now" said Lunie. "The whole idea is to get rid of things, not to create new places to put them."

Dayton dropped another armload of balled-up socks, and three horse statues that had been on top of the range, into the freezer, closed it, and sat on the lid.

"Look it, Lunie-moonie," he said, "Mother's stuff is half mine. I can't let you just throw it all away. She had lovely things—a lot of lovely things, and here you are with those big trash bags ready to toss everything without regard to value—especially sentimental value. I can see Mother now, shopping for bargains. Buying decorations and presents. Taking advantage of two-for-one sales and clipping coupons. Trying to make ends meet for us. She did everything for us." He was really worked up. Emotional.

"I know she would have straightened everything up if she had lived longer, and I could have helped her." He opened the freezer and took out tissues folded among the sweaters. He handed one to Lunie, who had no intention of sharing in his moment of grieving. He was avoiding the issue, just as he had avoided doing dishes as a child.

Maybe she should spend the $19.95 and have a quick session with Dr. Manngo. Then she remembered what she had read on his Web site—a sample counseling session from another patient that he had identified only as Mr. DP:

Dr. Manngo: Tell me about your problem.

DP: I have problems talking with my sister. She is very judgmental and doesn't understand me at all.

Dr. Manngo: How does she express her feelings?

DP: She doesn't exactly . . .

Dr. Manngo: Then you should say to her, "It sounds like you're angry." Then she'll say "yes" or "no" and you can talk about it. Yes?"

DP: Wow! You're fantastic. I'd recommend you to all my friends, if I had any."

Dr. Manngo: Time's up. We'll talk about the best way to find new friends. I call it friending. Making friends through social networking. Today it's on Facebook. Tomorrow, who knows--maybe Footbook or Kneebook--but friending will always be here. See you next time for $19.95.

Lunie reflected that Dr. Manngo had once again given sensible advice to his clients, so she decided to try it out. "Dayton, you sound, um, angry."

Dayton hung his head. "I didn't know you cared, Lunie. You sound angry, too."

Emboldened, Lunie said, "Frankly, I am. I'm angry at this mess. I'm angry that it's taking over our lives. I'm angry that we can't agree to work on it together."

Dayton said, "Lunie, you sound *very* angry."

Lunie gave him a hard look, took a black plastic bag out of the box, and stuffed it with bottles of lotion, umbrellas, and empty cereal boxes.

"I'll show you angry! This is going to the curb, Dayton, and don't you dare bring it back! It's from my half!"

Four

L UNIE'S ARMS AND BACK ACHED, but she jogged most of the way home, buoyed by a sense of accomplishment. After two hours, she had neatly stacked twenty-one giant black trash bags at the curb awaiting the Tuesday pickup.

She didn't care that Dayton hadn't spoken to her all afternoon, nor had she paid attention to what else he was storing in the freezer. She had filled her bags with the contents of the pile she had earlier that day tossed out the back door. When she returned the next time, she'd continue pulling trash out of the kitchen. Her goal was to reach Mother's stove within the week.

Lunie was planning to work on her novel for a couple hours. However, with the day's distractions, she was having difficulty imagining what Sue (she really needed to remember to call her Vivian Valencia while she was on the cruise) would be doing right now. Vivian wasn't in her stateroom, nor had she reached the Aguanaut dining room for a casual-night dinner where she would meet the five passengers who would have the early seating with her for the next week.

Where was she? On the Promenade Deck watching the twinkling Miami skyline disappear? No Vivian was—no, she wouldn't do that—*oh, my gosh, not Sue!* But there they were: Vivian and Bob, holding hands and barely balancing tall rum drinks (their third), had left the sail-away party while the

Caribbean band taught everyone the words and steps to "Hot Hot Hot." Worse yet, Lunie realized that Vivian's nametag had fallen to the floor when Bob had ripped off her blouse in a corridor marked CREW ONLY.

Vivian wouldn't go along with that, or would she? How well did Lunie really understand Sue from Minnesota? Maybe she was more of a sexpot than her glasses, mousy hair, and day-job at Beaver Crawl Elementary had indicated.

"But I can't write steamy sexy scenes," Lunie gasped with dismay when she reached her driveway. She realized that worse yet, Vivian's adhesive nametag was now stuck to the bottom of Bob's new waterproof sandals, which his wife had purchased for their cruise. (Deloris had a matching pair.)

Bob's tryst is going to be discovered once Deloris gets her head out of the toilet. But, of course, Sue isn't registered on the ship's manifold as "Vivian Valencia," so maybe she won't be suspected, unless the cabin steward finds them together when he goes through that door, without knocking, to get fresh linens, again, for Deloris' bed.

Lunie pushed the front door open. *Maybe I should move on to chapter 5,* she thought. *I can always come back to chapter 4 later when I can think this through.*

Phil was waiting by an empty ceramic dish inscribed TUNA BREATH near his water bowl. Lunie ignored his desperate plea for an early supper, and turned on her laptop.

She typed "Chapter 5" and stared at the screen. She placed her fingers on the keyboard, willing them to leap into action. She closed her eyes, waiting for a scene or character to appear. The only characters that she could conjure were her mother and Dayton.

Horribly unfair, Lunie thought. *They won't leave me alone.* As she tried to erase family from her thoughts, Agnes from Lucky Maids replaced them. *Ah, that's better.* What if Agnes is on the cruise, celebrating her fifth anniversary with the cleaning company? Agnes had done so well bringing in new customers, despite the economy, that she had won the cruise. She had picked her sister Maureen from Blarney Stone, Ireland, (Lunie would later Google that name to see if it was an actual place) to go with her.

Maureen, a former nun . . . No, Maureen, a gourmet cook at St. Lucy's Convent . . . Or, Maureen, a spinner, who raised her own sheep at Loch Ness.

Lunie wasn't sure about Maureen's background, but perhaps it didn't matter at this point. Just put the redheads together on the ship and see what happens. Lunie's inspiration lasted less than two minutes. She heard a crash from the front porch. A hanging terra-cotta planter, filled with frost-damaged begonias, had fallen and smacked her rocker, chipping the arm and covering the tapestry fabric with dirt. Or so she thought until she saw the golf ball. It had struck the pot with sufficient force to knock it off the galvanized hook screwed into the porch beam. Lunie's heart pounded; she stared up and down the street, squinting as she looked directly across into the new neighbors' yard. No one was in sight. She was about to pick up the golf ball, when she decided Dayton for once might be right. She used a tissue to lift it so that the fingerprints would be preserved, and once inside her house, placed it in a plastic bag as evidence. Evidence of what? A drive-by drive? She pocketed the bagged ball and returned to the kitchen, where Phil tried once again to get her attention regarding his empty bowl.

Lunie stared at the still-blank screen. Chapter 5.

> Agnes and Maureen, wearing orange life jackets, went to the information desk to get new key cards for their stateroom because they discovered when they came back from the muster drill they were locked out.

That had happened to Lunie after Mags had disappeared somewhere on the ship, tossing her vest for Lunie to stow on the shelf above the tiny closet. Lunie couldn't get back in the stateroom. Then she discovered to her embarrassment, that she was on the wrong deck, which is why the plastic ship's card didn't open the door.

Agnes and Maureen would benefit from her experience. Their keys really didn't work for reasons the information desk could not explain. For their trouble, they were given a free subscription to the daily *Shipboard News*, a compilation of headline news from all the wire services around the world. They would not read it. They were issued the Taiwanese version by mistake. Agnes would use it to wrap souvenirs.

Lunie knew she should change Agnes' name. If Agnes should read her novel, there might be a lawsuit. She'd have to put something in the front about how there was no relationship to people living or dead, even though everyone knows that novels are only 97 percent fiction.

Would Agnes and Maureen go to the sail-away party or to one of the themed-bars for the evening? Would they want to catch up on family gossip from across the pond (Lunie knew that was what some people called the Atlantic Ocean) or did they have mischief in mind? Lunie's fingers were frozen with apprehension. What would Agnes be thinking? Would she light a cigarette in the casino as soon as the ship was in international waters?

Lunie jumped when she heard steps in the hall. She had forgotten to lock the front door. She looked up; it was Dayton.

"Hey, Lunie, you'll never guess what I found today."

She stiffened. "I don't want to know."

"Money."

"Yeah, sure. Where was it? In a sock?"

He looked surprised. "How did you know? Yes, a black one, long and stretchy."

Lunie said, returning her eyes to the screen, "And I suppose the sock was under a mattress?"

His round face beamed. "Guess again."

"I don't want to. I'm busy, if you haven't noticed."

"Then, I'll have to tell you." Dayton paused, waiting for her to say something, but Lunie had put her motionless fingers back on the keyboard.

"You won't believe it, but the sock was in the laundry basket."

"The broken blue plastic basket on top of the three-legged chair on top of the counter that you can't see?" she said. It was less a question than a snapshot of that section of the kitchen.

"Yep, that's the one."

"That's nice," she said typing quickly.

Dayton leaned over her shoulder. "I don't think those are words," he said, reading "Xoopzi vonfge sloppgret."

"Go away, please," she said, wanting to cry. "I'll call you when supper's ready."

He spread his mail, mostly supermarket fliers and election campaign literature on the counter, succumbed to Phil's plaintive mews and opened a can of tuna-salmon supreme, which he put on the floor next to the empty cat dish, then left.

As soon as Lunie heard him on the stairs, she quickly closed out chapter 5 without saving, and typed Dr. Manngo in the Internet search field.

To her amazement, his Web site was back, with a notation that it had been undergoing "construction." He was still offering one free session. In addition to his sample discussions with a DP, he had a brief example of "dealing with issues" of "refrigerator fuzz." Lunie wondered if that might be of help to her, or was he using her problems to help others?

Although she realized it wasn't ethical, she decided to create a new e-mail account with a new persona. But using what name? Sue? No, there were too many Sue's out there. Phil? Maybe. No, better yet, Philma.

Five minutes later, with a new e-mail identity, she logged in to Dr. Manngo's site and clicked on the button called SOCIAL COUNSELING CHAT.

Welcome, Philma, he typed immediately.

What's today's problem?

This time she would not bring up the refrigerator. Lunie excitedly typed back:

My mother's house. SEND

What's the house problem?

Mother's a hoar. SEND

Lunie meant to type "was a hoarder" but hit SEND before she could change it.

A hoar? I counsel hoars in my new sexual addictions program. $19.95

Sorry, I meant hoarder. SEND

Hoarding's a hard problem. No one in my family is one. My sister drives me crazy, though. Her manners are terrible.

I didn't expect you would know Mother or anyone like her. I'm sure you have a very neat office. No clutter, not like Mother.

Lunie hit SEND but was concerned that perhaps she was getting too personal with this caring professional.

So, what's the real problem, Philma?

Mother has too much stuff. We can't get in her house. I want to throw it all away but my brother won't help. SEND

Philma, everybody has stuff. Deal with stuff and you'll deal with life.

Lunie sighed. Her time was up, but again she had a strange feeling of release. Deal with stuff and you deal with life. It was profound, in a curious, simple way. She wondered where Dr. Manngo's brick-and-mortar office was located, and whether or not she could afford weekly consultations in person.

She imagined he would have a very discrete receptionist, who knew the contents of each patient's file, but never looked knowingly or betrayed her feelings when one walked in the door. Of course, the receptionist would discuss the specifics— not using real names—with her hairdresser, but would swear her to secrecy in case they shared the same clientele. When her name was called, simply by initials, (Miss L.) Lunie would be escorted down a hallway to a small, but comfortable room—not the great Dr. Manngo's office with an imposing desk and walls of degrees in MBO, MIA, CON, FFA from all the best universities. She would be seated in an overstuffed (but not-too) chair. New Age music with the sound of waves lapping a tropical beach would play softly while she tried to relax, but worried if she was wearing a blouse that was cut too low or slacks that were too baggy. Should she have painted her toenails? Then there would be a quiet, but authoritative knock, and she would rise to greet the famous doctor.

"Please sit, Miss L.," Dr. Manngo would say, "and tell me what issue do you present?" His aftershave thrilled her; a scent not unlike the freshness of her favorite bleach spray cleaner. Lunie smiled.

"What's for supper?"

Lunie snapped her computer closed. "You keep scaring me, Dayton," she said. "Stop creeping around my house and leaving messes everywhere." She pointed at his mail.

"I thought you'd like to see the food flyers, Lunie-balloonie. Look, you can get ten boxes of cereal for $10."

"We don't need ten boxes of cereal."

"You can mix and match the kinds—sugar or healthy," he said. "Same with the canned vegetables."

"I already have a box of cereal. Healthy," she said.

"I'm trying to help you shop economically," said Dayton. "Take advantage of sales, and buy in bulk, like Mother did."

"I would rather buy one flake of cereal at a time," she said, glaring. "I'm happy with the empty shelves in my pantry. They are neat and clean and I can see exactly what I have and what I need." She was upset with herself for becoming so cross with her brother, who never had an unkind word for her or anyone. Fortunately, but also annoyingly, he seemed impervious to her sarcasm.

"Why don't I fix supper tonight," he said. "I found canned beef stew at Mother's. There's enough for both of us."

"Absolutely not. Nothing from that house." Lunie knew that the contents of unopened cans were probably still okay to eat, but it was the principle of the thing. The refrigerator principle. If Dayton weren't a factor, she'd just have frozen burritos—three minutes to heat two in the microwave. But Dayton *was* a factor, and he had consumed all her burritos and a frozen pizza on the night he had pulled in her drive just days ago. The peanut butter was gone; no jar in reserve. They were down to two eggs and a half box of bran flakes. That would have to do.

"I'm having breakfast for supper," she declared.

Dayton didn't answer. He was heating the contents of the can of beef stew directly on the left burner. "It's just like tent camping in the Targhee National Forest, next to a little brook," he said, reaching for a spoon so he could eat out of the can. "Lunie-moon, you should see the stars."

Five

A FTER INSERTING HER FAVORITE CARIBBEAN steel-drum CD in the player for inspiration, Lunie curled up on the sofa in her worn chenille robe. At the top of the new legal-size yellow pad that she had purchased at the Dollar and Dim, she wrote: My Novel by Lunette Pitts.

She would prewrite as Professor Finbarr had suggested. Her pen, removed from a motel that Dayton stayed at in Utah, moved across the pad and returned to her name. Should she write under a pseudonym? That would be something to discuss in an online chat with the professor. She wrote "my characters" on the next thin blue line. Well, there was Sue, aka Vivian Valencia aka ViVi. Bob from Ohio and his wife, Deloris. Agnes and Maureen. The steward would have a shiny bronze name tag with the ship's logo: José from Bali. He would have a thing for Maureen but knew he would lose his job if he flirted with a passenger.

Lunie wished her own cabin steward, Juan from Cancun, had said more than, "Good evening, Miss Pitts," when she passed him in the narrow hall on her way to the stateroom. He had left two mint chocolate squares on her pillow and had fashioned something different every night out of her towels. One night it was a monkey wearing her sunglasses. Another night Juan had twisted her pajamas into an elephant. No one had ever done that before. Mags, who came back to the room later and later each night didn't notice that Lunie had eaten her chocolates, packing her own to take home as a special souvenir.

While she was savoring the treats, Juan slipped the ship's activities calendar for the next day under the door. With the monkey or elephant beside her in the small bed, Lunie studied the information about Aruba, the first port of call, shopping opportunities in the gem shops, and the pedestrian or bus tours. Mags had already announced that she would be going to the beach.

The next morning Lunie got as far as walking down the gangplank, but rather than wander around the city by herself, decided to go back on board and read by the pool. Besides, she could see the roofs and distant shops from sports deck where joggers thundered past at all hours. The shopping district might be wonderful, but a woman might not be safe walking the streets alone, even in broad daylight with hundreds of other passengers disgorged into the tourist area.

So what was Sue doing down there, putting her passport in her shoulder bag and heading straight toward the market? Was that Bob from Ohio in a Hawaiian print shirt, white shorts, and flip-flops waiting for her by a stand of painted coconuts and shell necklaces made in China? Lunie was shocked. Now what?

"Write about what you know," Professor Finbarr repeated in the first, third and fourth lessons. Lunie realized with growing dismay that she knew nothing. Her characters knew more than she did and they were now shutting her out of their adventures. Maureen and Agnes were off snorkeling. Deloris was sleeping fitfully. José from Bali had left the ship for a few hours to use the Internet at a small café on a seamy side street where sailors bought cheap Viagra and American potato chips.

Prewriting. What else had Professor Finbarr said? Don't give up if your mind is blank. Brainstorm. If you have an idea, let it percolate. Set a kitchen timer for ten minutes and see what you can come up with before the buzzer goes off. And then on the www.writeanovelfastcontest site, which had all kinds of information about writing a novel in a month, they said to "silence your inner editor." Lunie gathered that meant don't worry if what you're writing sounds stupid or is filled with error. Keep going.

She would have been happy if that were her problem. She just hadn't gotten beyond the "mind-is-blank" issue. If her characters would just stay in sight, she might be able to focus, but they were always running off unexpectedly, doing the unimaginable.

She leaned back and closed her eyes, comforted by Phil hunkering down between her feet. I'll see what comes to my mind, and then, no matter what, I'll get up and type. What came to mind was Mother's thirtieth high school reunion. Dolce planned to attend and promised to bring her diaries, yearbook, scrapbooks, and prom dresses. Trunks of things she had saved from what she had called her happiest years when she was pretty and popular. Before she got married. Before she had children.

Dolce never made it to the reunion. By the time she unearthed her scrapbooks in the uncataloged piles in the attic, she had missed the reunion entirely. She moved her high school memorabilia to the dining room where she could locate it in time for her fortieth, she said.

I can't write about Mother, but I could write about a reunion. My characters could meet at their tenth high school reunion, just like I did. Where? At their former school? They'd walk the halls together looking for evidence of their lipstick graffiti on rest room stalls or milk-soaked straws hanging from the cafeteria ceiling. They'd recall the fun they'd all had, even though only a handful of kids in the senior class really had fun, and they'd pretend it still didn't matter that no one else had been popular.

Write about what you know.

Lunie couldn't write about the popular kids because she certainly hadn't been one. They dated, danced, excelled at football and cheerleading, drove their father's cars and stole cigarettes, which they lit up in the rest room while they wrote gross sayings on the stall doors,

Lunie had been a "good girl." She had lugged her books a mile to school, and three days a week, brought her stand-up bass.

Her mother had acquired the string bass cheap at a silent auction to raise money for the town orchestra. Although the bid price of donated violins, cellos, and even a viola, soared in $5 increments, there were no other bidders for the bass, perhaps because of a long crack in the front that resembled the flow of the Potomac River. Proud of her achievement of attaching the stroller wheels to the bottom of the case, Dolce sealed the crack with Kidz Gloo (she had a case of it in the upstairs bathroom) and stenciled pink hibiscus around it.

"I don't know why instruments aren't colorful," she told a dismayed Lunie. "You start a trend." It was the last thing Lunie wanted to do—stand out.

Dolce had no idea what a struggle it was for Lunie to maneuver the bass over the speed bumps on the next block. Nor did she care. She bragged to Wilma that Lunie had quite a career ahead of her because classical bass players were in high demand.

Lunie endured the bullying that school musicians had to go through—a series of viola jokes that were modified into jokes about string bass players and their instruments. She thought they were less funny than true: What's the difference between a string bass and an onion? No one cries when you cut up a string bass, was one that she remembered well.

Lunie did not feel that the bass was truly her instrument—her heart had been set on playing a flugelhorn—but the minimum bid for the horn was more than her mother wanted to invest at the auction. Dolce was also impressed by its size and said she had gotten more for her money.

Her mother had never forgiven Lunie for losing the bass on her way to her after-school job at the ice cream parlor. "How could you just lose something that large? I don't get it," Dolce ranted, while Lunie listened impassively. She had no intention of telling her mother about the homeless man in the park who needed firewood.

Lunie had lasted at her own high school reunion for three hours, long enough to tour the building and listen to the popular kids guffaw, as they passed the music room about a girl (they couldn't remember her name) who dragged a painted string bass wherever she went. Lunie had decided to skip the dinner at the country club and go home. There wasn't anyone she wanted to be reacquainted with anyway, except perhaps Fink, who had sat next to her in science. He had been too shy to ask her out, but he never made fun of her or her clothes, which smelled a bit like they came from a thrift store or yard sale, which they did. If Fink was at the reunion, she hadn't seen him.

Fink. She wondered what had happened to him. When the reunion materials had arrived, she had turned immediately to the "Fs" hoping to read current information about him. The reunion booklet included everyone's high school yearbook pictures, plus current photographs, if classmates had provided them.

Fink hadn't sent one, and neither had Lunie. She had updated her street address, making it clear to anyone who might care, that she no longer lived at Mother's, but Fink apparently hadn't returned his bio form. She ran her finger over the senior picture of his face, mulling his ever-optimistic smile, regardless of how their classmates treated him. She remembered when he had smiled at her that way.

Lunie decided Fink hadn't returned the personal information because he was terribly busy and likely married to a beautiful, talented woman. He surely had put high school, Mosby Gap, and mousy Lunie long behind him.

Now, if Sue went to her high school reunion, everyone would be astonished by the transformation since her teen years. They would look at her nametag that displayed her yearbook picture, then at her stylish pixie cut and would wonder if she colored her hair or if it was natural. They'd admire the fact she hadn't gained weight even though she had six children. The men would flock around her, offering to buy drinks, now that she was single again. In addition to teaching kindergarten, Sue would wow them with her national prestige as an author of a book about Minnesota corn crafts, her performances on the flugelhorn with the symphony, and her children's brilliant achievements.

> "You're so hot, hot, hot," whispered Bob, who had married his high school fling, Deloris. Deloris was back at the hotel suffering from a migraine. "Sue, you remind me of someone named ViVi whom I met on a cruise," he added. "Aruba, perhaps."

"Damn," said Lunie. "They're at it again."

Six

WHERE DO YOU WANT THIS, HON?"
The freight truck had pulled into the driveway shortly after Dayton had left for Mother's the next morning. He had had a bounce in his step, a cheerful sense of purpose on his face, and a Thermos of milky coffee,.

Still in her faded-lavender chenille bathrobe, Lunie had cautiously answered the doorbell, then immediately regretted her decision. Two large men, the type who would load a moving truck, but wouldn't be there later when the truck was to be unloaded, were shuffling on her porch.

"I didn't order anything," she said loudly.

"Is your name Lunette?" asked the man with the clipboard.

"Yes, but you must have the wrong house."

"Sign here, hon," he said, thrusting the clipboard inside the screen door.

Lunie shoved the clipboard back, without her signature, and hooked the door.

"Don't matter, hon," said the man. "We can verify you were here to accept delivery." He took a picture of her, staring through the door. "That'll do," he said, grinning at the picture before pocketing his camera phone.

With that, the men hoisted a crate the size of an upright piano onto the porch. "Want us to open it for you?" he asked, adding "hon" when she didn't reply.

"Let's do it," said the other. "I want to see her face."

Lunie closed the front door and watched them through the beveled glass.

The larger of the two large men went to the truck for a crowbar and hammer, and within moments they had knocked apart the box—cardboard, foam, and wood supports spilling everywhere.

The man with the phone took another picture and one of her closed door and what had to be a beveled blur of lavender. They drove off leaving the mess of packing materials. In the middle of the packing chaos, Lunie could identify, even through the distortion of the window glass, a full-sized moose. Stuffed.

Lunie leaned against the door and realized that her bathrobe sash had come untied, revealing cleavage and who knew what else. Before the truckers had gotten around the corner, the picture of her had probably gone viral on the Internet—as well as the mess and the moose.

Lunie quickly dressed in her jeans and sweatshirt and took a forty-gallon trashcan outside so she could remove the debris before the neighbors could see it. Getting rid of the moose would be trickier. She had never been that close to one; it towered above her, with baleful glass eyes. "I wasn't the one who shot you," she said. "Don't look at me like that."

Taped to its varnished hoof, she discovered a card. "Love you, Sis," it read.

I should have known. Well, Dayton you can just send that moose back where it came from if it takes a saw to hack it into mailable pieces.

Someone was calling her name. Lunie saw Omar Billings, with toothpaste-white hair poking out from under his blaze-orange hunting cap, stopping by her mailbox. He often walked after breakfast. It was a short walk, enough "to get the juices going," he always said.

Omar built birdhouses—his own modern design, that he marketed as inspired by Frank Lloyd Wright and I.M. Pei—

and sold them to a specialty catalog. He was working out a deal to have them manufactured in China despite picketing by six people in town who demanded that he keep his business local. He had offered them all jobs cutting perches and holes, but the picketing stopped when they declined to work part time for minimum wage. "Go get yourself some illegals," screamed a woman wearing a flag T-shirt.

"Morning, Lunie," Omar called again.

Lunie waved, hoping he hadn't seen the moose. She didn't want to try to explain. She was beyond explanations where Dayton was concerned.

"We're planning the annual neighborhood barbecue cookout on the sixteenth. If it's chilly, it'll be a cook-in," he said, laughing at his little joke, which he told every year. "You and your brother better be there."

"I'll check the calendar," said Lunie. She'd come up with an excuse later and send a regrets note to him and his wife, Edna.

"I'm leaving an invitation in your box, and one in the new neighbors' mailbox. I haven't met them yet—hope they'll be able to come," Omar called.

Lunie waved again, hoping that without contributing further to the pleasantries by talking, she would encourage him to continue his walk. But Omar seemed to be looking beyond her as she tried to block his view of the moose. For a moment it appeared as if he were going to come right up the walk, but after taking another hard look at Lunie with her arms outstretched and her head angled along the stiff lines of the moose's neck, he apparently thought better of it and ambled off.

After he was out of sight, Lunie swept up the remaining pieces of packing and dragged the trashcan behind the house.

There was no budging the moose, she soon discovered. She wasn't able to move it an inch. It blocked her rocker and its broad antlers covered the bird clock. Sparrows would soon screech 10:00 AM, followed by starlings cackling at eleven.

The moose's presence startled Phil when he dashed around the side of the house and up the porch steps. He hissed and backed into the railing, then jumped to the sidewalk.

Lunie debated covering the moose with a sheet, not a good one from her bed, but the old one she used to protect her vegetables from early frost. But that would stand out—a large moose-shaped ghost on her porch would quickly attract attention. Maybe a dark blanket would be better. The moose would blend into the shadows. She'd leave her porch lights turned off at night until Dayton removed it.

What could he be thinking? That was the problem, her brother wasn't thinking about her. Until his return, life had been relatively uncluttered. She even had had a sense of humor. Wit. Purpose. Satisfaction with having small tasks completed perfectly and on time. It was the way she had kept her desk at work. Neat. Orderly. She had been efficient, not like her co-worker, Rachel, who sipped from a coffee cup that she never cleaned and who updated her social networking sites every twenty minutes. Rachel was almost as bad as one of the supervisors, Lewis, whom Lunie had caught playing solitaire on his computer. No matter, Lunie prided herself on a dust-free house. A never-any-dirty-dishes-in-the-sink house. A clothes-neatly-folded-and-put-away house. A simple, nicely manicured house where its owner could sit on her front porch on a fall afternoon and write a novel without having to move a moose to get to her rocker. She turned and, with arms hanging at her sides, buried her face in the moose's withers.

"So, what do you think, Lunie-croonie?"

Lunie whirled around. "Get this thing out of here, Dayton! I'm not amused."

"But, Lunie, I bet you haven't discovered the trap door." Dayton patted her on the shoulders. He walked around her to the moose's butt, and lifted a well-concealed door, which made a sound not unlike a balloon losing air. Dayton beamed and said, "See? A secret compartment for storing your jewelry."

There were two times in Lunie's life that she couldn't think of a thing to say, and they had both been within the year. The first involved the reported circumstances of Mother's death; and the second was when Dayton attempted to explain the properties of the Trojan moose.

"And that's not all," Dayton continued. "There's a switch behind his ear. Here, flip it."

She refused.

"Okay, I'll show you just this one time then you can do it yourself. First, turn this little dial to moose sounds, or ducks, geese, loons, grizzlies, or tourists. Then turn it on and listen." Not surprisingly, Dayton had selected "moose."

Not only did the moose's jaw move, its eyes flashed, as from deep within its belly, a speaker broadcast its mating call. Loudly.

"Want to try?"

Lunie was beyond response. Dayton turned the dial to geese. The moose honked unconvincingly with an occasional skip in the recording device.

"Maybe that is why it was on sale," said Dayton. "Now if you push the button under its tail . . ."

Lunie turned and went in the house. "I'm going to call the police."

"Lunie, I don't think it's a good idea to leave the moose outside. It might get stolen," said Dayton. "It's really quite valuable. Wait until you see what you can do with the antlers." He stood back, admiring his gift.

But, what would she tell the police? Would they lecture her about being ungrateful for a large and special present from her only living family member?

Manngo. Dr. Manngo would understand.

She pulled out a chair, sat at the kitchen table, and opened a new e-mail account using the name Heva.

Dr. Manngo: Hey there, Heva, what's your issue?

Heva: My brother just gave me a moose. SEND

Dr. Manngo: What's the problem with that?

Heva: It takes up my entire porch and it has a butt safe for jewelry. SEND

Dr. Manngo: A butt what?

Heva: Place to hide jewelry. SEND

Dr. Manngo: What jewelry would you hide in the moose butt?

Heva: None. I don't want the moose. SEND

Dr. Manngo: Heva, I feel your pain. Deal with the moose and you'll deal with life.

Lunie would have liked more assistance, but she was relieved to learn that he felt her pain. It wasn't exactly pain—it was more like itching from where she had touched the moose. She looked in a mirror; her forehead was covered with a rash.

She had no idea what kind of ointment she should use, and she certainly wasn't going to call her doctor for advice.

"I really wish you'd help me," called Dayton from the front hallway. Lunie didn't like the sound of the scraping and scuffling.

"You can't bring that thing in here," she said, hurrying to the hall. "You just can't."

"Here, take hold of the antlers. They won't break." The moose had tipped to one side and was only partly inside. "I had to lower its head by raising the rear, then sort of pushed and pulled," he said, panting, "but now it's caught again."

The moose did not appear pleased. It reacted to Dayton's jostling efforts by emitting a series of alarming growls, followed by a recorded tourist voice saying, "Look at the moose, Dorothy."

"Eek," replied a scratchy treble voice.

"If you go outside and around, you can shove from behind, or would you rather pull?" asked Dayton.

"Neither," said Lunie.

"So, you don't want to use your front door anymore?" Dayton asked, with an uncharacteristic annoyance. "I'll just do it myself." He tugged on the antlers, but the moose didn't respond. "Stuck."

Seven

Dayton, assuring Lunie that the moose's location would be temporary, said he had to go to town for a job interview at the tourist bureau. It had something to do with promoting shopping locally during the holidays. He whistled as he took two steps at a time to go to his room to change his shirt and comb his beard, and tossed a baseball cap on an antler as he came back down. "See how useful it is?" he asked. "Coat rack. Hat rack. Towel rack."

"When you get back," his sister with all the firmness she could muster, "you better have a plan to move this thing out the door and back where it came from." She considered stamping her foot, but decided that would be childish, which is exactly how she felt. Like stamping her feet, slamming doors and scribbling. Throwing something.

"Turn the dial and listen to the coyote howl," responded Dayton cheerfully. "It's really neat. Mother would have loved it. And, don't wait lunch for me, Lunie-baloney."

Lunie turned her back on the gift blocking her front doorway and went back to the kitchen. There was no point in trying to write for a few minutes; her mind felt like an autumn windstorm with dry brown leaves blowing everywhere.

I've got to concentrate, Lunie thought, moving her chair so she couldn't see the moose's hostile stare. *Here goes.*

Chapter 6

Sue's mother, who lived in South Dakota, was a folk artist. She had taken up painting at age fifty-five while working at the bank. She was best known for her landscapes featuring cornstalks and silver windmills. Until she retired she'd been able to use the office copy machine (when everyone was at lunch) to reduce the size of her watercolors and reproduce them in color. She slipped the pages in her handbag, and when she got home, she'd use Kidz Gloo to make greeting cards. Sue's mother sold the cards at fall corn festivals. She was so busy that she forgot to clean her house and pretty soon . . .

Oh, no, not Sue's mother, too! Lunie decided to keep going. Maybe Sue's mother would be the key to the book's plot.

In addition to painting, Sue's mother made lots of crafts. She watched the Craft Channel to get ideas, particularly for months that didn't have obvious seasonal items. October was easy. She learned to cover toilet paper rolls with orange and brown fabric to make cute pumpkins. She made snowmen out of white socks filled with rice and tied off with rubber bands. In February, she made construction paper hearts and decorated them with doilies glued on with Kidz Gloo. Unfortunately, Sue's mother liked all her crafts so well that she didn't want to sell them or give them away. And she stopped selling her corn and windmill paintings. Pretty soon . . .

At least Lunie had words down. Progress. Now she would have to figure out why Sue left home at age seventeen and ran away to Minnesota with either a Bible salesman or a bootlegger. Or maybe he was a biker she met at a Sturgis motorcycle rally. Or maybe she just hitchhiked because she was allergic to construction paper and couldn't stand it anymore at home. Lunie was increasingly anxious about Sue's wilder side—the side the school board knew nothing about when they hired her. But, finally, a character was coming to life. She checked her e-mail spam for ideas for the name of the biker. He would be a premed or prelaw, because that's what she had heard about

Harley owners. She skimmed over the six or so names that weren't very nice, and wondered how Rolex would sound. An odd name, but it had a touch of upper class. She received a lot of spam messages from Rolex and Pfizer. Yes, Rolex would be the name of Sue's biker, helping her escape the House of Crafts.

> After Sue's mother made her a paper dress covered with construction-paper autumn leaves attached with Kidz Gloo, Sue decided to run away to the big city. She just couldn't wear that dress to school the next day with its poofy tissue-paper sleeves (left over from dress patterns) and a ribbon belt. "Be a trendsetter," were the last words Sue remembered her mother saying before she rushed to her room, packed her knapsack with clean underwear, her homework and her piggy bank. Sue jumped out the window and ran for the road, never looking back. When she reached the highway, a motorcycle screeched to a stop. "Going my way?" asked the handsome rider.
>
> "Why not," said Sue. "My name is Sue."
>
> "Hop on. I'm Rolex."

At last, her book was taking shape. Lunie was relieved. Her mind danced with possibilities. Starting with chapter 6 had been the right decision. Her fingers flew, transporting Sue, who was enjoying having her arms around Rolex, on roads that passed through the darkened cornfields, the moon shining on the slowly moving wings of the wind machines. By morning they had reached Fulda. Lunie had never been to Minnesota so she wasn't sure how to describe the setting. *I'll Google Fulda later.* Meanwhile, she could envision the sound of traffic, and the cars honking at the handsome couple.

The kitchen door creaked open. "Didn't you hear me beeping?" asked Dayton. "I need your help."

Lunie sighed and clicked SAVE. "Help with what?" she asked.

"Come see," said her brother. She followed him to his VW camper. A large carpet was rolled up and tied on the top. Dayton cut the ropes. "What's in it? A body?" asked Lunie.

"Grab an end," he answered. The carpet dropped to the ground and relaxed, revealing an oriental pattern and what looked suspiciously like the skeleton of a small rodent. "What are you going to do with this dirty old thing?" asked Lunie, wary of what further unrolling might reveal.

"It will look nice in my room after I hose it down," he said. "It might be valuable."

"Dayton, are you not hearing anything I've been saying? This is *my* house. I like it the way it is, I mean was, before you starting bringing in all the stuff. Take the rug away. Get rid of the moose. You're driving me crazy." This time she did stamp her foot. Dayton unfurled the rest of the carpet, kicking off a mound of something that resembled congealed, partially digested kibble.

"Dayton, I can tell you're not listening."

"I'm not listening, Lunie."

"Listen to me."

"I'm not going to listen. I'm a calm person."

"Just listen."

"I'm not listening. You are not calm. You sound uncalm. Very uncalm."

Lunie picked up the bucket of soapy water he had just filled and hurled it. Dayton stepped aside and the suds spilled on the carpet.

"Thanks for your help, Lunie. And I really mean it." He took a long-handled scrub brush and worked on the carpet. Lunie didn't wait to see him rinse and drag it into the sunshine to dry.

She slammed his camper's door closed and hurried toward the street. A walk might help. After a few strides, she began jogging, wishing with every step that she wasn't still wearing her fuzzy pink bunny slippers. When she reached Mother's house, Lunie ducked into the backyard where she could sit on the back steps.

Dayton's right. I am very uncalm.

The new shed was padlocked, as was the chest freezer—a safety measure, to keep children out, figured Lunie. She wondered how much cleaning he had done. She tugged the door open and stepped in the kitchen. Indeed, she was able to see part of one counter. *If we get Mother's house emptied out, Dayton can move in. I'll even give him my share of the house just to get my life back.* With new determination, Lunie grabbed a box of old yellowed newspapers, and hurled it out the door. Then a sack of grocery bags, and another of picnic plates—dirty. Two plastic bins of 45 records were next. She paused only briefly to note that she remembered hearing some of them when she was young. She hurled a carton of cracked flowerpots, unwashed, then a pile of moldy towels.

Uncalm was transitioning into calm. Lunie picked up a small blue box that she found on the floor near the kitchen table. It looked vaguely familiar, like something her mother had treasured and kept on her dresser. She shook it and was puzzled by the sand-like sound.

"Lunie, please give me that!" said Dayton. "That's mine." Her brother stooped in the doorway, his hand outstretched.

"You crept up on me again," said Lunie. "Stop doing that."

"Please, just give me the box. I can see you've been getting rid of things without looking at their value."

Lunie shook it again. "Did Mother go to the beach?"

Dayton said, "Don't you remember her dirt collection? She has little film canisters filled with dirt from every state and six foreign countries. All her friends brought her dirt from their travels."

Lunie hadn't seen that particular collection, prized by their mother, in years. "Is this part of it?"

Dayton shook his head. "You probably won't appreciate it, but Mother was very sentimental. She loved us a lot."

"What's in here?"

Dayton extracted the box from her hand and mumbled, "Nail clippings. But only from when we were too little to clip our

Eight

LUNIE STRODE PAST MOUNTAINVIEW Park on the next street. A single-fathers' support group was meeting in the gazebo, keeping watchful eyes on their toddlers in the sandbox. The next fenced play area was the dog park, named for Sparky-Munroe, a beagle that had rescued his elderly owner when she had fallen asleep on her couch with a lit cigarette. There had been no fire, other than a scorched nightshirt, but Sparky had barked and barked until the paperboy named Munroe, hearing the commotion, had broken the door open and rescued both of them.

The snarling and growling behind the holly bush indicated that Harvard and Yale were playing. A woman with a quaking Maltese was waiting outside the fence for them to go home so her dog could romp without fear of attack.

Lunie didn't stop to talk with Cara Newton, and hoped she wouldn't be noticed.

She walked past Mosby's Market, which had been sold three years earlier to a family from Pakistan (Mosby's now sold curried chicken as well as fried chicken gizzards with gravy over grits), and Raiders Dixie Bistro. Lunie wasn't sure what the difference was between a bistro and a café, but Raiders offered speciality coffees, lattes, and biscotti all day, and served wine with a light supper. It was a popular spot for local poets. Wilma often recited her new poems there at Tuesday's open mic.

Next was Cotton's Curios, which was rarely open. Supposedly Howard Cotton, uncle to the mayor, traveled out of town much of the year to run antique auctions. Perhaps she could engage him to run an auction at Mother's, if there was anything of value under all that trash.

Just beyond it was Varina's Book and Bridle—a used-book store, with a tack room in the back. "You gotta make a living," Winston Berger, the owner had told her. For a long time, his was the only retail outlet for Mother's watercolors and cards. Winston let her keep them there on consignment. Then Dolce took them all back without a word and refused to sell her art to anyone. Winston had told Lunie, "I couldn't figure it out. They didn't sell much, but people liked to look at them."

The door to the Book and Bridle opened and a familiar figure wearing a tweed golf cap stepped into the street. "Good afternoon, Lunie," said Professor Finbarr, glancing quickly at her feet. Lunie felt her face flush. "How's your novel coming along?"

"Really well," she said. "Making progress. I'm working on Chapter 6 right now, thank you."

"I'd like to have a look, when you're ready," he said. "Speed writing is one thing. Polishing it carefully is another."

"Thanks," said Lunie, wondering if she should address him as professor, mister, or Hobart, because although she was taking his class, he was also a neighbor.

"But don't forget your writing assignments. I haven't received last week's exercise on writing humor." He shifted his brown paper shopping sack to his other arm. "How's that brother of yours? If he has the time, I could use help painting several rooms."

"I'll tell him, Professor Finbarr."

He didn't say, "Oh, Lunie, you may call me Hobart," so she was glad she had been formal herself. Perhaps, after she was finished with his class, that might change. He looked at her slippers again. "Would you like a ride home?" he asked. Lunie would. Her feet hurt. "No thanks, I need the exercise," she said, quickly continuing along the sidewalk.

The reason she hadn't written about "The Funniest Thing That Ever Happened to Me As an Adult" was because nothing funny had happened to her as an adult. She couldn't even remember something funny that had happened to anybody that she could adapt as her own story. She'd have to take a failing grade. The only person she wanted to talk with about her family was Dr. Manngo. He wouldn't mark her grammar or correct her spelling or tell her that her syntax was wrong. He'd listen patiently, say something comforting and help her deal with her problems.

She passed the Tidey Dry-day Cleaners that had been closed by the EPA, and Two Bits Barbershop, which charged women more than men for the same cut. Lunie asked about it once. Edith, at the third station, told her it was just the way things were industrywide. After Edith had received a cell phone earpiece for her birthday, all she did was talk on the phone while she trimmed, so Lunie had switched to Roger, Edith's nephew, who was trying to build his customer base. He had been a carpenter, but with the downturn in the economy, took an online cosmetology course, and was hired by Two Bits. "It's an apprenticeship for six months," he told Lunie. "But it's all the same. Cutting angles and planes." He had cut her hair so short the first and only time that it was months before she needed another trim.

The Dollar and Dim was next. There was only one bin now of odds and ends for either a dollar or a dime. Everything else was at least $9.99, plus tax. The last shop before the gas station and garage was Kissy's Krafts and Karamels. The owner's name was really Krissy, but the sign painter had erred, and the shop's name was now more easily remembered. It was not a shop for children. Too much breakable bric-a-brac. The aisles were narrow and it was easy to knock something off a shelf, especially during the winter when everyone wore bulky coats.

Lunie rarely went in after her jacket hood had swept three angel figurines to the floor where they shattered. She had offered to help sweep up the pieces, but in turning around with the broom, knocked off two large elf candleholders. Porcelain. The mishap cost her almost $100, with nothing to show for it. From then on, she preferred to shop online. Her only regret was not having an occasional homemade Karamel.

Beyond the garage was a large vacant lot where Birdie's "Cheep" Motel used to be located. It had closed down when the state had built the bypass, and two chain motels opened near the highway exit. After Birdie moved to Florida, vagrants had torched the boarded-up building.

Beyond the lot was the older of two Methodist churches. There had been a falling out fifty years earlier among members of the congregation, and The Fallen, as they called themselves, built a new, identical church next door. "It tore the town apart," Wilma told Lunie and Dayton one night. "People still aren't speaking and they don't know why." Wilma had speculated that it had something to do with the pastor and the organist, and then pretended to zip her lips.

Lunie hadn't known which person of the cloth she should ask to officiate at Dolce's simple, nonreligious memorial service; she didn't want to stir up trouble. So she had asked the new rector at Gray Ghost Episcopal, just four miles out of town, if he could handle the service. The priest was near retirement, agreeable, and didn't ask questions other than if it was all right to pray. "God would prefer that," he said. He hoped that his willingness to help out would tug at Lunie's heart and she would come to a service. She hadn't.

Lunie's feet ached and she wished she had thrown on a jacket before going outside to "help" Dayton. Time to go home.

Climbing back up the hill, she saw Wilma coming down. Wilma looked hard at Lunie's feet, then asked, "Lunie, dear, I'm wondering, um, what sort of remodeling project are you doing? I didn't see a permit. Honey, I would hate for you to get in trouble with your own building department if you want to be called back to work."

"A project?" Lunie could not contain her alarm. Despite her aching feet, she hurried up the street to her driveway. She saw Dayton on the front porch, standing back with a stance of satisfaction. He had taken four interior doors that had been leaning against the back of Mother's garage and used them for his entryway construction.

"Pretty neat, huh," he said, when he heard Lunie padding up the porch steps, bunny ears flopping.

"What are you doing?" she asked sharply.

"Now we have no security problems and no drafts," he said, "and, look at this." He pulled the door open, revealing the back end of the moose and lifted open the butt safe. "We can put beer in here in cold weather, or Halloween candy. Extra storage."

"Dayton, get rid of the doors. Get rid of the moose. Get rid of everything that doesn't belong in my house. It is my house. *My* house."

"Lunie, do you want burglars, murderers or wild animals to crawl through the moose's legs and break in while we're sleeping? I'm just trying to help." As if to prove Dayton's point, Phil dashed in the open door, ran under the moose and toward the kitchen. Dayton closed the outside door and locked it with a padlock. He taped a sign with an arrow that indicated that the entrance was around the back.

"There," he said. "C'mon inside. Let's warm up those bunnies." He smiled so sweetly that she wanted to hurl her slippers at him.

Once inside, Dayton said, "Sit down, Lunie-cartoony." He handed her black support hose. "These will make your feet feel better." Lunie was too tired to object, although she regarded the hose and their faint musty smell with suspicion. "I'll put the bunnies back in your room." He slipped them on his hands and waggled them like dancing puppets, but Lunie didn't smile.

When he returned, he made her a cup of tea. "You didn't ask me if I got the job," Dayton said, pulling out a chair.

Lunie considered the bubbles on the surface of the tea. "Don't you want to know?" he asked.

When she still didn't answer, Dayton said, "Well, they hired me."

"To do what?"

"I'm going to be Mosby Gap's walk-about."

"A what?"

"It's better than wearing a sandwich board to advertise things," he said, "although I might do a little of that, too. I get to wear really fun costumes and walk about, get it? Walk about. And I'll pass out fliers, menus, free tickets to events, and sell discount tickets to shows, just like they do on Broadway."

"What do you know about Broadway?"

"I know a lot about a lot of things, Lunie. Do you want to hear about my costumes?"

Lunie didn't answer. She put the warm mug against her forehead.

"My first one is a squirrel suit with a big bushy tail. I'll be advertising the fall festival sponsored by the Southern Sons of Nutcrackers. At Thanksgiving, instead of a turkey, they've got a cornucopia made by someone who used to help out with floats for Macy's, and at Christmas . . ."

"Let me guess, you'll be a tree."

"Yes, but guess what will be around my ankles."

"I can't imagine."

"C'mon, imagine."

Lunie really couldn't.

"Okay, I'll tell you, but you've got to keep it a secret. Promise? Presents. They have huge square presents that fasten with Velcro. It's really cute—a walking, talking tree with presents under it."

"And you get paid for this?" Lunie closed her eyes, trying *not* to imagine Dayton dressed as a squirrel or Christmas tree.

He had liked wearing costumes when they were children. Dolce encouraged him by buying secondhand capes and tutus at yard sales after Halloween. His closet was filled with outfits, not just the super heroes, witches or princess gowns, but also her old shoes and hats. He'd put on something outlandish, parade to wherever Mother was sitting, and the two of them would laugh uproariously.

"Yes, and I can keep the tips."

"Why would tourists give tips to a Christmas tree?"

Dayton looked at her with a poker face, then, when she rubbed her feet, apparently losing interest in the conversation, he said, "They'll give me tips about how to get warm. Get it?"

Lunie dropped her feet to the floor and stood up. "Dayton, I'm going to fix supper. Pasta. Then, after we eat, we're going to talk. We're going to have a serious conversation."

A flicker of concern crossed his face. Dayton looked at his watch. "Pasta sounds great, but I can't talk tonight. I have an appointment."

"An appointment? What kind of an appointment?"

Dayton's feet shifted and he looked at the ceiling. "Sort of a social appointment. Several of them, and—" He looked uneasy about sharing. "With my social, uh, counselor."

Lunie sat back down. "Your what?"

"Lunie, I don't like to hold out on you, but some things are private, and I'm not ready to share. I'll set the table."

Lunie shook her head and stood. "Fifteen minutes until supper." She went to the cupboard. The single jar of tomato sauce and box of spaghetti were gone. The only thing on the shelf was a can of pork and beans with a five-year-old expiration date from Mother's. Cold cereal would have to suffice once again.

When Phil heard her open the refrigerator door, he begged on his hind legs. "I'll give you milk when I'm done," she said, wondering what Dr. Manngo would say about people who talked more to their cats than to people. Phil understood her need for order. He seemed to realize that tabletops should be clear of clutter, and demonstrated his agreement by pushing books or pencils to the floor. Phil had a sense of time, which corresponded mostly with Lunie's. Phil would not leave a wet towel or necktie on the bedpost, or draped over a moose's antler. Lunie squinted at the darkened hallway. There was a hat on one antler, and a beach towel now on the other. Phil was focused only on milk. Lunie put her almost empty bowl on the floor. She would sterilize it later.

She decided to contact the good doctor. In her desperation for immediate assistance she forgot to use an assumed identity.

Lunie saw that Dr. Manngo was still modifying his Web site. He had a new button for SOCIAL COACHING. His sample dialogue with a client again showed his helpfulness.

> Dear Dr. Manngo, what is the best way to meet new friends?
>
> Dr. Manngo replied: As I say to many lonely clients: Friending. Make friends on the Internet. Join Facebook. Twitter and Tweet or whatever. Just be careful what you send.

Lunie wasn't sure that was for her, but logged in:

> Lunie, because you've been here before, you get bonus time today. Ten minutes bonus.
>
> Thank you, Dr. Manngo. SEND
>
> What would you like to discuss?

Lunie hesitated. She wished she had thought about her most pressing problem before logging in, but even with bonus minutes, she couldn't waste the doctor's time. Impulsively, and immediately regretting her decision, she typed:

> Bunny slippers. SEND
>
> Bunny slippers?

My mother gave me pink slippers that look like bunnies. They have a face, a puffy tail and big floppy
ears. SEND

Why do you wear them?

My feet were cold and I put them on when I went outside to help my brother with a rug and then I got mad
at my brother and went for a walk. SEND

She realized she was rambling. What must he be thinking?
Dr. Manngo didn't answer immediately. Was he consulting reference books or a colleague about her case? Perhaps he thought
she was crazy.

Sorry for the delay. I was looking up bunny slippers.
They're not recommended for a long walk. You should
wear good shoes instead. What else is troubling you?

Lunie was relieved that he was nonjudgmental and even
wanted to talk further. She decided she'd spring for extra time
when the bonus minutes were up. She had already mentioned
some key issues in her life—her mother's refrigerator and
hoarding, the moose butt safe, and her painful walk through
town. It was time to get to the heart of things. Dayton. She
typed:

My biggest problem is my brother who is living with
me and making my life very difficult. SEND

You don't like your brother?

I like him, but he's messing up my house and my life?
SEND

How does he make you feel on a scale of one to ten?

Lunie was finding it hard to explain. She loved Dayton. He
was kind and protective. Brought her presents. Gave her support stockings for her feet. At the same time, he ate all her
food, was making a mess of her house, and certainly wasn't
helping her clean out Mother's, at least not in the way they
should to get it done. What number could she assign to her
feelings for him? If she gave a low number, Dr. Manngo might

get the impression that she didn't like Dayton. If she came up with a eight or nine, he wouldn't understand why she was upset. She decided to play it safe:

> Five. SEND

> Your feelings for your brother are a five?

> Yes. SEND

> Interesting. Very interesting. Deal with your feelings
> and you'll deal with life.

A smiley face appeared on the screen—something new—and the session ended.

Lunie savored the moment. Dr. Manngo had actually used the word "interesting" in his responses. He hadn't rejected her because of her bunny slipper indiscretion. He had asked about how she felt and listened uncritically. Uncalm and depression were being replaced by a new sensation. Lunie had only felt this way one other time in her life. It was when Fink, the boy she sat next to in biology, had told her that she had nice feet. She remembered that moment clearly. It was the first really warm day of spring and she had worn sandals without the fuchsia anklets that her mother had laid out for her. Their teacher, Miss Savannah Pembroke, opened the window halfway through the class letting in both fresh air and a swarm of yellow jackets. While her classmates swatted and dove for cover, Lunie and Fink had calmly remained at their desks, and continued to take notes. They were perhaps the only students in the room who appreciated Miss Pembroke's taking advantage of the situation by turning it into a teachable moment. She switched from her discussion on the difference between arteries and vessels to one on the birds and the bees.

Fink leaned over and whispered, "Yellow jackets aren't really bees, but Miss Pembroke's amazing." It was then that Lunie realized that Fink was studying her feet, which were sticking out slightly in the aisle between their desks. Fink quickly wrote a note and slipped it to her while Miss Pembroke drew ovaries and sperm with a red marker on the whiteboard.

80

Lunie opened it: *You have beautiful feet.*

Lunie's heart beat so fast that it drowned out Miss Pembroke's impromptu lecture. She glanced at Fink, the boy with slicked-back hair, friendly brown eyes, glasses, and a blue button-down shirt. He smiled again. He might have winked. Lunie couldn't remember for sure, but the moment certainly would have been right. She was in love.

Fink never mentioned her feet again. Then, the next day and the next, he avoided eye contact.

Lunie borrowed some of Mother's hot pink nail polish. It was a clumsy application effort with ragged edges of color on her toes as well as the nails. If he saw the flashy, uneven color, when she edged her feet near his desk, he didn't say a word.

Distracted by longing, Lunie's grades suffered, and the next year, Fink was in advanced biology II, while Lunie had to go to summer school just to pass biology I. Then she heard that Fink had applied to all the best colleges and planned to study medicine.

She wondered what she had done wrong to end the relationship. It haunted her. Was it the note that she had handed back? In retrospect it was bold: *I like your feet, too.*

Or had she read something into his note to her? Was his note kindness, or simply clinical? She would never know.

Unfortunately, Dr. Manngo was stirring the same feelings, a ten on the feelings chart. If she were visiting him for a therapy session in his actual office, this would be the moment of truth. She would find out how he felt about her. It wouldn't be the first session—maybe the tenth or twelfth, after he had probed and solved her real problems. As the sessions continued through the years, he would be amazed at how well she had coped—no, truly dealt with life's challenges. He would admire her resilience, a survivor of the House of Hoarding. How she had followed his counsel, found friends, and moved away from her hometown in the Blue Ridge piedmont.

Sessions would no longer be through the anonymity of the Internet. She would be one of his special patients. She would awaken from her hypnosis session to find him leaning over her, reaching his hand out for her face. "Of all the people I have ever met, you are the most unique. You have beautiful—"

Embarrassed, she would cover his mouth with his hand, then he would take her hand and touch it to his lips, then . . .

"Lunie."

"Stop creeping up on me, Dayton!"

"I wasn't creeping. I was walking, like this."

"Stop walking like that, too."

Dayton kept walking on his toes and stopped behind her chair. Lunie quickly closed her laptop. Her brother rubbed her shoulders. "Pasta ready?"

"I think you ate it a few days ago. There's nothing left in the pantry."

"Lunie, that's my point. You should have more supplies."

Lunie pushed his hands away. "I like my house the way it was." She wanted to add, "Before you moved in," but Dayton was whistling "Ain't She Sweet." He returned to the table with her box of healthy cereal and the carton of milk. "Care for some?" he asked pouring a bowl for himself.

When she didn't answer, Dayton continued, "You know, Lunie, Mother was very worried about you. She said you were so fanatic about not having any stuff in your house you'd probably clean shells off a beach." He waited for a reaction but got none. "Well, if you're not going to converse, I'm going out. Don't wait up, and, thanks for dinner." He patted her on the head, and left, leaving his dish, milk and cereal on the table.

Nine

SHE HAD CAREFULLY AVOIDED looking at the moose when she passed it in the front hall on the way to her first floor bedroom. Phil found Lunie's feet shortly after she slipped between sheets. As Phil aged, he rarely attacked her feet during the night, but once in a while when she rolled over her toes must remind him of something in the wild and he would draw blood. Still, he was good company, not like the dog her mother owned when Lunie and Dayton were little.

Lunie wrapped her arms around her extra pillow and thought about Puddles, a black cocker that her mother had received in trade for a stuffed musical parakeet that cheeped when you wound it with a little gold key in its back. After it cheeped three times, more like a wren than jungle bird, the little blue-and-green toy warbled "The Blue Danube." Lunie, about nine at the time of her mother's trade, would have preferred keeping the *ouiseau mechanique*, as her mother called it to make the toy sound more impressive. Instead, the bird was traded for the cocker.

The bird was not one of a kind; Dolce had acquired a case of them, but it was the only one in the batch that worked. Lunie and Dayton knew that when Dolce had her heart set on a trade, she became very creative, relying on conversational French at times to make her sound knowledgeable about antiques in her bargaining. Mother had never taken conversational French, but had swapped a Martha's Vineyard cookbook for a book and tapes called *Learning French in Twenty EZ Lessons*. Lunie remembered her mother sitting at the kitchen table studying the first lesson until she could say "bonjours," and "avez-vous" something. But, Dolce lost interest after the second lesson and the book soon became covered with craft projects. *It's probably still under them,* thought Lunie. She wondered if there might be some useful terms for her to be able to throw into dialogue in her novel in case Sue decided to head for Quebec instead of the Caribbean.

Puddles, not surprisingly, had never been housebroken and was often damp to the touch. She smelled like Mother's rarely-laundered dish cloths. Puddles adored Lunie and tolerated Dayton. Puddles lasted about six months, until Dolce traded her for a mechanical monkey that was able to swallow pieces of real banana, as long as its throat was rinsed after each "meal." Neither Dayton nor Lunie protested the trade. Puddles had developed an extraordinary ability to determine what was valued or treasured and then leave her mark. Lunie cleaned up all the scraps of clothing and toys from Puddle's carnage in her room, only to discover the next day that her mother had rescued the trash bag saying, "Lunie, you never know when you'll need a doll arm. Waste not, want not." And then, to further make her point, Dolce praised Dayton for saving the pieces of plastic soldiers and socks with holes. Lunie remembered the delighted look on little Dayton's round face.

She vowed that very moment that she would never ever be like either of them.

A woman with three little girls came for Puddles, cooing over the leaky dog and handing Dolce a set of muffin tins and a jar of prickly pear jam made from a recipe in the Martha's Vineyard cookbook, and the mechanical monkey.

Lunie was positive that the scrap bag, plus the monkey full of decayed banana, were still buried deep within that house, along with the jar of jelly.

The gibbous moon didn't cheer her. The moon never did. Too many people, including Dayton, had made fun of her name.

"Did you know that Mother named you Lunette because she thought it was French for little moon?" he asked in an e-mail when he was out West. "It is that, but it also means eyeglasses. Pretty funny, huh!"

Lunie hadn't heard the eyeglass part. Maybe he was just teasing her. Dayton continued, "I bet you thought she named me for Uncle Dayton, didn't you?" When Lunie didn't respond to either e-mail, curious as she was, he wrote again: "I was named for a city in Midwestern state where Mother met a man she really liked." She didn't respond to that either.

Lunie wished she had closed her curtains to block out the moon's icy glare. She rolled to her right side; Phil rolled with her. She needed a plan. A plan that would work. She had read in a magazine that when you had problems, first list them in order of importance, then list possible solutions. Try to imagine what action would lead to what reaction. The author made it sound so easy.

The first problem that kept rising to the top of her mental list was Dayton. She could think of no solutions, only Dr. Manngo's wise counsel. "Deal with your brother and you'll deal with life." *Tomorrow,* she thought. *I'll make a plan tomorrow.* She pulled the soft blanket under her chin and closed her eyes, but only for a second. There was a thud in the hallway, and the sound of footsteps, then voices. A door opened and something was dragged across the floor. Another thud.

Lunie froze. She had never had burglars before—there was nothing to steal in her immaculate home. Her mother never did either for the opposite reason. And no one else in the neighborhood had ever mentioned crime, even Wilma, who had admitted that her poem about being the target of a terrorist plot had been inspired by a newspaper article, not her own personal experience. But then there had been the golf balls and neighbors who hadn't been seen in days.

Lunie tried to think of something she could use as a weapon. Her table lamp was small, but she might be able to throw it and frighten the intruders. She was reading a heavy book. That might work. Perhaps she should quietly hide under her bed or in her closet. Should she put on her robe or change out of her pajamas? The intruders were walking around the front hall. She listened as the footsteps went up the stairs and back and forth in the room above hers. While they were upstairs, and hoping that there weren't more—a gang, perhaps—skulking about in her living room and kitchen, Lunie made her move. She decided she'd rather die in her favorite jeans and sweatshirt than her pajamas. She dressed quickly in the moonlight, and, without thinking, slipped into her bunny slippers. Lunie armed herself with her copy of the complete works of Heloise. She would try to get out of the house and run for help, but if that was not possible, if she was outnumbered, she'd go down with a fight.

She heard footsteps coming back downstairs. Lunie carefully opened her door and crept toward the front hall, shielding herself with Heloise, but forgetting about the moose. As she bumped into it in the dark, the moose let out its mating call. Lunie ducked under it just as the hall lights were turned on. She could see two pairs of legs, a man's and a woman's.

"Lunie, is that you hiding? I can see your bunnies," said Dayton with an alcoholic giggle.

"That your sister?" asked the woman, peering under the moose.

Lunie tried to make her feet less visible. "Dayton," she hissed, "what the hell are you doing?"

"I could ask you the same thing," he said, still sounding silly.

"Who is that woman and what are you doing in my house at this hour of the night?"

"Your sister always talk to her guests that way?" asked the woman.

Dayton whispered something to her in response and they both laughed.

"I'm counting to ten, and I want you both gone," said Lunie. "Gone. Out-the-back-door gone. Never-come-back gone." She wished her voice wasn't trembling and nonauthoratative. She heard shuffling and for a moment thought they might be leaving. Instead, they'd moved a few feet away to whisper.

Dayton's feet moved back toward the moose.

In a more sober voice he said, "I can't do that, Lunie. Rhoda is my new friend and I promised her that she could spend the night."

Lunie crawled out and stood up, knocking Dayton's towel off the antler. "She cannot stay. Absolutely not. Must I remind you whose house this is?" She refused to look at the woman.

"Just tonight, Lunie. It's late. She can stay in my room and I'll sleep on the couch."

"No."

"Is she always this rude?" Rhoda asked. "I don't know if I want to stay where I'm not welcome."

Lunie glared at her brother.

"One night, Lunie. I already put her things in my room. One night."

Without waiting for Lunie's response, Dayton said, "C'mon, Rhoda," and they went upstairs.

Lunie trembled, partly from the draft coming from the makeshift doorway surrounding the moose, and partly from rage. Her mother always said she wasn't assertive enough. A dish rag. Doormat. Yet, when she tried to be firm about things that mattered even in her own house, she was ignored.

She picked up the towel, folded it and put it back on the moose. The grandfather clock alerted her to the hour. It was 12:30 AM and she was beyond wide awake; she was mad awake. There was no point in returning to bed. She decided to have a cup of tea, something Dayton didn't care for so he probably hadn't used up her supply. Phil darted past her anticipating a unexpected late-night meal. When she turned on the kitchen light, she saw that instead of waiting next to his empty bowl, Phil had bounded to the top of a pile of four boxes and five bulging shopping bags in front of the refrigerator. The boxes were not closed well, and the bags, filled with what looked like shoes, a hair curler, and cosmetics, a stuffed bear and a jewelry box, hadn't been packed with care.

Lunie returned to the bottom of the stairs. "Dayton!"

"Shhh," he said from the upstairs landing. "Rhoda's sleeping. I'm coming down."

"Well, I'm not sleeping. I'm shouting! And I'll continue to shout until you wake her up and get that stuff out of my kitchen."

"Shhh," whispered Dayton reaching the bottom. "I told you Rhoda's just here for tonight. She got kicked out and had nowhere to go."

"I don't believe you!" shouted Lunie, who discovered that at that decibel level, her voice didn't tremble.

"I know you are uncalm again," said Dayton, soothingly. "Let's talk for a couple of minutes and then get a good night's sleep. Mother always said—"

"I don't care what Mother said." Lunie felt herself being steered toward the kitchen.

"Sit," said Dayton. "I'll fix you tea." He looked in her cupboard above the microwave. "And where would I find a single bag of tea on your empty shelves?" When she didn't answer, he said much-too-sweetly, "Then how about a cup of hot water, with perhaps a spoon of sugar and a dash of peppermint extract? Mother used to make that for us after school, remember?" He took two mugs out of the cupboard, the Grand Canyon mug with the chip, and one with a picture of a hoodoo from Bryce Canyon. It had had a crudely glued handle when it had arrived in the mail for her birthday.

The microwave peeped and Dayton set the mugs filled with his concoction in front of each of them. "I liked to stir mine and see if I can make wishes on the bubbles like we used to do. Remember?" He captured four bubbles, squinted his eyes closed, then opened and blew across the spoon, spraying Lunie with peppermint mist.

"Want to know what I wished for? I made a wish about us, Lunie. I wished you were happier. I know I am now that I met Rhoda."

Without making a wish on the bubbles, Lunie took a sip. It was more soothing than she had expected and she was encouraged that Dayton sounded like he finally wanted to talk.

"I'm not unhappy when I'm alone in my house," she ventured. "It's the way I like it." It wasn't what she meant to say and immediately Dayton pounced.

"I think you are, and so did Mother—unhappy, I mean. She said that people who live like you do may have deep psychological problems that make them clean all the time."

Lunie knew there was no debating the issue, especially at this hour of the night. This conversation shouldn't be about her, but about Dayton, and now Rhoda.

"Where did you meet that woman?" Lunie asked, studying the mug's interior with its startling 3-D image of the canyon.

Dayton said, "Her name is Rhoda. I was trying to meet people, like my social coach had suggested, and discovered you could have a lot of friends if you joined Facebook. If you have even one friend, then you can friend their friends—you should really try it, Lunie. At first I didn't know who or what to be friends with, but then I saw companies, like the hardware store or my favorite cereal wanted me to be their Facebook friend, so I did that. My counselor was right. Friending makes the world a happier place. People send me messages all the time. I know all about new products and sales—" Dayton rubbed his beard, then stared at his sister's chin. "Your zit is really red. You ought to pop it, Lunie-soony."

Lunie quickly covered her chin with her hand. She wasn't going to let him change the subject. "What about Rhoda?" She wondered if the little black dot in her cup was part of the 3-D image—a mule or hiker perhaps in the canyon, or something else that had invaded her kitchen since her brother had arrived.

"Oh, Rhoda friended me on Facebook because we both know some of the same people, and it turns out she lives in Mosby Gap. Or used to."

"So, when did you actually meet her?"

"Tonight."

"Dayton, have you lost your mind? You meet a stranger tonight and bring her home to my house with all her stuff. She could be an axe murderer."

"Shhh," her brother said. "Your voice is so out-of-control sometimes, Lunie. It isn't *all* of her stuff. We have to get the rest tomorrow. And, if it will make you feel any better, I asked her if she was a murderer and she said no."

"She can't bring more things here."

"She has nowhere else to go. Everything's going to be fine," said Dayton. He took a long last sip. "I'll show you how to create a Facebook page in the morning after Rhoda helps me at Mother's. Then we can all friend each other. Good night." Dayton headed for Lunie's sofa, followed by Phil.

Ten

LUNIE AWAKENED TO THE SOUND of footsteps, going up, coming down, going up, coming down. She rolled over and looked at her clock. Eight-thirty. She never slept that late, even on New Year's Day.

She ran her fingers through her hair and realized she was still wearing her jeans, sweatshirt and slippers—also a first. The footsteps had disappeared in the direction of the kitchen. Without making her bed, which she always did immediately after getting up, Lunie opened her door, walked briskly past the moose and down the hall to the kitchen, where she lunged at the kitchen table.

"What are you doing?" she yelled at Rhoda.

"Calm down," said Dayton. "She's checking her e-mail."

"She's using my laptop!" said Lunie.

"Tell her I'm almost done," said Rhoda.

"She's almost done," said Dayton to his sister.

"Tell her that I like her novel," said Rhoda.

"She's been reading my novel?" Lunie's voice stuck in her throat like an aspirin swallowed without water.

"Needs more action," said Rhoda. "Your characters get trapped in scenes, like you don't know what to do with them."

"She's critiquing my novel?"

"Only the part I've read so far. There. I'm done checking in with everyone. They're all worried about me, especially because

I'm staying where I'm not welcome," said Rhoda. She closed the laptop and pushed it in Lunie's direction.

Dayton said, "My sister would be nicer if she knew your laptop had been stolen."

"I doubt it," said Rhoda. "She doesn't seem impressed by people's hard-luck stories. Did she care that your laptop was trampled by bison?"

"Not a bit," said Dayton. "She never said a word. Not one tiny word of sorry."

"I can't believe it," said Rhoda.

Ignoring them, Lunie gripped her laptop and looked around the kitchen. To her relief, only one sack crammed with stuff remained. Perhaps Dayton's van was loaded with Rhoda's things and they would be leaving soon.

"What's for breakfast, Dayton?" Rhoda asked.

Lunie took her first long, studied look at the woman. Perhaps late thirties. Coltish. Gracefully awkward. Thick dark hair that she twisted into a ponytail and pulled through the back of a mustard-colored cap emblazoned with a green logo of Zion Canyon. A face that reminded Lunie of Mount Rushmore. Rhoda's hazel eyes hardened when they caught Lunie's stare. The stranger's height and self-confidence made Lunie immediately feel oafish and crumbling. She *was* crumbling. Her world was out of control. It gave her the same sense of fear and bewilderment as the first time she entered a ladies room where everything was automated. The toilet flushed as if it were observing her every movement; the water came out of the faucet and the soap dispensed itself. Paper towels anticipated her need and dropped down before she could reach for them. She was no longer in charge. It was the toilet, though, that continued to unnerve her. What made it flush? What did it know about her? Was nothing sacred?

Dayton answered, "Let's see, we have lots of cereal. Any kind you want. Have a look in the pantry."

"Wow!" said Rhoda. "It's just like a grocery store."

Lunie pulled out a chair and quickly sat. She tried to think but couldn't. Her mind was empty. For a moment, "empty" was comforting.

"Want breakfast, Lunie?" asked Dayton.

She shook her head.

"Is your sister anorexic?" asked Rhoda, splashing milk on her granola and dried fruit.

Lunie shook her head again, but Rhoda didn't notice. She crunched her cereal.

"She's having a hard time dealing with Mother's passing," said Dayton.

He can't be serious! Lunie thought.

"Sorry about your mom." Rhoda talked while she munched with her mouth open.

"We didn't call her 'Mom,'" said Dayton, "but maybe we should." He sounded silly again. "Guess what, Lunie, we're going to *Mom's* house today. Rhoda can't wait to see *Mom's* house."

"Take trash bags," Lunie said.

Rhoda picked up the bowl and slurped the remaining milk. "Where's your dishwasher?"

"I hand wash," said Lunie.

"Nonsense, if you have a dishwasher, you should use it. More sanitary and less work." She opened the dishwasher and placed her spoon and bowl inside. *"Voila!* See, done!" She adjusted her ponytail, draped a sweatshirt of Dayton's over her shoulders, and said, "I'm ready. Dayton told me about all the wonderful things in your mom's house. Can't wait to see them."

The brown paper sack was still in the kitchen when Rhoda and Dayton went out the door. Dayton was whistling.

When they didn't return after a few minutes, Lunie took Dayton's bowl to the sink, removed Rhoda's from the dishwasher, and washed them.

She looked at the wall calendar, one that had pictures of grizzlies, bighorn sheep and elk. She would receive a failing grade for this three-week period from Professor Finbarr for

93

not completing her humor paragraph. She hadn't purchased the newest book for book club, and she was behind in yoga and Spanish. Worst of all, time was running out for finishing the novel, or even making a reasonable effort. She wished she hadn't signed up as a participant and had taken the pledge to write 1,666.6666 words a day. She couldn't even think 600 words a day or parts thereof.

She needed an extra-long session with Dr. Manngo. Buoyed by his astute, compassionate mind, she'd become her own woman again.

She found his site, and before logging in as Hana, read his recent postings of conversations with and testimonials from other clients.

In the testimonial section, a person identified only as "Happy Now" wrote:

> Dr. Manngo, how can I ever thank you enough for changing my life. I listened to your advice, friended many people, as you suggested, and now have met the love of my life.

Lunie wished she'd be able to write something like that some day. She had a lot of life-dealing to do first.

> Hana, so what's your problem?

Lunie had intended to ask for help dealing with Rhoda's arrival, but instead listened to her fingers as they typed:

> My brother and his girlfriend are going through my mother's house. SEND

> How does that make you feel?

> I don't like my mother's things, but half of her stuff is mine. SEND

Why on earth had she said that?

> You want your mother's stuff? My sister wanted all my parents things. We had a terrible argument. Had to get lawyers.

> I don't want stuff. I just want my house back. SEND

> You had a tornado, too? A tornado took away my uncle's house.

> It's just a manner of speaking. My house isn't gone, it's been taken over by other people. SEND.

There, that was better. She needed to be more careful in her choice of words. But, no matter. What was important was that Dr. Manngo understood her issues. He had had the same problem in his family—a parent's death and the division of property with a sibling.

Dr. Manngo didn't respond for forty-five seconds. Lunie glanced at the clock. She was running out of time for her session.

> Sorry for the wait. My sister Sissy called. Sounds like you need to deal with homestakers and Mother's stuff. That's important if you are going to deal with life. I have a special holiday offer $19.50. You can save forty-nine cents and we can talk again.

Yes, Dr. Manngo had once again zeroed in on the real problem. Lunie wished he had expanded the how-to of dealing with the homestakers, as he put it. That should be her question the next time. Perhaps Dr. Manngo had written a book that explained in detail the business of "dealing." Or perhaps he needed a ghostwriter to help him put his theories in readable, nonacademic form. *I've never done that, but I could learn,* thought Lunie. She would be seeing Dr. Manngo in his office—by then their final session because she would have successfully dealt with absolutely everything. Her mother's house would have been cleaned out. Dayton would be gone somewhere, taking the moose and Rhoda with him. Her novel would be picked up by a publisher. Dr. Manngo would enter the room without knocking. He would carry a bouquet of lilies, and say, beaming, "I'm more proud of you than any of the others." His hand would touch hers as he gave her the bouquet and a certificate for successful dealing. "You're strong. A good writer. Ghostwrite for me," he would say, handing her a retainer for

$1,999. "There will be more after you finish each chapter." He would then give her two boxes of detailed notes. "Your new office is just down the hall," he would say, to let her know they would be working on this closely. Together.

Phil jumped on the table and lodged himself on the keyboard.

"Didn't you get breakfast?" Lunie rubbed his ears, realizing she was quite hungry herself. Phil led the way to the refrigerator, which Lunie realized with horror, was crammed with food. So was her pantry. She discovered two bags of canned goods on the back porch. She extracted a note tucked in the top of one. "May you have better times ahead." It was signed "Your friends."

What friends? She didn't have friends, especially any that would drop off food—food she didn't want or need. She left the sacks on the porch and tripped over Phil who was rubbing against her leg. She found a can of cat food shoved at the back of a shelf now strangely full of cans of soups, children's pasta dinners, sardines, jars of mayonnaise, peanut butter, jellies and bags of dried beans. Lunie's stomach churned with disgust and growing hunger pains. This would never do.

Phil gulped the albacore tuna, which Lunie had mistaken for his seafood paté and rubbed her leg for more.

"Do you usually eat cat food?" Rhoda asked.

Lunie spun around, realizing too late that she was spreading the chicken-salmon blend on a slice of bread.

"Don't come into my house without knocking," Lunie blurted, shoving the half-sandwich back in the bread bag. "And what are you doing with Mother's lamp?"

Rhoda placed the lamp on the kitchen table. "Isn't it a piece of work? It's going upstairs in Dayton's room. He needs more light." Rhoda studied the desk lamp, one of Mother's favorite craft projects. It was made from men's belt buckles, lovingly glued into a pyramid surrounding the metal shaft that carried the cord and held the socket. The yard-sale shade was decorated with scraps of belt leather and artificial petunias. Mother liked the way the light peeped through the holes in the belts and the petunias cast floral shadows around the room.

"You should see the treasures we're finding," Rhoda continued. "It's really fun." She reached in her right pocket and pulled out a handful of plastic buttons and dropped them on the table. She then removed two golf balls from Dayton's sweatshirt hood. "I didn't know you were a golfer," said Rhoda.

"Where did you find those?" asked Lunie in alarm.

"One was on your car next to a little dent, and another was on the ground. Why?"

"No reason." Now her stomach was beyond begging for food. Lunie realized that not only had she missed breakfast, she hadn't eaten supper last night. She eyed the chunk of thick white tuna left in Phil's dish. Phil was wiping his whiskers with great satisfaction. But, before Lunie could disgrace herself by snatching it, Phil stretched, returned to his dish and savored the last morsel.

"Oh, Dayton said to tell you that he's expecting packages today. He'd like you to sign for them," Rhoda said. "I'm going back to your mom's house. See ya!"

The moment the door closed, Lunie snatched a spoon out of the drawer and grabbed the new jar of peanut butter.

Eleven

Lunie shoved the buttons aside and moved the buckle lamp to the kitchen chair. While her laptop downloaded e-mail, she ate three more gobs of peanut butter, even though this was the chunky variety and she always bought smooth. Her in-box showed three notes from Professor Finbarr. The first was a reminder to members of his online class that the humor assignment was due—no exceptions—by noon. The second was an extension to the five students who hadn't sent their paragraphs, with the notation that they would automatically receive a deduction in points for tardiness. And the third, which had arrived at four this morning, about the time that Lunie was hiding from the intruders, was more personal. "Miss Pitts, I see your light is on. I'm wondering if everything is all right. You've never missed an assignment before."

Lunie was so touched that her neighbor cared that she placed her spoon in the pile of buttons. She replied: "I'll write it today, Professor Finbarr. I've had unexpected—"

Unexpected what? Unexpected everything. She sent the message without finishing the sentence.

She had two e-mails from members of her book club asking why she hadn't joined in their chat about this month's selection. "I'm sorry, I've been—"

Been what? "I'm sorry, I've been writing a novel," she typed. There, that would sound important to a book club.

She saw a reminder from the bookstore of how many calendar days were left until the manuscripts would be collected, words counted, and prizes announced. She also had an invitation from a Mr. Alam Salmon to be her friend on Facebook. She knew no one by that name, nor did she have a Facebook page; she deleted his message. Before logging out, she checked her spam messages. Rolex had sent her four; Pfizer, two.

I wonder what Sue and Rolex are doing? Lunie opened her word program and typed "Chapter 8."

> The sun was rising above the corn when Sue realized she needed to go to the bathroom. But there was no porta-potty in sight, and no convenience stores. Just miles of cornfields and wind farms. Sue couldn't wait until they reached the big city. She tapped on Rolex's leather jacket and

"Working on your book again?" Rhoda was back with an armful of moldy sofa pillows. "I need to wash these."

"That stuff doesn't belong in my house. It's awful," said Lunie, turning the laptop so that Rhoda couldn't see what she was writing.

"Dayton says they remind him of Mom. Burnt-orange and blue were her favorite pillow colors. I bet you didn't know that." Rhoda opened the louvered doors that hid the washer and dryer. She dumped Lunie's white load from the dryer on the kitchen floor just as the doorbell rang.

"I'll get it," said Rhoda. "Just add the soap powder."

Lunie heard her tell someone to leave the boxes on the porch.

"There," Rhoda said, "I signed for them." She returned to the washer. "Hey, you didn't add the soap and I almost started the load without it."

"You're standing on my underpants," said Lunie in a childish voice that was uncomfortably familiar.

"Sorry," said Rhoda, sliding them out of her way with her foot. She pushed the start button on the washer. "Hey, Dayton would like me to bring him lunch." She moved the open jar of peanut butter to the counter. "Yuck! What's with your bread? It stinks like dead fish."

Lunie flushed with embarrassment. Rhoda studied the slice slathered with cat food, then dropped it in the trash. She found a jar of seedless strawberry jam in the refrigerator and made four thick sandwiches with the peanut butter and jam. She cut the crusts off the edges, wrapped the sandwiches in paper towels and shoved them in Dayton's sweatshirt pockets. "Come see the progress we're making," she told Lunie on her way out the door. "And, if you don't mind, put the pillows in the dryer when they're washed."

Lunie's left eyelid twitched as she surveyed her unrecognizable kitchen. Phil jumped to the counter to check out the crusts and crumbs. He ignored the open jars and gooey knife before hopping, without reprimand, on the kitchen table. He landed in the middle of the buttons, which caromed in several directions taking Lunie's spoon with them. He purred when he reached Lunie, her face buried in her hands.

I've got to keep writing. Lunie rubbed Phil's ears and moved the laptop screen where she could see it once again. The twitch made it hard to focus, but Lunie decided she had to find a way to help Sue. From the time she had learned to read, Lunie was puzzled that authors ignored their characters' body needs. Nancy Drew never went to the bathroom when she was solving a mystery. How realistic was that? Her characters would be different. She wasn't sure how far she should go with that, but Sue would at least duck into the cornfield, out of Rolex's view, and pee.

> Sue tapped on Rolex's leather jacket and he pulled the big orange Harley off to the side of the road, carefully avoiding the prairie gopher holes (Google later to learn more about Minnesota wildlife). Rolex removed his helmet, his white teeth gleaming in the morning sun, smiled and said, "Take your time, sweetie." Sue darted into the field of waving corn. Rolex dismounted,

stretched and called, "Ready or not, here I come," and the stalks parted between his eager hands.

"Hot, hot, hot," called Sue.

Not again! Rhoda was right. Lunie's characters had gone off by themselves. Lunie needed to take control. She reread the scene. Perhaps the word "eager" was too strong. "Eager" implied that Rolex had something on his mind besides bringing toilet paper to Sue, who hadn't packed any in her knapsack. And perhaps she'd been wrong to describe his teeth as "gleaming." Professor Finbarr would raise his eyebrows and ask if that indicated that Rolex was leering and planning to take advantage of Sue, who was underage. Perhaps she should make Sue older when she left home so that readers wouldn't think she was writing kiddy porn, not that she even knew what that would be like. Sue would be eighteen and a half, and would definitely have at least a box of tissues with her, or would remember from summer camp how girls should use leaves. Should Rolex ride an orange Harley or a steely blue one? Lunie deleted the paragraph and started over:

> Sue tapped on Rolex's leather jacket and he pulled the big steely blue Harley off to the side of the road, carefully avoiding foxholes. Rolex removed his orange helmet, his tobacco-stained teeth reflecting the morning sun, smiled and said, "Take your time, sweetie." Sue darted into the field of waving yellow corn. Rolex dismounted, stretched and called, "Hot, hot, hot," and the stalks parted between his calloused hands.
>
> "Bring toilet paper," called Sue.

There, that was better, and she had added another seventy-four words. Lunie didn't really want to know what was going on in the cornfield, but soon Sue and Rolex emerged, giggling. Lunie was suspicious about what they'd been up to and wasn't terribly pleased. After all, Sue was destined to become a kindergarten teacher. But maybe she needed to have a fling—sowing wild kernels—before she settled down. Should they reach the Harley only to discover that a sheriff's car had pulled up behind it, was checking the plates and asking Sue if she was the same Sue whose family had reported her missing?

No, Lunie would let them continue on to the big city and deal with the missing person's report later. Lunie didn't like the look of Rolex's teeth. Perhaps they weren't stained from tobacco. Maybe Rolex had a fatal dental disease that he hadn't told Sue about. Yes, he would die soon, and then the heartbroken Sue would decide she really needed to get that degree in education. Then, after years of teaching and unrequited love, Sue would decide to go on a cruise and would meet Bob. Now, if Lunie could just think of a way to make the kindergarten classroom interesting to adult readers, she would have the middle section worked out.

Lunie paused. Phil was on the counter again sniffing the knife she had used for cat food. If she were really going to do a reality novel, there could be a lot of situations where Sue would let the children go to the lavatory and would teach them to raise their hands for number one or number two.

The door slammed and Phil jumped down, taking the open bread bag with him.

"I'm back," said Rhoda, depositing a box of empty but not well-washed canning jars and partly burned Christmas candles on the kitchen table.

"I asked you to knock," said Lunie, her eye twitching more frequently.

"I don't think that's necessary since I am staying here. How many guests do you know that have to knock or ring every time they go in and out, but if that's what you want, you got it," Rhoda said, walking over to the washer. "Hey, I thought you were going to put the pillows in the dryer. Never mind. I guess you've been too busy. Writing."

Lunie didn't like the way she said "writing," as if it couldn't possibly be true.

"Look it, Rhoda," she said, mustering her courage, "my brother said you were only staying last night."

"Well, he's changed his mind," Rhoda said. She put her hands on her hips. "Dayton's my friend and he needs my help. As your ma always said, 'A friend in need is a friend in deed.' We're both in need, and I'm doing deeds."

Lunie's eyelids twitched furiously. "Mother never said that. Her friend, Wilma, said that."

"Dayton said Ma said it all the time. She was worried about you, too. You were so rebellious, locking them out of your room."

"It's none of your business," said Lunie.

"Dayton says you're still rejecting gifts and that you don't understand the value of all the treasures Ma saved for both of you."

"Dayton would never call her 'Ma.'"

"And just how well do you know your brother?" Rhoda pulled out a chair, and placed the buckle lamp on the floor. She sat and waited for Lunie to answer.

"I don't need to answer you," said Lunie, trying to hide her frantic eyelid.

"Go ahead. Tell me about your brother," ordered Rhoda. "What does he do for a living?"

"He's a park ranger out west during the summer, and he's going to be a walk-about for the tourist bureau during the holiday season."

"Did you ever notice the yellow shirt he wears during the summer?" Rhoda asked.

With one eye covered, Lunie noticed that Rhoda's face appeared oddly beveled, without the benefit of glass.

"His park ranger uniform." Why did her response have half a question mark at the end?

"Actually, it's his uniform for the parks' Lost-and-Found Departments," said Rhoda. "He had worked his way up to regional supervisor two years ago." She sounded smug. "And do you know what that means? After all the visitors have gone home, and before the snows close the parks, he gets first pick of everything that has been lost and found during the season. It was a perk he preferred to a cost-of-living increase. Ma was so proud."

The boxes. Those boxes. All the boxes. Mother had signed for them when they were delivered to her place, and now he was sending them to Lunie's. The chip in the rim of her Grand Canyon mug suddenly made sense.

"He never told me," Lunie stammered. "I thought he—"

"He was afraid you'd be filled with . . . scorn. That you wouldn't understand how he was helping reunite people with cameras, and water bottles, cell phones, and baby pacifiers. But if he couldn't make that reunion of lost-and-found happen for tourists from all over the world, he was ensuring that the lost would have a new home." Rhoda watched Lunie's face, waiting for a reaction. "It's rather biblical when you think about it."

Lunie couldn't respond. Her brain felt leaky. Empty. However, the boxes on her porch, and perhaps in Dayton's room, and at her mother's house, were not empty. They were filled with extreme clutter. Broken, tossed, lost, unclaimed. Unclean. She had been drinking coffee from just such a mug. Yes, she might have felt scorn, if she had anything left to feel.

"I think you need to apologize to Dayton," Rhoda said. "Make amends. You'll feel better."

"For what?" Lunie whispered in bewilderment.

"Oh, the moose, for example. Dayton said you didn't appreciate it. His feelings are hurt." Rhoda stood up. "I'll leave you with that thought to ponder while I get back to work at Ma's." She went to the back door, knocked loudly, and said, "See ya."

Lunie didn't watch her leave. She moved the white shirt buttons to spell LOST, then the mixed-sized ones to spell out FOUND. She didn't answer the next series of knocks. Rhoda would come in anyway.

"Lunie, what on earth?" It wasn't Rhoda, but Wilma.

"What has happened to your house?" asked Wilma. "I probably shouldn't put things indelicately, but judging from the, well, condition of your kitchen, I'm just wondering if . . ."

Lunie swished the buttons into a vague cloud-like formation. "I'm fine. I just have company." It sounded like a lame excuse for the canning jars, the buckle lamp, and her underwear on the floor, but it would have to do.

"Are you sick? Do you need help?" asked Wilma. "I can stay for a few minutes." She set the lamp on the counter, and wiped up the morning's cat food mess with spray bleach on a sponge.

"I'm okay. Just, uh, busy at the moment."

Wilma didn't look convinced. "Lunie, dear, you've never let *busy* get in the way of *clean*."

Lunie didn't answer. She wished Wilma would just go away, but her mother's friend seemed to have something on her mind. Wilma opened the dishwasher, loaded it with the canning jars, then said, "Actually, I just came by to ask you about the new fence at your mother's house."

"A fence? What sort of fence?" Lunie asked, panicked.

Wilma unzipped her quilted vest. "It's not your typical fence—I mean like the kind you order from a fence company, and *you, of all people,* should know what needs a permit or doesn't." She took a few careful steps toward Lunie, as if to calculate her reaction, then said in a soothing voice, "Lunie, I know you've been under stress since dear Dolce's passing. It's not easy dealing with an estate and property, especially when there is well, so much of it."

"It's okay to say hoarder," Lunie interrupted. "That's what Mother was, you know."

Wilma continued walking slowly and talking gently as if not to cause alarm with someone delusional. "You know you can call on any of us to help you, but you must also know that there are certain things that the neighbors get concerned about."

When Wilma reached the kitchen table, she carefully pulled out a chair, moved the lamp shade to the floor, and reached out to Lunie. Lunie pushed the buttons to one side and quickly put her hands in her lap.

"What don't the neighbors like about the fence?" asked Lunie, gazing at her chewed fingernails.

Wilma leaned forward trying to get Lunie to look at her. "The fence is a problem. And your new entryway is a problem. As you should well understand, none of it will pass code. You must be aware of how particular this neighborhood has always been about such things. Even your mother kept her 'stuff' behind closed doors with sheets covering the windows."

"I don't know anything about the fence," Lunie said, hoping that Wilma, an apparent delegate from the neighbors, would believe her. "I really don't."

"You'd better have a look, then. A woman I saw for the first time today going in and out of your house said you had approved it," said Wilma. She surveyed the kitchen again. "Are you sure you are okay? I've never seen such a mess in your house. You were always the neat one in the family."

Then Wilma looked down the hallway toward the front door. "You're not being held hostage or something? Should I call the police?" Wilma whispered, pretending to hold a phone to her ear.

Lunie shook her head. "I'm okay," she mouthed back. Okay was not how she felt.

Wilma closed the door quietly behind her after taking one more puzzled look down the front hall. The moose was pretty well covered with Dayton's jackets and a towel, and Rhoda had wrapped a red scarf around his long head like a turban.

Lunie considered walking down the street to see the fence. The neighbors would be coming home soon from work or shopping, and she'd rather have a private viewing than to be part of their gawking.

She thought about going in disguise, but she had few clothes in her closet and everybody knew them well. Perhaps she should just drive by—pretend she was going on an errand. That way she could just keep going if Wilma was watching or if there was a crowd. That was a better plan.

Lunie slipped into her loafers, threw on a hooded sweatshirt, and pretended not to notice the sacks of food and boxes for Dayton on the back porch. She got in her car. It wouldn't start. The empty light shown brightly. Lunie rested her head on the steering wheel. "Dayton," she muttered.

Unwilling to walk down the center of the street, Lunie darted through the yards and woods, concealing herself behind the larger trees. When she reached the lot next to Mother's, she saw what Wilma was concerned about. Mother's back and right side yard were now fenced with an assortment of doors and boards.

Dayton and Rhoda, and several people she didn't recognize were in the front yard, surveying their project. Wilma, Cara, and Omar, were on the other side of the street with digital cameras. Forgetting her plans to remain clandestine, Lunie barreled across the yard at Dayton. "Get that monstrosity out of here! Right now!"

"Lunie, you don't like it? It's fence art. All the rage in parts of the country."

"Me and my friends worked on it all day," said Rhoda. "I think you're being rude again. To all of us, including your sweet brother."

"Look what you've done! I'll never be able to get my job back at the building department," Lunie shouted.

"Hey," said Dayton, calmly, "just tell them it is on my side of the yard. See, no art fence on yours." He pointed to the uphill side of the house.

"Who are these people?" Lunie asked. There were six men and four women sitting on boxes on the lawn. One was leaning against the front porch post.

"My friends," said Rhoda. "I have lots of friends and I can tell you, that with that kind of shouting, they don't feel very welcome here."

"And what's she doing here?" Lunie was surprised to see Agnes, dressed in jeans and a denim jacket, come out of Mother's house carrying the family Bible.

"You can't have that, Agnes," said Lunie. Agnes stopped next to Dayton.

"Lunie, you said you didn't want anything from Ma's house," said Dayton. "Besides, I'm not getting rid of it. Agnes just wants to borrow it."

Lunie felt dizzy. Someone took her arm and led her across the street. "Lunie, dear," said Wilma softly. "You really don't seem well. Would you like to sit on my porch for a bit?"

Lunie allowed herself to be steered to Wilma's. Her mother's friend removed the rainproof cover from the double glider, and patted the seat next to her. "Let's just rest here together for a few minutes, dear," Wilma said, much too kindly. "Would you like a ginger snap? I have some that just came out of the oven before . . ." When Lunie nodded yes, Wilma disappeared into the house and returned with a small plate with four cookies.

"Comfort food," said Wilma. "It's important always to have comfort food handy. I've written a poem about that."

Lunie quickly ate her cookies and mumbled a thank you. She was trying to figure out what to do. A dike had broken in her life. The floodwaters had surged through the breech. They were threatening to drown her and there was no rescue boat in sight. Across the street she could see Dayton, Rhoda and their friends in a huddle. They gave a rousing cheer, clapping shoulders and slapping hands before her brother and Rhoda went back into Dolce's house. The others piled in two cars and drove off honking.

Lunie was so engrossed in their activity that she only half listened to Wilma.

"Perhaps you'd like to tell me, dear, what's going on?"

When Lunie didn't respond, Wilma sighed. "You know, you need to stop blaming yourself for your mother's death. It was a shock, but it wasn't your fault."

Lunie rocked, deep in thought.

"Well, stop by anytime," Wilma said, and went back into her house.

How could Lunie tell anyone what was going on when she didn't know herself? The glider squeaked as she rocked more vigorously. The only thing she knew for sure was that she was upset. When she was near tears as a child, Dolce always had a remedy for that. Her mother would say without sympathy, "Get a grip." Lunie needed to get a grip right now. She thought about the mess in the kitchen. She'd go home, and get a grip on that. It was time to reclaim her house. *Be assertive. Get a grip. Be assertive. Get a grip.* Lunie practically marched back up the street. It felt good to have a plan—and without consulting Dr. Manngo first.

Twelve

"KNOCK, KNOCK," SAID RHODA, walking into the kitchen carrying the sofa pillows that had been washed earlier. Dayton was right behind her clutching the buckle lamp.

"Lunie, you didn't throw out Ma's lamp?" her brother asked in a pained voice. "I found it at the curb along with the pillows."

"I did indeed, and that's where they belong." Lunie stopped sweeping and glared at both of them.

"And where are my buttons?" asked Rhoda, raising what Lunie realized were quite bushy eyebrows. "You didn't throw them out, too?"

"I did. I'm cleaning."

"Lunie, you're not being considerate," said Rhoda. "I told you Dayton wants the lamp and pillows for his room."

"It's not his room. It's my house. He's leaving. You're leaving." Lunie was surprised at the new forcefulness in her voice. *Get a grip. Get a grip.*

Dayton handed Rhoda the lamp and motioned for her to take it upstairs. She said, "See if you can find out where she hid the buttons, Dayt."

He pulled out a chair, sat down and watched Lunie sweep. She then sprayed her countertops with bleach and wiped them until they shone. She washed Phil's cat dish and refilled his water bowl. The washer beeped and she took her rewashed white load out and tossed it in the dryer. She used her favorite degreaser to scrub the stove, then wiped fingerprints off the refrigerator. The tic, which had vanished when she began cleaning, threatened to return.

"Looks nice, Lunie-cleanie," said Dayton.

"It's the way I like it and the way it's going to stay," Lunie said. She filled a mop pail with a pine cleaner and vigorously swished the floor.

"It'll look really nice for the party," he said.

"What party? There will be no party here," said Lunie, fear seeping into her voice.

"That's what I wanted to tell you. You're invited, you know. But you don't have to do any cooking or anything, unless you want to make a dip—you know, a spinach or onion dip. Enough for thirty or so."

"Dayton, you can't be serious."

"They'll be here about eight," he said, pushing back from the table.

"There will be no party. Tell them. Tell them all. No party. None." The shrillness of her voice caught Lunie by surprise.

"I can't, and won't," said Dayton. "They are Rhoda's, and now my, new friends, and I know you won't understand this, but I haven't met them yet, so I can't tell them. They can be your new friends, too. My social counselor encouraged me to have a party, you know."

"Dayton, does your social counselor know this isn't your house? Does he know that you didn't ask permission? Does he know that the person who owns the house doesn't want a party? Does he know anything?" Lunie hurled the mop at her brother, but missed, splattering gray suds on the side of the refrigerator.

"Lunie, you don't even know that my social coach is a he. He might be a she, but there you go making assumptions. You assume that I like staying here. You assume that having the party was my idea. You assume that—" Dayton stood up, and threw his hands in the air. "Lunie, oh, never mind. Let us know when supper's ready. And, if I were you, I'd cover that zit with makeup. It gets pretty red, especially when you're upset."

"I'm not fixing supper," said Lunie, but she knew her voice had not carried beyond the kitchen table.

Dayton patted the moose's leathery nose on his way up the stairs.

Get a grip. Lunie wiped down the refrigerator and the floor where the mop water had slopped. *Get a grip.* Should she call the police? Warn them there was going to be a wild party, with who knows what going on? They'd probably tell her to call back when the who knows what turned into the actual "what," and by then it would be too late. The party would be going on. And if they came, they'd have questions. Cops always have questions. They'd probably ask about the situation involving access to the front door. Then they'd come in the back door and flash their badges. Rhoda would give them chips and dips because cops always like free food, and Dayton would offer them wine or beer. Instead of breaking up the party, they'd decide to come back when their shift was over at midnight.

Lunie's eye twitched like a flickering fluorescent light. She had hoped to get a grip on her own, but it wasn't working. She opened her laptop and logged on to Dr. Manngo's site. She clicked on COUNSEL SESSION.

> Dr. Manngo: What would you like to discuss?
>
> Lunie: How do you get a grip? SEND
>
> Dr. Manngo: Get a grip?
>
> Lunie: I mean, how can I get my life back? SEND
>
> Dr. Manngo: Hmmm. Another tornado?
>
> Lunie: I mean, how do I learn to take charge. Be in control. SEND
>
> Dr. Manngo: Grip. Charge. Control. Powerful words. My mother told us never to say hate because it's such a strong word. I sometimes think hate about my sister, though. Grip's not bad. Get a grip.

That sounded pretty simple and very assertive, but what was the process?

> Lunie: How do I do that? SEND
>
> Dr. Manngo: Do what?
>
> Lunie: Grip. Take charge. Get control. SEND
>
> Dr. Manngo: Hmmm.

Dr. Manngo might need more information. More details.

> Lunie: My brother's having a party in my house. SEND
>
> Dr. Manngo: I see. Have a good time.
>
> Lunie: But, I told him he can't have the party. SEND
>
> Dr. Manngo: A sleepover can be fun for boys.
>
> Lunie: He's not a boy. He's grown-up. Late thirties. SEND
>
> Dr. Manngo: Adult parties are fun, but I must work late tonight. What time is it over?

Oh my gosh, Dr. Manngo thinks I'm inviting him. She flushed deeply and ended the session before her $19.99 time was up. *How can I ever talk with him again?*

Lunie checked the stove's digital clock: 7:18. Dr. Manngo doesn't know where I live, unless he looks up my credit card billing address. I hope he lives far away—California at least— so there's no way he could get here tonight. How unprofessional of me.

"Lunie, you should see how nice the pillows look on your sofa," said Rhoda. "They brighten your room."

"I don't want them on the sofa," said Lunie, covering her flickering eyelid.

"I think we'll put the drinks on the table, and the dip and chips on the counters," Rhoda said, extracting plastic cups and foam plates from a brown paper sack. "I think it's wonderful the way Dayton recycles everything. All you have to do is wash 'em." Rhoda filled the dishpan with soapy water. "I don't think they should go in the dishwasher. Plastic might melt."

Lunie's stomach churned. "Did he find them along the side of the road? Is that what you're telling me? You're washing trash and will use it at the party?"

Rhoda said, "You obviously aren't thinking about saving the planet. Dayton is tuned into nature. This is reuse with a capital R, Lunie. REUSE!" She dumped the cups and plates into the sink.

Lunie's stomach threatened to erupt like Old Faithful. She wouldn't stay. She couldn't be around when Dayton's so-called friends showed up and were served food and drink on and in items her brother had found along the roads and campgrounds. She grabbed her jacket, tucked her laptop under her arm, opened the back door and shrieked.

Standing in her doorway were five space aliens. "Dayton home?" asked one with large pointed ears. "We're early."

"Oh, Norton, come on in," said Rhoda, before Lunie could compose herself. "You really don't look much like Spock, but it isn't too bad."

"So you're Norton," said Dayton, emerging from the hallway. He shook his hand, and then noticed Lunie cowering by the pantry. "I became a fan of the Enterprise Trekkie Club on Facebook," said Dayton, as if that would be a satisfactory answer for his sister. "It's a great way to friend people."

"And you invited these people to my house?" Lunie whispered. She didn't wait for Dayton's response but continued out the door. Shadowy costumed figures were headed toward her.

There was no getting a grip. She had to get away. Her car was blocked by Norton's pickup. She didn't want to go back in to ask him to move it. Lunie walked down the driveway, ignoring the partygoers' hellos.

There was a light in the upstairs right bedroom in the house across the street and she thought she saw a small animal leaping at the window. That couldn't be. Nobody's home.

Professor Finbarr's lights were on, including his porch light. Wilma's kitchen was lit up, but not in the front of the house. Like Lunie, she always turned out lights when she left a room.

Oddly, there were also several lights on at Mother's. Lunie found herself walking to the back door. She'd turn them off before continuing her walk, perhaps to the coffee shop; it was open late and offered free Wi-Fi.

Mother's back door was open. Lunie flicked the kitchen light switch. If Dayton had been cleaning out things, it wasn't evident. In fact, the small path she had cleared was now an obstacle course. She pushed aside boxes and climbed over a chest of drawers stuffed with beads, yarn and dried out permanent markers. She gingerly stepped on a pile of medicine cabinets, and found herself blocked from further travel by a parrot cage, two mannikins, a weather balloon, partially inflated, and several rusty file cabinets filled with sewing patterns, gift wrap, and ten boxes of ribbon candy that Dolce had retrieved from the trash at the Dollar and Dim after their post-holiday sale ended in January 1986. It was as appealing as the chocolate chips covered with a chalky coating that her mother had found in the trash at an ice cream parlor. "I know they're stale, but I can glue them on a wreath at Valentine's Day," Dolce had told her.

Lunie still hadn't reached the source of the light, and wondered how Dayton and Rhoda had navigated the remainder of the house.

If she sat on the medicine cabinets and pulled out one of the dresser drawers, she'd be able to fashion a little desk for herself. It would be a place to write in peace for a few hours; there was no going home during the party. That hadn't been her plan when she left her house, but it now seemed like a good idea.

She checked the battery—two hours and sixteen minutes left. Lunie gingerly pulled an orange crocheted afghan from between two chairs, wrapped it over her shoulders and hunched over the computer. She wasn't sure what to do with

Rolex and Sue, so she decided to work on chapter 10. She'd skip over the part about Sue's failed marriage to the town butcher, and write about her teaching career.

Lunie remembered her own first day in kindergarten when Mrs. Simpson, who wasn't very nice, made the children march around the room to an opera—*Carmen*, to be exact. Lunie liked the music, though, and told Mrs. Simpson that she wanted to be a gypsy when she grew up. Mrs. Simpson told her that was a stupid idea and that she should aspire—she actually used the word "aspire"—to be a nurse, or a secretary, or a teacher like herself. Lunie decided that Sue would be kind and gentle with the children.

> Sue (the children knew her as Miss Coley) arrived at the Beaver Crawl Elementary School early on Monday morning. She brought two extra boxes of tissues (on sale with a coupon because it was flu season and school funding had run out for such supplies), and her new bulletin board materials. Even though it was in the middle of winter, Miss Coley was already thinking about spring and how she wouldn't have to help twenty-three six-year-olds with boots and mittens every day—not that she minded, of course, because she was a kind and gentle teacher. A very very kind and gentle teacher. However, she didn't really like wiping those red, drippy noses. Her students, especially Wayne, had chronic drips. Gooey, awful, nonstop threads of boogers . . .

I wonder if I should talk about boogers in an adult book, Lunie wondered, *but nasal discharge sounds too clinical, and this is fiction.* She decided to deal with the booger issue later. It was time to write and write and write.

> Miss Coley stepped out of her fake-fur-lined boots and slipped into her comfortable brown, laced support shoes. She checked her hem, discovering with horror that her wool skirt had shrunk in the wash (she had realized too late that she should have put it in with the pile of dry cleaning). She stepped on Wayne's sticky little wooden chair and reached high on the bulletin

board to tape the yellow spring flowers to green construction paper. She was so engrossed in her decorative design that she did not hear Mr. Pfizer, a third-
grade teacher, who aspired to be the assistant princi-
pal at Beaver Crawl Middle, enter the room.

"Ah, Miss Coley, are you not aware of the dress code?"
His tone was not that of a reprimand. Sue felt his hands,
strong from catching the basketball when he helped
out with after-school sports, encircle her waist.

"I don't want you to fall, Miss Coley."

Sue felt like she was about to faint. She was glad that
he was helping her down. Only his hands didn't return to his pockets. They spun her around and pulled
her close. She inhaled his aftershave.

Lunie stopped typing. Why can't Sue stay out of trouble?
She shouldn't be fooling around at work. She'll lose her job.

Mrs. Simpson would have slapped Mr. Pfizer's face. She
would have made him dress like a toreador, and march with
the kids. But Sue was nice and kind and gentle.

"Mr. Pfizer, the bell is about to ring," Sue said, removing his hands. "My little cherubs will be here soon."

"Will you join me for a drink later?"

Sue said, "Yes, I'd love to, Mr. Pfizer."

There, that was better. When they went out to the Golden
Prairie Dog after Mr. Pfizer was finished coaching basketball,
Sue would just order a Shirley Temple. Lunie was pleased. She
would make every effort to look after Sue. She checked the
battery level on her computer, wishing she had stuck the power
cord in her pocket. One hour and forty-eight minutes left. She
stretched and rewrapped the musty afghan that was coated
with animal hair. Lunie didn't know if her mother had acquired
it that way, or if the white fur came from one of her thirty-six
cats. The animal welfare people had removed most of them
(after receiving an anonymous tip). The "nice lady," as
Dolce described her sarcastically, said she could keep two
cats, but Dolce said they were all littermates and belonged

together. "Take them all," she said furiously, and two days later came home with Phil, who within a week dashed up the street and took refuge with Lunie.

"Dolce was heartbroken about her cats, you know," Wilma told Lunie at the calling hours. "I think that helped contribute to her cravings and her tragic end." She quickly broke off the conversation when she saw Lunie's fearful eyes morph into a blank stare. "I'm sorry, dear, I didn't mean to bring it up," said Wilma. "The memory must be painful for you. I hope you'll seek out help. I can give you a name."

Dolce's demise was only moderately painful. Lunie could only remember what the police told her and she had to accept their word, typed into an official report, as The Truth.

A box behind her shifted. The floor creaked. The clutter seemed to be cloning itself. Reproducing. What could her mother have found important in this mess? Then a light came on in the hall.

Thirteen

Lunie looked for a place to hide. There were plenty of places that could conceal her if only she could fit under or behind them, but she would likely initiate a cascade of papers, ornaments, and bric-a-brac covered with black nylon men's socks. There was a thud, and another, and an "Ouch!" Lunie pulled the afghan over her head trying to blend in with the mess. She could hear the intruder shoving things as if to try to clear a path into the hallway where she crouched, her face in her keyboard.

"Damn," said a male, only a few feet away. She lifted her head to have a look. "Good gawd, a crocheted ghost," said the voice and the accompanying body turned to try to leave the hallway. It became wedged, however, between two six-foot cartons containing pre-decorated artificial Christmas trees, which had shifted an hour earlier.

"Stop right there," said Lunie, as if the intruder had any other choice, at least not for a few moments.

"Who are you?" asked the voice.

"Who are you?" Lunie replied, wishing she had something other than a feather duster for a weapon. Her mother had a box of them in various colors.

"I'm the caretaker of this house," was the reply.

"The heck you are!" said Lunie. "My brother and I are the owners."

"I know. Dayton lets me stay here. I look after things."

"Get out," said Lunie. She was greeted with silence. "Did you hear me? You can't stay here."

"I'm stuck."

Lunie tossed the afghan on the dresser and crawled over boxes until she reached the intruder. She helped him push until he was free. She still couldn't see his face. "Who are you?" she asked again.

"Clive Turkel."

"Clive from the Dollar and Dim?"

"Yep. Little ole me. Bird-dog."

She could envision him now. Small, always in need of a shave, knit cap even in the summer. He stocked shelves, did in-town deliveries. He was the only person she knew who whistled, mostly out of tune. When he wasn't whistling, he sniffed a lot, earning him the nickname Bird-dog.

"I'm only here at night," said Clive. "Your mother hired me several years ago, and Dayton let me stay."

"Mother did what?"

"She was afraid of break-ins," said Clive, sniffing. "Someone might take her valuables."

"There's nothing of value in the House of Junk," said Lunie.

"You might be surprised," said Clive. "Collectors often save wonderful things. I bet you have no idea what's in this place. Can we sit down somewhere?"

"You tell me if that's possible," said Lunie.

"Follow me," said Clive, sniffing. He nimbly navigated his way. Lunie, carrying her laptop, struggled to keep up. They reached her mother's living room. Clive flipped on a bug-filled overhead light. Someone had cleared off one end of the sofa and a barrel-shaped brown, leatherette hassock next to it. It was the first time Lunie had seen either one in more than five years—one of the last times she had been inside to visit her mother.

"Sit," said Clive, pointing at the sofa. Lunie pushed the dusty artificial flowers farther to one side and sat. Clive eased himself on the hassock. Why am I doing this? wondered Lunie. This is insane.

"Nice in here, isn't it?" said Clive. When Lunie didn't answer, he sniffed and said, "Like some apricot brandy?" He reached under a table covered with broken packages of candy canes and garland, and pulled out two small glasses and a flask. He wiped the glasses on his jacket, then poured a brownish liquid in them. "Don't worry," he said, when Lunie recoiled. "Alcohol kills the germs." It was something Dolce always said.

Although her mind vehemently declined Clive's offer, to her surprise, her hand accepted the drink and raised it to her lips. She closed her eyes, realistically fearful that the rim would have a bead of ancient lipstick.

"Dolce vita," said Clive, clinking his glass against the flask.

The slightly thick, fruity liquid warmed Lunie's throat. She had meant to take only a polite sip, but gulped it down.

She blinked and watched as Clive extended the flask, and poured them both a second glass before she had a chance to chip off the lipstick crust.

The second glass warmed her brain; she smiled.

Clive reached under the sofa and pulled out a bag of pretzels. He blew the dust off the bag and popped it open. "Here," he said. Lunie grabbed a handful, spilling some on the floor, and handed Clive her glass for a refill. She didn't want to know whose pretzels they were or how long they had been in the house.

"Dayton says you're writing a novel," said Clive. "I like to read, so put me on your list for a copy. I have a box of graphic novels in the other room. Your mother gave them to me."

Lunie leaned back and studied Clive Turkel. "How long were you living here before Mother died?"

"Oh, just a few months. I used to bring her groceries and things. One day, she asked me to come in and I kind of felt sorry for her—living here all alone. She told me I could sleep wherever I'd like."

"And you actually found a place to stretch out in this mess?" Lunie's voice reconnected with her brain.

"Oh, eventually. Then after the accident—" Clive hesitated. "I'm sorry. I didn't mean to bring it up." He topped off Lunie's drink.

"It's okay," she said, sipping the brandy. "I really don't remember anything."

"You blocked it out. That's what Dayton says."

"What's that noise?"

"Sounds like the kitchen door," said Clive. "She often comes about now."

"Who comes now?" asked Lunie. She placed her glass between the seat cushion and the arm of the sofa.

"Agnes."

"Lucky Maids Agnes?"

"Did I hear someone say my name?" Lucky Maids Agnes, obviously knowing her way around, deftly crawled over cartons and bins.

"What's she doing here?" Agnes asked Clive.

"This is my mother's house, in case the rest of the world has forgotten," said Lunie. "I think you both need to leave."

Agnes smiled sweetly at Lunie, then turned to Clive and said, "I left it there and brought one back."

"Another big Bible?" he asked.

"Where did you leave my family Bible?" asked Lunie, wishing she hadn't quickly downed three glasses of brandy.

Clive pulled from under the couch and filled it for Agnes. "Don't fret, Lunie. I'll bet you didn't know that your family Bible wasn't from your family, did you? Your mother got it at a rummage sale, along with photos of guys with handlebar mustaches and ladies in petticoats. She said, 'Every family Bible needs a family.' I figured that was pretty thoughtful of her." Agnes tossed back her bronze curls and leaned against Clive's hassock.

"Who did you give it to? I might have wanted to look at it," said Lunie.

Agnes looked conspiratorially at Clive. "Should I let her in on my little cleaning joke?"

"I don't know," he said, glancing at the tipsy, nodding Lunie. "I don't know if she can be trusted."

"You're right," said Agnes, quickly swallowing the remaining liquid in her glass and holding it out for a refill.

"Look, Bird-dog," whispered Agnes, "guess she can't hold her brandy. Wouldn't Dolce be surprised to know that Lunie was napping in her house after all these years!"

"Well, what's it going to be for the trade tonight?" asked Clive, sniffing.

"As long as she's snoozing, I'll look upstairs if I can find my way through these trails. I'll find something interesting."

WHEN LUNIE OPENED HER EYES, Clive and Agnes were gone, their sticky brandy glasses tipped on the floor next to the couch. Someone had covered her with a second afghan. It smelled suspiciously like cat pee. She threw it aside. Her eyelid had stopped twitching, but her eyes were having trouble focusing. It was difficult to tell the time because the sheets her mother had tacked over the windows obscured the light as well as neighbors' disdainful, but curious, eyes.

Lunie struggled to her feet and tried to figure out the best way to get out of the house. More piles had shifted in the night, and the way was not as clear, especially with the overhead light turned off.

She tucked her laptop under her arm, a handicapping condition when trying to move around. For a moment she considered leaving it behind, but she knew there was a good chance she'd never find it again.

Her left foot became entangled in a beaded necklace. Trying to kick it off made things worse and caused a ballerina on top of a music box to dance for ten chilling seconds.

Lunie wondered briefly about her former bedroom—the one she had painstakingly protected from clutter as a young girl. She tried to picture it. Pristine. Dust-free. No teen heart-throb posters tacked to the walls. Everything in its place. Her clothes arranged by color in her closet. Her shoes neatly lined up. Even when Lunie had moved out, she had begged her mother not to wreck her room. Mother had simply given her a hard look and said, "When you go, I have plans for the space."

Why were those words troubling now, so many years after she had moved out? Lunie paused to get her bearings.

She left the room, and was relieved moments later when she saw a shape that looked like the refrigerator, and near it, the back door cracked open. Crisp fresh air gave her new life when she stepped outside, took a deep breath, and walked briskly up the street. Wilma was still asleep (she didn't rise until seven-thirty) but Professor Finbarr's living room light was on. There was no sign of the little animal leaping in the window of the house across the street. Lunie's eyes searched for evidence that the party was over. She shifted her laptop to under her left arm.

To her relief most of the cars that had been parked in front of her house were gone. Lunie was not surprised that her back door was unlocked, nor was she surprised that the kitchen was a mess with spilled beer and soda, food underfoot, and part of a cheese ball hanging precariously from the refrigerator door, as if someone had hurled it in a food fight. She *was* surprised, however, that two Klingons were sleeping on the floor in her living room while Dayton snored on the sofa. Dolce's ugly pillows covered his head like large ravioli on a bed of curly pasta. *Get a grip. I've got to get a grip.*

"Wake up!" Lunie said loudly, flipping on the light.

"Go'way," mumbled Dayton. "I'm sleeping."

"Not anymore," said his sister. "Time to clean up."

She touched the nearest Klingon with her foot. "Party's over."

He opened an unfocused eye, gazed at her, and closed it.

Lunie looked around in growing dismay. Worse than the mess, everyone was ignoring her. The grandfather clock struck five-thirty. Lunie decided to go back to bed. She was relieved that the bedroom door was closed. She opened it, and turned on the light only to discover that a large lump under the covers appeared to be the fully clothed Rhoda, Norton, another space alien, plus Phil. "Out," she shouted. None stirred.

Lunie went into her bathroom, checked it for inhabitants, locked the door, sat on the floor, and leaned back against the white porcelain toilet. She wished she had brought her laptop with her.

Fourteen

Hey, who's in there? Will ya hurry up?" The male voice, perhaps Norton's, awakened Lunie. For a moment she couldn't remember why she was locked in her bathroom, but then it came back with a repulsive clarity. The party. Sipping apricot brandy from a dirty glass at Mother's; the aftermath of the party. The bodies everywhere.

"I gotta go!"

"Me, too." That sounded like Rhoda.

Lunie didn't want to face them. Not like this.

She heard Norton suggest that maybe the door had locked on its own—it had happened once when he was a kid, and they should try to break it down if they couldn't jimmy the lock.

Lunie looked at the small frosted-glass window above the tub's fiberglass shower walls. She stood on the edge of the tub, cranked open the window, hoping she'd be able to gather enough spring in her knees to propel herself out of the window. The discussion about the lock became louder and more agitated. Lunie crouched, jumped, and made it halfway through the window before the door popped open, her lower legs and feet still inside.

"I knew it. A burglar," shouted Rhoda. "Norton, grab his feet!"

"I've gotta go first," said Norton. "Give me privacy." Lunie could hear a minor scuffle as her feet slipped through the window and she fell onto a bush and then to the ground. She caught her breath, heard the toilet flush, and got to her feet. When she reached the back door she could hear excited voices in the kitchen. She opened the door and nearly bumped into the space aliens on their way out.

"Lunie, I'm glad you're back," said Rhoda. "There was a burglar in your bathroom. Do you want me to call the police?"

Lunie was momentarily touched by Rhoda's concern, then remembered the scene in her bedroom; the mess in her kitchen.

"Rhoda, I want the kitchen clean by noon. I want everyone gone who's not cleaning. If not, I'll call the police and charge you all with trespassing." Lunie wondered if her voice sounded forceful enough. It didn't to her.

"Oh, Lunie-goonie, there you go again," said Dayton, appearing in his Buffalo Bill Cody boxer shorts and Capitol Reef T-shirt, followed by Klingons. "Of course, we're going to clean up. It would be rude of us not to clean up. It would be totally thoughtless of us not to clean up." He looked around at his friends. "But first, we must offer our guests breakfast, and thanks to Rhoda, we actually have food to serve our guests, and enough to share with you, Lunie."

"Dayton, you don't sound like you mean it—about cleaning up. You sound like you are just saying it. Say it like you mean it." Lunie thought of all the times he said he was going to help with the dishes, then disappeared.

"How can you talk like that in front of our guests?" Dayton pouted and rubbed his eyes like he was going to cry. Rhoda and the Klingons laughed. "See, I'm helping right now." Dayton licked at the dab of cheese ball, then peeled it off the refrigerator, used his elbow to wipe the smeary residue, and tossed the ball in a bowl. "Watch me help," he said. He picked up two plastic cups from the floor and threw them in the sink. "Look, I'm wiping a spill." He tossed a wad of paper towels into a brownish puddle and swished them around with his foot.

Lunie grabbed her laptop and power cord and brushed past Rhoda on her way to her bedroom. She yanked the sheets and blankets off her bed, and piled them in a corner, pushed her dresser against the door and flopped on the bare mattress for a moment, closed the curtains except for a crack and positioned herself so she could see if anyone was coming up the street toward her house. A cold draft reminded her that the bathroom window hadn't been closed, and she quickly cranked it shut. She gingerly picked up a wet hand towel used by Dayton's friends and threw it on top of her dirty bedding, located her favorite spray bathroom cleaner, and relaxed for the first time in several days as the little foaming bubbles coated all surfaces. She loved the way they slid like jolly miniature skiers down the sides of the shower stall, capturing every germ and trace of soap scum along the path. If she had to live in the sanity of her bathroom until she could figure out a plan to reclaim her house and life, she would.

While the bubbles did their job, Lunie sat on the floor and plugged in her laptop. She had another e-mail from Professor Finbarr and a reminder about the bookstore novel-writing countdown. (Just thirteen days left.)

> Miss Pitts: I hesitate to pry into your private life, but I am concerned as a teacher and neighbor, although I always separate the two. You have showed such promise with your creative writings. I was delighted to give you a B three weeks ago for your description of your favorite food—granola. It was one of your best paragraphs to date, but all of a sudden you have fallen behind in your work and I fear you are ill. There is still time to make up your work. Get me your paragraph on humor by the end of the day and I'll still be able to give you credit. The next assignment is to write about a vacation you'd like to take. A mere 300 words, due Friday.
>
> Now, as a neighbor, I must express the concern of all of us that—

Lunie didn't want to read about his concern as a neighbor. She would like to take a vacation to anywhere at the moment but she couldn't think of a specific location. Perhaps Sue could help her. There was no point in writing about how the drink with Mr. Pfizer went. Perhaps Sue should go to counseling for her libido. Lunie wasn't exactly sure what libido meant, but it sounded clinical and she'd look it up later. She typed: "Chapter 13 or maybe 15." She was uncertain where to continue.

But nothing came to her. Nothing. Lunie tried to envision Sue at age twenty-seven, several years of teaching kindergarten, always looking out the window across the snowfilled cornfields, hoping that Rolex would return, if not on his bike, because of the weather, then on a snowmobile, or snowplow.

> Sue saw a quickly moving dot in the gray distance, her heart magically pounding with knowing. Sue looked at all the little blond children, struggling to tie their shoes, and Wayne, his gooey face glistening. She glanced at the clock. Its big hand was on the ten and the little hand was at twenty-five. "Time for a nap," Sue told them. She knew that if any could tell time they would know that naptime came at eleven-thirty, right after early lunch. But they couldn't yet translate time on the old-fashioned clocks. All the homes now had digital timepieces. The children dutifully rolled their mats out and lay down. The dot sped closer. "Close your eyes, little ones," said Sue. They all did, except for Wayne, who was checking the size of his newest booger. (He would tell the principal when the closing bell rang and their class was still asleep, that he saw Miss Coley put on her winter coat and mittens, boots and snowshoes, open the window and leave.) Her snowshoe tracks would be covered by the time the principal, Mr. Pfizer and the school crossing guard noticed them; Rolex's snowmobile tracks were swept away in the howling gale-force winds.

Lunie rubbed her temples. Why was it so hard to come up with even a few words to write? Did Hemingway have moments or days like these? Is that why his old man was on the sea rather than in a city where there was a lot of action to imagine rather than just drifting along behind a big fish?

The sound of feet scuffling upstairs reminded her that she couldn't stay barricaded in her room and bathroom forever. She needed to work on her plan to move Dayton out and reclaim her house. It was time to have that talk.

Lunie concealed her laptop under her sweaters in the center drawer of her dresser to remove it from Rhoda's prying, shoved the dresser away from the door, and gathered dirty linens to take to the washer.

The moose, now wearing a cone-shaped party hat, seemed to follow her with his glassy eyes as Lunie walked past. She tried to remain calm even when she saw that not only had the party mess not been cleaned up in the kitchen or any other room, but also that someone had cooked breakfast and left the egg-encrusted frying pan on the stove, and sticky dishes on the table. She could leave home until Dayton and Rhoda got around to cleaning, which was likely never, or do it herself. Her eyelid twitched slightly as she ran the hot water and filled the dishpan, adding extra liquid detergent. While the dishes soaked, she collected plastic cups and plates strewn around the kitchen, and threw them in the garbage along with leftover bags of chips and the dips. Gone. In minutes all would be gone. She threw out two pointed rubber ears that she found next to the stove, and with an inner strength she didn't know she had, she tossed Dolce's sofa pillows someone placed in a corner into a large lawn bag, and emptied sloppy kitchen garbage on top of them. "There," Lunie said, triumphantly.

Her refrigerator door and counters once again sparkled, the floor was swept and washed. "There," she said again. "I got a grip. I'll tackle the living room next."

"Knock, knock," said Rhoda walking through the back door with a yellowed stuffed pillowcase. "Hi and bye," she said, passing Lunie and headed toward the stairs.

"Rhoda, tell Dayton we need to talk. Now," said Lunie.

"He's busy," said Rhoda. "I'll tell him you want an appointment."

"I don't need an appointment to talk with my brother in my own house."

"'Fraid so," called Rhoda from the stairs.

Lunie waited a moment, then followed her—the first time she had been on the second floor since Dayton had arrived. The bathroom door at the top of the stairs was open. Lunie gasped at the mounds of towels and spilled bottles of shampoo and soaps, and closed the door. Boxes and bins filled the hallway. The doorknob to the room Dayton was staying in had a DO-NOT-DISTURB sign from the Where the Deer and the Antelope Play Motel in the Grand Tetons. She heard unfamiliar voices inside, but was afraid to open the door.

The other, smaller bedroom to the left of the bathroom had a large poster board sign taped on it that read: OFFICE HOURS BY APPOINTMENT ONLY. She heard Rhoda and Dayton laughing.

Now they had gone too far. This was her Empty Room, her special place of solace. When Lunie had moved into her house she debated using the extra room for storage, but she had nothing to store in it other than a small blue overnight bag. So, rather than clutter up the ultimate clean space, she kept the bag in her bedroom closet, on a shelf above her three pairs of shoes, not that she planned to go anywhere anytime soon. At least once a week prior to Dayton's return, Lunie would go into the Empty Room, vacuum the beige carpet, and wash the window with a view up the street. In late fall through winter, she could make out the red stop sign at the top of the hill. Sometimes she counted the number of vehicles that slowed but didn't fully stop because the drivers didn't think anyone was watching. At first Lunie would also open the small closet and dust the five plastic coat hangers, but when she realized that she would never need them, she threw them in the trash and hoped her mother would not retrieve them on garbage pickup day. She winced as she remembered her mother's weekly forays into neighbors' trash bags and recycle bins, filling a small wagon that had been discarded when a family with small children had moved out of the house now occupied by Professor Finbarr.

This is the way I wish all rooms could be, Lunie had thought recently, as she unconsciously ran her hand over the window-sill, her fingers looking for evidence of freshly settled dust.

Now her fingers made a fist and she knocked hard on the door—so hard that the sign slid off.

"Who's there?" asked Rhoda.

"Open up," said Lunie, pounding harder. The door suddenly swung in, and Lunie fell forward against Dayton.

"Lunie-kaboomy," he said, "how do you like my office?"

He had made a desk with bookcases out of cement blocks and boards that he had brought from behind Mother's. Two folding chairs leaned against the desk. Three of Mother's man-nikins were garbed in his walk-about suits: the Christmas tree, the cornucopia, and the squirrel with the big bushy tail. Old newspapers spilled out of a brown paper shopping bag. Phil was exploring another bag.

"I hate it," she said. "This is my—" She was going to say "Empty Room," but it wasn't anymore and perhaps Dayton and Rhoda would find it silly that she wanted it that way.

"I told you she wouldn't like it, Dayt," said Rhoda. "It needs art, like some Ma painted."

"Not those old paint-by-numbers," objected Lunie.

"You're absolutely right, Rhoda. I like the one she painted of the white fluffy cat," said Dayton. "The orange eyes are a nice touch. It was one of Ma's most dramatic paintings when she first started. She told me that the cat was supposed to be gray with gray eyes, but she wanted to prove to people you don't need to use the recommended colors as long as you stay within the lines. She even wrote the company about her ideas."

Lunie's eyelid twitched dangerously. She stumbled over a box marked ORNAMS and two red glass balls rolled out. She was tempted to stamp on them, but didn't want to ruin her carpet. Instead she stepped over to the window and saw a county pickup round the corner and slowly come down the hill. It parked, and a man and a woman wearing tan shirts with the county's patch on their pockets got out and studied Lunie's house before walking up her driveway.

Oh, no! It was her former boss Larry, and Stephanie from Code Enforcement. Lunie didn't know if she should pretend she wasn't home or answer the door like everything was okay.

"Doorbell, Lunie," said Dayton.

The door to her no-longer Empty Room locked behind her as she walked down the stairs. The bell rang several more times at the front, then, she heard knocking at the back. She opened it just as Stephanie tucked a notice on bright yellow paper inside the storm door.

Had she waited one more minute, they would have been gone, but Larry had spotted her in the kitchen and knocked once more.

"There you are, Lunie," he said, concern on his face. "May we come in?" Lunie nodded and opened the door. Larry had a short beard for stroking thoughtfully during department meetings; eyes that had always reminded her vaguely of someone— someone like an adult Fink, perhaps. Larry wore his tan cap with the county logo, which he respectfully removed when he walked in her kitchen.

"You remember Stephanie? She brought me along and frankly, we hope you can answer, uh, questions the neighbors have raised."

Code Enforcement Stephanie, hardly out of high school, wore a tan shirt that barely buttoned and long blond hair styled to look perfectly windblown. Lunie was positive she knew why Stephanie had gotten the job, but she didn't like to be snide so she had not added to the gossipy office undercurrents.

My neighbors? My neighbors called the county? About what? Why? Lunie couldn't imagine who would report anyone if they were neighbors. People just shouldn't do that to each other. Why hadn't they spoken just spoken to her first?

Stephanie swirled her hair and glanced at Larry, then handed Lunie that yellow paper that she was going to leave at the door. Lunie knew that a yellow paper from Code Enforcement would list violations at a property. She had seen them typed and ready for delivery many times. Property owners in violation would be given notice, then warnings, and more notices and threats of fines and court action, and maybe in a year or two, if ever, depending on attorneys and who knew whom in the county administration, nothing would happen—unless maybe someone called a newspaper and a reporter had nothing better to do when the editor received the complaint.

Neighbors, usually the people lodging the complaint, would continue to protest, but nothing would happen for a long time. Lunie, along with other county employees used to decry such a system that let offenders get away with overgrown lawns, illegal fences and sheds, or roofing done without a permit on the weekend, or swimming pools dug too close to a property line. Lunie's heart pounded as she read the typed list.

1. Front entryway improperly constructed and without a permit at 4027 Bilgewater. Property owner, Lunette Pitts.

2. Illegal fence at property owned by Lunette Pitts and Dayton Pitts, heirs of Dolce Pitts, 4073 Bilgewater.

3. Shed at 4073 Bilgewater installed without permit.

4. Excessive trash in yard at 4073 Bilgewater, to wit, large chest freezer, two refrigerators and twenty studded tires.

Lunie wasn't sure if the county could regulate trash on a property, but they had added it to the particulars.

The notice said she had thirty days to deal with the infractions or face a series of penalties. Stephanie handed her a pen with the logo of an interstate motel. "Sign here," she said, staring at Lunie's twitching eyelid.

"Is everything okay, Lunie?" asked Larry, stroking his beard. "Frankly, we were worried about you when we had the call. It just isn't like you to, uh—"

"Thanks for stopping by," said Lunie, wanting them out of her kitchen before Dayton, Rhoda, or anyone else who was upstairs came down.

"We'll be checking on your progress," said Stephanie. "I know you'll want to get it all taken care of rather than endure the publicity or shame."

"That's enough," Larry said curtly. "Lunie's been an excellent employee. I know we can count on her." He smiled warmly and said, "Lunie, we're hoping that we'll be able to bring folks back to work at some point, although it might not be at the end of the month."

"Thanks, Larry," said Lunie, knowing he hadn't said anything that would give her grounds for thanks, but it sounded polite, like the model employee she had been. She watched them walk down the back steps. Thirty days. Thirty days. She was supposed to finish her novel in thirty days, and was challenged to deal with Dayton in the same block of time. How could she do that when she couldn't get a grip that she could hang on to?

And what about her neighbors? Who would have reported her? Wilma, who had befriended her mother all those years? But Wilma had recently reminded her that her mother's stuff was hidden behind sheeted windows, not out in the open. What about Professor Finbarr? Doubtful. He seemed to be too much in his own world. Cara Newton? Omar Billings? Or was it the family building a four-bedroom house on a two-acre lot just downhill from Mother's?

Progress had been slow on the Townsends' new home, even with downturn in the housing market. No one could understand why it was difficult to get subcontractors to stay on the job when work was so scarce. Wasn't the Townsends' Dumpster surrounded by tossed cans on the property a bigger eyesore than Dayton's nonfunctioning freezer, fence, or shed? Besides, when they placed it on the edge of Mother's property line, no one complained to the county about the lack of a setback.

The thought of that Dumpster made Lunie shudder as if it were haunted instead of containing construction debris. The Dumpster recently filled her dreams, a giant gray box oozing with bitter rotting fruit and spilled rum, creeping into her house, looming near her bed, rats steering it until it located the cowering Lunie. Did anyone else have Dumpster dreams?

Lunie studied the official yellow paper. It was something she definitely wanted Dayton to see. They would have to have their big discussion now. She placed the paper on the counter near the refrigerator.

Hearing no sounds from upstairs, she plugged in her laptop, found a bookmark for Dr. Manngo's Web site and read the new sample conversation he posted on his homepage.

>Dr. Manngo: So, how was the get-together?

>DP: Great. My new friends came. Thank you, thank you, Dr. Manngo for giving me new social courage and a new life. I'm so happy now. I probably won't need to talk with you for awhile.

>Dr. Manngo: You are a good learner. Keep friending.

Lunie wished she could boast of similar results. *I'm not even an inspiration to me.* Without thinking, she logged in as herself, realizing with immediate dread that the last time she had consulted him she may have stepped over the line of acceptable conduct between a professional and client. Fortunately, he seemed to have forgotten.

>Dr. Manngo: What concerns you today, dear?

>Lunie: I have nightmares about Dumpsters. SEND

>Dr. Manngo: About what?

>Lunie: A big box that you throw away things in, like trash. SEND

>Dr. Manngo: You had a dream about a Dumpster? What were you throwing away?

>Lunie: It was filled with lots of other boxes. The big box frightens me because it follows me in my dreams. SEND

There was no response for several moments, then,

> Dr. Manngo: I've been looking up the meaning in my dream book. The box means control; restraint. Deal with the box . . .

Why hadn't she thought of that? The Dumpster—certainly a box—was a symbol of trying to control her world. How simple. How pure. How helpful he was as always. She typed a thank you, and with still no sound from above, checked her e-mail. If things stayed this quiet, she might be able to work on her novel.

Professor Finbarr had posted a new assignment for his unseen class: Write a one-page description of a happy childhood moment—not your childhood, but of someone close to you. Describe the weather, the people, the emotions. It will be due in a week. This will improve your interviewing skills, he had noted.

Lunie was relieved that the happy moment did not have to come from her own childhood. With Dayton her only close living family member—at least that she was aware of—she supposed she could ask him. Perhaps that would be a way to settle him down at the kitchen table, where after the casual "interview" for her assignment, she could shove the yellow paper into his hands and she would say, "Reality time," and they would finally talk. Should she let Rhoda sit in? No, this was between her and Dayton.

It would be like the old days when she was nine and he was six and they brushed away the newest layer of clutter on Mother's kitchen table so they could fix cocoa after school. On the days when the cocoa tin was buried beyond excavation by their little hands, they'd "fix" it topped with whipped cream in imaginary mugs. She would make Dayton giggle when she pretended to blow it cool. Pretend cocoa tasted better than pretend tea, they decided.

Dayton rarely seemed to mind the ever-growing heaps and mounds of junk in Mother's kitchen. But when they couldn't find the cocoa for the third week in a row, Dayton's eyes filled. Lunie grabbed his pudgy hand. "Let's run away," she proposed.

"Where?" he asked, alarmed and intrigued.

"Far," said Lunie, "To the Land of Nice and Clean. To the Land of Real Cocoa."

"That's sounds like fun," he said. "I've got to give Mother a kiss good-bye."

"Don't tell her it's a good-bye kiss. Tell her it's a hello kiss because you just came home from school."

"Okay," said Dayton. He returned a few minutes later. "I could hear her but I couldn't see her, so I made a paper-airplane note."

"A note?"

"I told her it wasn't a good-bye note because we were running away, but a hello note because we just came home from school."

Lunie wasn't surprised that Dolce had hollered for them to come back before they reached the curb. She was almost relieved because she hadn't figured out where they would go, and it was already getting dark.

Yes, she'd see if Dayton had any happy memories.

Fifteen

RHODA ANSWERED LUNIE'S KNOCK on Dayton's office door. "Do you have an appointment?" she asked.

Lunie briefly debated arguing about it, then said, "I'd like to make one, please, with my brother."

"Your name?"

"Lunie."

"He's free at three-thirty."

"That will do," said Lunie.

"Three-thirty tomorrow," said Rhoda.

"I need an appointment today," said Lunie.

"He's rather busy at the moment."

"I need an appointment now," said Lunie, adding, "I have a busy schedule, too."

The door opened. Dayton dressed in his Christmas tree walk-about costume, without the presents strapped around his ankles, said, "Rhoda, you didn't tell me it was my big sister Lunie." He reached out to hug her, his cloth branches dangling with shiny fabric ornaments. "Please come in." A five-inch star, powered by a hidden battery, twinkled on his head.

"Lunie would like to see you. Now," said Rhoda. "I told her you were busy." She was beginning to sound like Evelyn, the receptionist, who answered phones for the Mosby Gap Building Department. Evelyn had cultivated a pleasant but officious manner, which earned her marks on her annual review for professionalism, but let customers and co-workers know that she was the gate-keeper, the troll at the bridge, the dragon at the moat.

"I always have time for my sister," said Dayton. "I'm not totally set up yet, but please have a chair."

Lunie followed his gesture to a folding chair. "I didn't bring a writing pad," she said.

"I have one of Ma's in my supply cupboard," said Dayton. Rhoda quickly opened the closet door, found a pad and handed it to Lunie.

"I need a pen, too."

Rhoda muttered, "You should have asked for it at the same time."

Dayton sat at his desk, his bearded face encircled by garlands and a hood that looked like pine branches.

"What is it, Lunie-dearie? You seem so distracted lately."

Lunie looked at Rhoda, then turned to her brother. "Can't we talk alone?" she asked.

"Rhoda's my confidential secretary. It's okay for her to stay," said Dayton. Rhoda slid to the floor and leaned against the brick and board shelves filled with what appeared to be objects from the park's lost-and-found collection. There were mugs, four binoculars, fifteen digital cameras, ten baby pacifiers, two full water bottles, several dog-eared AAA guidebooks to the West, a pile of maps, three hunting knives, and a canvas-covered canteen.

"First," said Lunie, "my creative writing professor has given me an assignment that I need your help with."

"Sure," said Dayton. "And second?"

"I want to do the first thing first."

"That's your problem, Lunie," said Dayton, cheerfully. "You always go in order. You create order. You thrive on order and you're miserable. If you want to have more fun in your life, you need to do the second thing first. Eat your dessert before your soup. Start at the last chapter of a book and read it backwards."

Lunie realized that Rhoda was taking notes.

"Order doesn't make me miserable. It makes me happy," said Lunie.

"I guess I won't be able to change you in one appointment," said Dayton, "so we'll do it your way today."

"First," Lunie began again, "for my creative writing class, I'm supposed to interview a family member about a happy childhood memory. It's just a one-page essay, so it doesn't need to be a long memory." She watched the Christmas tree's face. It went from smiling to puzzled, then troubled. Dayton turned off the switch to the twinkling star. He pulled his hood off and ran his fingers through his thinning hair.

"Lunie, you may have short happy memories, but I have really long ones. Let me think. What would be a fun one to tell." She watched his face for a sign of happiness, but his brows furrowed. Maybe prompting would help.

"Do you remember when we ran away because we didn't have cocoa?"

"I do," he said with a smile. "Yes, we ran away because Mother had given us a dollar each to go to the store to get cocoa, or maybe we borrowed the money from her purse. Yes, we ran away and had a great time."

Rhoda scribbled.

Lunie didn't remember his version at all. She decided to ask about something else, "What about pets? Do you have a happy memory of a pet? I just need one happy memory."

"Yes, let's see. Yes, I remember Sparkly 27, my favorite of all the black cats named Sparkly. Yes, he was lots of fun." He looked desperately at the clock and then Rhoda. "What was the second thing you wanted to know, Lunie?" he asked.

She was so stunned that ever-cheerful Dayton apparently couldn't remember anything happy that she momentarily lost her resolve to bring up the code enforcement paper. But she might not be able to get another appointment with him, especially if Rhoda thought it might be upsetting. Secretaries have a way of shielding their bosses from people who want to make appointments. Evelyn had kept angry contractors from talking to Larry on more than one occasion. "Have a seat," Evelyn would say. And then an hour later, she would announce that Larry was still on a conference call and could they come back another day.

"The second thing is this." Lunie removed the folded yellow paper from her pocket and handed it to Dayton.

"Lunie, this is terrible. Terrible. What kind of people would write you up?" He handed the paper to Rhoda, who raised her eyebrows and notes on a legal pad.

"You see, we must take care of everything. We have a time limit now. Thirty days. The fence has to go. The front entrance made out of doors must go, and we really should clean out Mother's," Lunie said.

"How does my calendar look?" Dayton asked Rhoda.

"Busy," she said. "Very busy."

"There you have it," he said. "Busy."

Lunie felt a twitch in her lip, pulling it slightly to the right. She hoped it would not be misinterpreted as a flicker of a smile. She was not smiling. She reached for the yellow paper.

"I will need a copy for the files," said Rhoda, looking at her large watch with a fake-fur band that barely covered a tattooed bracelet of hearts and daggers. "I believe that your time is up. Dayton's next appointment will be here momentarily."

"My house isn't zoned commercial," said Lunie.

"I didn't see a complaint about Dayton's Rent-a-Walk-About listed on your paper from the county," said Rhoda. "I'd think you'd want to support your brother in his new business endeavor."

Dayton was fidgeting, folding and unfolding his hands. "Maybe my favorite pet was Harley, the goldfish," he said. "I don't think he ate a lot. He swam well, though."

"That's because he was plastic. You wound him up," said Lunie, remembering that Dayton played with Harley in the toilet, an improvised fishbowl, watching him swim and make bubbles.

"Harley was very real to me, Lunie," said Dayton, slipping the Christmas tree hood back over his head. The two short branches on the side of his head received a slight lift from the angle of his ears.

"That's all for today," said Rhoda.

Lunie absurdly wondered if she should thank her brother for his time. Instead, she simply left the room, hating Harley, and glad that Dayton didn't remember that she was the one responsible for Harley's disappearance with a deliberate flush.

"Close the door, please," said Rhoda.

Lunie ignored her and went down the stairs.

Sixteen

THE MOOSE'S PARTY HAT had disappeared, but hanging over his nose was a small, scrawled sign that indicated that the walk-about business was to the left at the top of the stairs. Lunie removed the sign and tore it up. "This will never do," she said to the moose. "I won't have more strangers traipsing all over my house."

Lunie absently wandered into her living room, still a mess from the party. She gathered the cups, cans, and papers, vacuumed popcorn and chips, wiped drips from drinks off the coffee table, and straightened the lamp shades. She also removed and ripped a poster of Spock that she found taped to the back of the door. Just before she sat on the sofa, she snatched Dolce's orange afghan that Dayton had brought over from Mother's and stuffed it in a garbage bag. It was a reminder of the seemingly unending task at a house near the bottom of the hill and her mother's lack of decorating taste or cleaning.

Lunie curled up and watched twilight stalk the fading afternoon sun outside her window, then deepening shadows crept into the room. She knew she should be writing up her interview with Dayton. Professor Finbarr would be surprised and pleased if she finished it not only on time, but early. What to say? Dayton hadn't told her anything remotely happy. Maybe she should just make up something. She thought hard. Perhaps she could come up with a happy memory from someone else's childhood. Who did she know who had been happy when she was in elementary school? It seemed like everyone else had been happy. Happy mothers. Happy fathers. Happy siblings. Happy real pets. Happy trips. Happy presents.

Happy presents? Lunie uncurled and put her feet on the floor, ready for motion. She remembered that one day during show-and-tell, Fink's father had arrived with an enormous locked wooden crate. Throughout the school year everyone else had brought in small objects or pets to talk about. Frankie had a dead snake; Bev had new makeup; Eve, her grandmother's Valentines; Harvey, a potato masher he said had belonged to Thomas Jefferson. That had set off an impromptu unit on foods served during the Revolutionary War.

Lunie had squirmed with worry. She was afraid that her classmates would make fun of Fink in front of his father. No one had arrived with an object this large, and no one else had needed parental help with their ten minutes in the show-and-tell spotlight. Lunie had been astonished at how similar Big and Little Fink looked. Both had slicked-back hair, glasses with thick frames and soft brown eyes. Beaming, Little Fink had gone to the front of the class and the two of them carefully opened the crate that stood almost as tall as Little Fink.

Inside was the happiest present Fink had ever received, he told the class. A vintage wooden Buster Brown Shoes Fluoroscope Machine that still worked. He and his father demonstrated how, when you stood on it in just the right place and looked down a tube, you could see the bones in your feet. The actual bones! Through your shoes. Fink said, "That way, you knew what size shoes you should wear and how they'd fit!"

Little Fink placed his feet in the machine, looked down the tube, and said, "Wow! This is so cool!" All the kids wanted to try it, too, but Mrs. Braxton said notes were needed from their parents because you could get an overdose from X-rays and then you'd never be able to have children and your hair might fall out before you were twenty. So, all the class could do was watch Fink happily wiggling his feet and saying, "Wow! I can see my talus and my medial cuneiform." Lunie watched Mrs. Braxton's heavy-lidded eyes flicker with obvious concern when she heard those words. "That's enough, Fink," Mrs. Braxton said, much too sweetly, as she quickly gazed around the class to see if anyone might react inappropriately. "But, thank you for sharing."

Fink and his father carefully packed up the Buster Brown Shoes Fluoroscope Machine while several boys whispered "cuneiform" and "talus." Fink's popularity had soared from about two, on a good day, to a ten. It had to be one of his happiest educational moments. One of the happiest days of his life.

Yes, Lunie would write about the day that Dayton brought his Buster Brown Shoes Fluoroscope Machine to school and all the children got to look at the bones in their feet without taking off their shoes and without notes from their parents. She would write about how she and Dayton—no, Dolce and Dayton wheeled the crate down the street on Dayton's shiny red wagon to the school. How proud her mother was to stand in front of Mr. Humpert's class so that Dayton could show off his best birthday present ever. Dolce would have her hair combed back and would be wearing the brand-new orange dress with white polka-dots that she bought at a department store. Dayton, wearing a starchy navy shirt and pressed khaki pants, would beam happily.

Lunie would then write about how she had helped her mother pick out the amazing machine at an auction and how she and Dayton played shoe salesman every afternoon after school. And then, when they were tired of looking at their talus' or cuneiforms, they would have hot cocoa. Real hot cocoa in a real cup. A clean cup.

And she would end her story with a few sentences that revealed how this single happy event had inspired Dayton to become a collector of oddities, including all things mechanical.

Lunie's anger was slowly ebbing as she saw Dayton in this new light—her happy little brother wanting to share with his classmates his excitement of owning a special device. And then, he would be popular.

But, Lunie frowned, the story would need to stop there, because Dayton would never be able to bring his classmates home. He'd have to enjoy his collection of oddities, including windup toys, if they worked, all by himself.

She was about to stand up and go to the kitchen when someone flicked on the overhead light. "Whatcha doing sitting in the dark?" asked Rhoda.

"Thinking," replied Lunie, even though she didn't feel Rhoda deserved an explanation.

Rhoda plopped down on the beige recliner and put her feet up. "Got a moment?" she asked.

"Not really. I have work to do," said Lunie.

"I'd like to ask you a few questions," said Rhoda, taking a pen and small spiral pad out of her pocket. When Lunie didn't respond, Rhoda continued. "In addition to helping Dayton with his secretarial needs, I've offered to ghostwrite his life story, so I'd like to ask you some questions."

Lunie gulped. "Dayton has a life story?"

"I don't know why you're so surprised. Everyone has a story in them. I bet even you have one, too."

Lunie didn't respond; couldn't respond.

"I might need to borrow your laptop from time to time so I don't have to use Clive's," said Rhoda.

Lunie's voice returned. "Absolutely not!"

"That's what Dayton said you'd say," said Rhoda, sighing. "We'll locate your mom's computer soon. It was almost new. A gift from Agnes. Meanwhile, I have good handwriting."

"I have to go," said Lunie. She stood and banged into the coffee table with her shin, then hobbled into the kitchen.

"Tomorrow then," called Rhoda. "We'll start with happy memories, and then we'll get into the good stuff."

Seventeen

THE CONTENTS OF LUNIE'S refrigerator and cupboards were so foreign that she felt like she had wandered into a stranger's kitchen. Bags of groceries from "friends" remained unopened; her shelves were filled with varieties of cereal, canned goods, jams and jars of peanut butter. Her refrigerator bulged with barely covered plastic-wrapped containers of what looked like party food that had been left out overnight. She longed for a little container of plain yogurt, or a package of turkey bologna with a future, not past, expiration date.

Her stomach was complaining about lack of nourishment, but not wishing to venture downtown to the café for a bite to eat, Lunie studied the cans in the cupboard. She decided to have chicken noodle soup for supper, hoping it was the can she had purchased a week earlier, not something from Mother's that Dayton or Rhoda had placed on the shelf.

While the soup heated, she plugged in her laptop and began writing her essay titled "Dayton's Happy Memory." Her fingers jogged along at a satisfying pace. By the time she finished the can of soup and a sleeve of salty crackers topped with peanut butter, she completed the assignment and felt proud of Dayton's show-and-tell, and how nice her mother had looked that day. Lunie even mentioned that she loved him. That made the memory sound even happier. After checking the spelling and rereading the piece one more time, mouthing the words, Lunie e-mailed the essay to Professor Finbarr.

She felt a sense of peace and creativity for the first time in several days and decided to work on her novel.

She wasn't sure she knew where Sue and Rolex went in the storm—that could be explained later. Did they marry? Did they part? Did Sue get pregnant and have a child out of wedlock? No, not Sue.

Lunie decided to start at a different point in Sue's life and then figure out how to connect all the pieces later.

> Chapter 17.
>
> Sue went back to teaching kindergarten, this time near the little town of Starbuck, because she liked the name and knew no one there. The little school was desperate for teachers and didn't check her past record. Sue was grateful for the opportunity to start over, without questions being asked, and vowed she would give her class the same benefit of the doubt if little Lars snitched on little Ollie. She would teach them how to spell "second chance" and "redemption" for their first vocabulary words.
>
> On her second day of teaching, shortly after Lars freed the grasshopper from his lunch box, Sue saw the principal, Mr. Olsen, observing her through the glass pane in her door. He had blond wavy hair, deep blue eyes, and ruddy cheeks, even in August. He smiled and opened the door. "I'd be happy to help you catch the grasshopper, Miss Coley," he said. He joined her crawling between the little desks, their hands occasionally brushing as the insect stayed a leap ahead.
>
> Little Ollie ended the chase by smooshing the grasshopper, and thus creating loud wails from Lars and his friends.
>
> "Let me help you up," said Mr. Olsen, taking Sue's hand. "Do you think it's hot in here?"
>
> "Hot? Yes, hot," she said, flustered.

Lunie said, "It never ends."

"What never ends?" asked Rhoda, pulling out a chair.

"Nothing," said Lunie, hitting "save," then closing the laptop. "Nothing ever ends."

"Hmm," said Rhoda, "I was hoping we could have a little chat."

"I have nothing to chat about," said Lunie.

"Did you know that your brother makes his squirrel walkabout debut tomorrow to kick off the festival?"

When Lunie didn't respond, Rhoda said, "I didn't think you knew. It would make him very happy if you'd come downtown and watch him."

Lunie thought for a moment and shook her head no.

"Dayton needs your encouragement," Rhoda said softly, ready to pounce. "He's a very sensitive person, you know. He feels you have had nothing to offer but criticism since he came home." She leaned forward, "It's important that you be there. Do it for Dayton. Do it for Dolce." Her eyes were dewy with emotion.

Lunie blinked. Her lip twitched. Was that the way Dayton really thought about her? Someone who didn't care about him? Someone critical and selfish, as Rhoda had inferred?

"Okay," she said without enthusiasm.

"Wonderful!" said Rhoda. "We need to go in your car because his costume won't fit in his camper until he has time to clean it out and I'll have my costume, too."

"Huh?"

"I'm an acorn, and we have a sunflower seed costume for you."

"Never!" said Lunie.

"Never say never!" said Rhoda. "I'll tell Dayton, but first put on your coat and come with me."

"Where?"

"I think we need to check out the house across the street. Dayton's worried about it."

"At this hour of the night?"

"It's only 9:15," said Rhoda glancing at her large wristwatch.

"They might be in bed," said Lunie.

"Then we'll find them at home. Dayton says nobody's seen them in days. Neighbors should check on neighbors."

Lunie did not want to go across the street. She did not want to walk up to the door with Rhoda and knock. It wasn't their business to butt into the new neighbors' affairs. The new people hadn't been particularly friendly and their decision to cut down so many trees had upset more than just Lunie. It was possible that they were involved in illegal activities, such as making bathtub gin, or running a diaper service without a permit.

"From my room," said Rhoda, "I have observed lights on in different parts of the house. Don't you think that's odd?"

Lunie was about to object to Rhoda calling the guest bedroom "her room," but said, "People do turn lights on in different rooms at night."

"Yeah," said Rhoda, holding out Lunie's green jacket, "but factor in the golf balls, and we've got a real mystery here." She looked down, "Don't forget your shoes."

"Is Dayton going with us?"

"He's going to watch out my window, and will call the police if need be," said Rhoda. "That way, if we're overpowered, we have backup."

Lunie didn't like the sound of that at all. Overpowered by whom?

Rhoda went to the bottom of the stairs, put her fingers between her teeth and whistled like she was calling a cab. "That's the signal that we're ready to go out the back door," she said.

Lunie followed Rhoda as she ducked behind bushes and darted across the street. Rhoda looked back and saluted Dayton's silhouette holding binoculars in the upstairs window.

"C'mon," Rhoda whispered, "and be quiet on the steps."

Lunie reluctantly followed. "Knock," whispered Rhoda. When Lunie didn't move Rhoda said, "All right then," and she let the door knocker fall.

"Let's go," said Lunie. "Nobody's home."

"Shhh, I hear voices." Rhoda put her ear to the green wooden door. "Two voices."

"Let's go," repeated Lunie. "Somebody *is* home."

Rhoda found the doorbell and pushed twice.

"Why didja do that?" Lunie stepped away into deeper shadows.

The voices were closer, arguing. Lunie could hear the deadbolt turn and then the doorknob. The door opened four inches, the length of the security chain.

"What do you want at this hour?" asked a man. "Didn't you see the no solicitation sign?"

"Not selling anything," replied Rhoda. "I'm Lunie from across the street. We just wanted to invite you folks for dinner Friday night."

"I'll talk to the wife, but the answer is no," said the man. They heard whining at his feet, and saw a long thin nose sticking out the door about three inches off the ground. "Back, Scooter," said the man. But Scooter didn't go back, the tiny dog slipped through the door, scurried over Rhoda's shoe and down the steps.

"Damn, look what you've done!" shouted the man. "You let my dog out. If anything happens to Scooter, the only person who will be at your house on Friday is my attorney." They heard him yelling for his wife to get him a coat.

"We've got to catch the dog," said Lunie. In the distance they could hear the yipping of an unnaturally small animal.

"I hope we can," said Rhoda, "but it's very fast."

LUNIE TRIED TO SORT OUT THE rest of the evening's events when she awoke at five-thirty. Squad cars had come from both ends of the block—the ones dispatched after Dayton's frantic call for help, and the others arriving at the request of the neighbors whose little Scooter had escaped and was still missing. The neighbors wanted the valuable pedigreed and trademarked dog found immediately and Lunie arrested for disturbing their peace and causing their pet, which they had planned to use as a stud, to get loose in the dark of night.

Their names, Lunie had learned when the rookies were gathering information for their official report, were Stubb and Alaina Sanders. When the cops radioed their names into headquarters as part of a routine check, they discovered they were wanted in Idaho for shooting potatoes through a PVC pipe at animal control officers who were investigating their dog-breeding business. Animal rights activists had claimed it was inhumane to reduce the noble greyhound to a creature as small as a squirrel so that it could be raced on a Ping-Pong table track. The Sanders' claim that they had a right to bear potatoes did not impress the law, and they had left town before their court appearance.

Lunie had remained hidden behind a tree while the cops interrogated Rhoda, who continued saying she was "Lunie." By now Rhoda knew enough about the family to sound convincing. Lunie decided it was better to remain out of sight than to correct her on particulars, such as the date of her mother's death.

The rest was a blur. There were ugly murmurs from the Sanders as they got in the patrol car that they would get even. The flashing lights went off as the car turned to go up the street, then it stopped and the cop at the wheel lowered his window. He asked Rhoda-Lunie if she'd call them if she found the dog. "Sure nuf," Rhoda replied and took the officer's card.

"Guess the Sanders won't be going to Omar's neighborhood potluck," said Rhoda, reading the invitation that Omar Billings had handed out to everyone at the scene, including the cops. "I'm making brats and sauerkraut. What are you taking? Your mother's jelly bean gelatin? It would probably make a better Easter salad."

"I'm taking an aspirin and going to bed," said Lunie, walking home quickly.

Lunie had forgotten that she hadn't remade the bed after washing everything that morning. She folded her favorite tan sweater for a pillow and curled up under her soft chenille robe.

Eighteen

WILMA WOLENSKI WAS SIPPING coffee out of a Grand Canyon South Rim mug, one Lunie had noticed in Dayton's office the day before.

"There you are, Lunie," said Wilma. "I was just about to leave. I didn't realize you were such a late riser."

"Wilma stopped by with a new poem for you," said Rhoda, "and then she wanted to know what was going on last night. It's all over the block—how you stood up to those awful people and rescued their dogs."

"What?" Lunie looked at Rhoda in bewilderment tinted with newfound rage.

"I guess I missed all the excitement—my Bunco night, you know," said Wilma. "Rhoda says she wants to learn how to play the game."

"I just love Wilma's poems," said Rhoda. "She's going to give me a copy of each of her little chap books."

Wilma took a long sip, studied Lunie's unwashed face, uncombed hair, rumpled clothes, and said, "Well, I'd best be going. I'm proud of your fortitude and helping nab those criminals. And I'm so glad Rhoda is here to help you with everything. What a precious friend." She dabbed at her eyes with a paper napkin stained with a ring of coffee from the brown seeping crack in the canyon wall. "Your mother and I were friends like that." She handed the typed poem to Rhoda who handed it to Lunie, who was still standing near the kitchen table.

"It's titled 'Make New Friends'," said Rhoda. "Aren't you going to thank her?"

"Thank you, Wilma. I wasn't expecting company," said Lunie. She ran her fingers through her hair.

As soon as her mother's friend left, Lunie slapped the poem on the table. "Rhoda," she fumed, "you can't keep telling people you're me and that I am doing things that you did. You are not my friend. You don't belong here. I want you out." Her voice trembled. She grabbed the back of a chair to keep from throwing something. The toaster. The mug. The poem.

"You'll feel better after you have a cup of coffee," said Rhoda. "Don't forget to get things done this morning because we all have to be downtown by two when the Southern Sons of Nutcrackers assemble. And we'll be discussing our role in the Harvest Festival. The city decided not to call it Thanksgiving anymore because someone on the city council said that not everyone is thankful and he didn't want to alienate anyone."

"I'm going for a walk," said Lunie, pouring her coffee into a travel mug.

"Dayton would like some crime scene tape for his office," said Rhoda. "Could you ask the officers for a few feet?"

Lunie slammed the porch door and immediately regretted the fact that in her haste she had forgotten a jacket and her shoes. She went back in. Rhoda had already gone upstairs.

When she went back down the driveway she realized that indeed the cops were still across the street, taking pictures, measuring, writing, talking. Cara Newton was attempting to drag Harvard and Yale away from the 4030 Bilgewater driveway. They barked and snarled at a sniffer dog being unloaded from the K-9 truck. "Take them away, please," said the sniffer dog's handler.

Cara yanked the leashes. "Our hero!" she called across the street.

"I didn't do anything," said Lunie.

"That's what all heroes say," said Cara, jerking at the dogs' choke collars as they wrapped themselves around each other.

"If it hadn't been for you—"

Lunie broke into a jog, then stopped to take her first sip of coffee when she passed the professor's house. He opened his front door and waved. *He must be going to class,* thought Lunie.

"Oh, Miss Pitts," he said loudly, "may I have a moment of your time?"

Lunie paused, then walked up his drive.

"Miss Pitts, I was most impressed by your story about your brother's happiest memory. It's one of your best essays, and frankly, the best I've seen on the subject in this class. Nice descriptions. Strong verbs. Good action and intrigue about what was in the large crate."

Lunie blushed with pleasure.

"But, Miss Pitts, I am puzzled by one entry. You refer to Dayton at one point as Fink. Did you mean that? You know the word has certain connotations, and it was a bit jarring when you wrote that you had never loved Fink more."

Lunie's blush deepened, now with embarrassment. "It was a typo. I meant 'think.' It should have read that I think I never loved Dayton more. May I change it?"

"Certainly," said the professor, "especially because you got your work in so early. I'd still like you to write your piece on humor. You have quite a flare—it's a pleasure to have you in my class. Good day."

As Professor Finbarr backed out of his driveway in his black 1996 Chevy sedan, with only a few dents in the left rear fender, Lunie stood transfixed. "Good day," she had replied after he had climbed in his car. "Good day," she repeated as he drove up the street.

A flare. A pleasure.

A typo. Fink.

Oh my gosh! She'd fix that as soon as she got home from her walk and resend her essay. Maybe she should ask Professor Finbarr about her novel. She took another swig of coffee, noting that the travel mug didn't hold the heat very well. She looked at it again. It was not her travel mug; it was a similar one that Dayton must have picked up from who knows where. Yuck! She set it on a stone next to Mother's driveway. When had Dayton gone from being a boy who picked up litter because of Earth Day, to someone who kept all the litter he found? Litter wasn't like coins, something you collected!

Lunie heard Mother's back door slam and a car start. Clive sped past her down the driveway, narrowly missing the travel mug as he took the corner close.

"Come back!" shouted a woman, and another vehicle started. Agnes also drove around from the back of the house, took the driveway corner much too closely, apparently not noticing Lunie. The rear tire ran over the travel mug, shattering the plastic. She honked and honked as she chased Clive's old Ford pickup.

I've got to change the lock, thought Lunie. *As soon as I get home, I'll call somebody.* She decided not to go inside Mother's until later in the day, until after the locksmith had shown up. She'd give one key to Dayton and keep one for herself. And that would be that. Then the cleaning out would begin.

The walk around the block boosted her spirit and energized her. Lunie even stopped to talk with Omar, who asked what she planned to bring to the potluck. Without thinking she blurted jelly bean gelatin salad, and he smiled with curiosity and wrote it down on a little notepad he always carried in his jacket pocket. She hadn't meant to go to the Billings' party, and certainly hadn't planned on making that dish—one of Dayton and their mother's favorites, but its name had been rattling around in her head since last night and it just spilled out. *Ha!* she thought. *Spilled the jelly beans. See, I haven't lost my sense of humor.*

She remembered why she hated the salad—the one her mother made for Dayton's fifteenth birthday. Her mother had bitten the jelly beans in half because she couldn't find a paring knife, and dropped them in the yellow gelatin. The concoction remained runny because the refrigerator wasn't working properly. The red, green, and white jelly beans resembled citron in fruitcake, something else her mother tried to make on several occasions. *Tried* was the word. The oven didn't function well, and the fruitcakes (dozens of little loaf pans that Dolce had purchased at a baker's going-out-of-business sale) looked like the runny jelly bean gelatin. Lunie detested both. Dayton ate, well, slurped, both their shares hungrily.

"Children are starving in Wongo," her mother would say, glaring at Lunie.

In later years, Mother purchased fruitcake, half-price or at a 90 percent discount after Christmas. The front hall closet was full of fruitcake boxes. "It's better when it ages," Dolce told a complaining Lunie a decade ago when her stash threatened to spill into the hall, and Dolce mentioned extras would go to Lunie's former room.

There was something about the thought of Dolce's fruitcake stockpile that made Lunie uneasy. Gloom returned. The third thing she would do when she got home would be to call Omar and decline the potluck invitation.

Nineteen

WHAT ON EARTH HAVE YOU DONE?" asked Dayton, bustling in
the back door an hour after Lunie had returned from
her walk. "There's a locksmith at Ma's and she wouldn't give
me a key."

"Too many people have keys. I don't even know who they
are," said Lunie. "Here's your key, and I have one, and that way
we'll be able to control access."

"Why would we want to do that?" asked Dayton. "It's my
place, too, and if I want my friends to visit, then it's my right."

"Did you know that Clive has been staying there?" she asked.

"Yes. I gave him permission. He guards the place."

"And Agnes comes and goes, taking things in and out?"

"What of it? Ma really liked her gifts."

"Agnes' gifts?"

"See, there's a lot you don't know about, Lunie-ruiny. Agnes
and Ma were friends, just like Clive and Ma. Just ask Agnes."

"I can't believe Agnes would enjoy going in that house. She
cleans for a living. Mother's house is appalling."

"That's what I mean, Lunie, you don't know a lot. But ask
me questions and I'll fill you in." Dayton smiled. "Rhoda can
make an appointment for later today—perhaps after we get
back from downtown or we can talk in the car. I'm going to my
office now to pack our walk-abouts. We should leave in about
forty-five minutes."

The walk-about debut. Lunie had forgotten. While she tried to figure out how she could get out of it, a loud knock startled her.

"Come in," she said. Two officers she had seen across the street took off their caps and wiped their feet on the WELCOME TO DEATH VALLEY mat that Dayton had placed inside the door.

"We'd like to speak to Lunie, ma'am," said the taller cop, flashing his badge.

Lunie quickly realized that they didn't mean her. "Just a moment," she said, and hurried upstairs. "Rhoda," she called through the Dayton's office door. "The cops want to talk with you."

Rhoda, wearing her acorn suit, said, "You take it, Lunie."

"Hey, that's not fair. They think you're me," said Lunie.

"I'm done being you. I'm Alice Acorn at the moment." The door slammed.

Lunie's left eye twitched furiously.

She returned to the kitchen where the cops were petting Phil.

"Nice cat," said one.

"Ah, Lunie's taking a nap," she told them, averting her gaze and hoping they didn't have a secret polygraph machine that was evaluating her response. "She didn't get much sleep last night. Could she call you later or may I give her a message?"

"Sure," said the other officer. "Please let her know that we appreciate her help last night. It was courageous to confront those folks. We found quite an arsenal in their upstairs—potato guns of all diameters, and rounds of golf balls, potatoes and even rocks. Who knows what they were planning. Let her know that the other dogs are safe—there were quite a number of the little critters. Strangest case we've seen in a long time. Don't forget to let us know if you see Scooter. He's the valuable stud, they claim."

"I'll tell her," said Lunie, wondering if she should offer them the remainder of the box of donuts that the Klingons had left behind. She decided not. She didn't want to offend them by feeding into a stereotype. She heard them close the screen door quietly. Lunie realized she had forgotten all about Scooter. He had probably been carried off by a fox by now.

"Tah-dah! What do you think?" Rhoda flounced into the kitchen, the tallest acorn Lunie could imagine. Her lanky legs were covered by green fuzzy tights; the round body of the shiny nut was poofed out with crumpled newspaper, and a little brown crown was perched on her head and secured by a thin chin strap of rubber cord. "I decided to put it on here. You can do the same or change when we get to the tourist bureau, like Dayton's going to do."

"I will drive you, but I won't be getting dressed up," said Lunie.

"No one's going to recognize you after we apply makeup, if that's what you're worried about," said Rhoda.

"Are we ready?" Dayton asked. He carried two parcels, one marked Nutley Squirrel, and the other, Sally Sunflower Seed. He and Rhoda walked to Lunie's car and climbed in the backseat.

Lunie sighed and slipped into her jacket.

"So, ask your questions, Lunie," said Dayton as they pulled out of the driveway.

"I have no questions," said Lunie, coming to a complete stop at the stop sign at the top of the hill.

"That's not what Dayton said," Alice Acorn replied. "You wanted to know about Agnes."

Lunie did want to know about Agnes, but she said nothing. She turned on her blinkers and eased out on the highway to the county seat in Mosby Courthouse where the tourist bureau was located. She merged carefully at the speed limit.

"She needs to know," said Alice Acorn, adjusting her chin strap. "Tell her, Dayton."

Dayton thought for a moment, as if he were considering the wisdom of revealing secrets to Lunie.

"Agnes's like a sister," he finally said. "Clive brought her along to visit Ma when he delivered groceries one day. Ma felt like she didn't have a daughter when you stopped coming to see her."

Lunie hit the brakes and pulled off the road. "That's not true, and it's not fair."

Dayton continued, "Agnes brought Ma presents, like the computer. It's one of her pleasures in life. She borrows something from one house, and takes it to another. Most people have no idea what's in their house anyway," he said. "It's clothes or books, statues, paintings or even jewelry. Ma thought it was great fun and sometimes gave her things to use as 'gifts.' People are always so surprised and pleased."

"That's terrible," said Lunie. "And illegal. Stealing."

"Wrong," interrupted Alice Acorn. "Stealing would be keeping it for yourself. Agnes just rotates treasures around. People might be curious about where something is, or why their dishes look different, but they've never called the police. Consider your Mr. Finbarr. He's constantly surprised to find a book he didn't know he had on his reading table. He always compliments Agnes for her cleaning and ability to find the lost."

"Lunie, could you keep driving. We're going to be late," said Dayton.

Lunie grimly stepped on the gas and swerved back into traffic, narrowly missing a tractor trailer. She ignored the driver's honking and the hand gestures made by the passenger in a sedan behind her.

"Watch it!" exclaimed the acorn. "Are you trying to get us all killed?"

There was no answer from the driver's seat. Lunie sped on, just two miles over the speed limit so she wouldn't get stopped, until they reached the town. "Turn left at the second light," said Dayton. "They said to park in the little lot beyond the bureau."

"I'll wait in the car," said Lunie.

"You can't do that," said Dayton. "We've contracted for three walk-abouts today. Want me to lose my job?"

"I really don't care," said Lunie. "I don't care if you make a fool of yourself in a nut suit, or go west in the middle of winter. I just don't care."

"Lunie, that's a terrible thing to say," said Alice Acorn. "Besides, I'm in the nut suit and he's the squirrel. We've both got to help him out. He would do the same for you. He always has. Here, go inside and put this on. I'll do your makeup in a minute."

By the time they returned to 4027 Bilgewater, Lunie's feet hurt from wandering the streets without her good walking shoes. Rhoda assured her that special creams would remove the yellow-and-black stripes on her face, and that she'd speak to Dayton about not charging Lunie for dry-cleaning the sunflower seed suit on which she had spilled a cup of coffee. It wasn't her coffee. A tipsy tourist was singing "You are my sunshine, my only sunflower, you make me happy . . ." and Lunie had "accidently" goosed him with her sunflower wand when his wife, with coffee, wanted their pictures taken with the walk-abouts.

"I think we've had a very successful first day," said Dayton. "Unzip me, please." He peeled off the squirrel suit in the front hall and hung it, carefully draping the tail, over the moose's head. "They want us back on the weekend, ten to three. I said fine. We get paid at the end of the month." He returned to the kitchen and sat at the table.

"Dayton, I'm not part of this walk-about project. I'm not your little sunflower, as you sang all the way home." Lunie tossed her wand on the table and yanked at the Velcro securing the side seams of her costume.

"I was just trying to jolly you up after the cops stopped you for erratic driving. You were lucky not to get a ticket. The stripes on your face would have made for a weird mug shot," said Dayton, barely concealing a smile. "I can't believe you would feel that nothing about this afternoon was fun. Better than working at the building department—if they call you or anyone else back."

Rhoda offered Lunie a flowered orange hand towel that looked suspiciously like one from Dolce's house, and the cold cream for removing theater makeup. "You know, Lunie, some people would do anything for an opportunity like this. Dayton already has applications from his Web site from lots of people. I can't believe you would say no."

"Can we talk? Really talk?" asked Lunie. She pulled out a chair facing Dayton. Rhoda also sat down and said, "Sure. It could be like a reality TV show. 'Family Talk.' I'll moderate."

Silence. Dayton and Lunie simply looked at each other. Finally Dayton, without blinking said, "Lunie-boonie, remember when we used to play the staring game and the last one who blinked or laughed won? I'm playing it now. Rhoda, time us."

Lunie said very evenly, "I'm not playing. I'm blinking. Watch my eyes, I'm blinking very hard to get this game over so we can talk seriously about my house and my life."

Dayton said, "I see you blinking, but I'm not blinking. I'm holding out so Rhoda can time me. When we were little I didn't blink for sixty seconds once and you could only go to fifty-five. Now your silly excessive blinking is going to make me giggle. I'm giggling inside now without blinking."

The center of Lunie's lip twitched. She realized that it wasn't a regular pulsation, but a twitch, then a pause, then random little twitches, and then another bigger one—perhaps like a prelude of seismographic tremors before a quake. She looked at the ceiling and tapped her fingers on the table.

"Sixty-one seconds!" said Rhoda. "Fantastic. We should enter that in the world record books. Have you ever tried to outstare a cat? They are usually pretty good at it."

"Let's try. Where's Phil?" asked Dayton, looking around the kitchen. "Here, kitty, kitty."

Lunie pounded the table with both fists. "Will you listen to me! I'm trying to have an adult conversation."

Neither Dayton nor Rhoda answered immediately. Both looked at Lunie with shock. "Lunie, have you thought of therapy?" asked Rhoda. "Anger management?"

"I'm not the one with problems." Lunie pounded on the table again. Phil skidded through the kitchen and out the cat door.

Dayton said gently, "Just remember, we're here for you, Lunie. Don't worry about the coffee stain. We'll take care of it."

"You may need to use the cream more than once to get the stripes off," said Rhoda, as she and Dayton pushed away from the table. "I wouldn't go outside until you get your face clean. The seed stripes have no context without the costume." Rhoda and Dayton walked softly down the hall so as not to disturb her.

For the first time in her adult life, Lunie wished she had spent a few minutes talking with her mother. She would have asked her what she meant by "get a grip." Had Dolce ever gotten a grip, or had the hoarding blanketed that opportunity?

She wiped her face with the makeup remover, and threw the gooey hand towel in the trash. Without getting out of her chair, she kicked her sunflower seed suit toward the washing machine. Phil returned from the now-dark outside and sat expectantly by his dish. When she didn't get up immediately, he padded over to her side and stared—without blinking. She looked away, then pulled her laptop across the table, and logged on. She fixed the typo in the story of Dayton's childhood memory, and sent it to the professor. He had a new assignment: Write in six hundred words about someone you know who has triumphed over adversity. She was in no mood to work on that one. Instead, almost involuntarily she found Dr. Manngo's Web site. He was now offering camera sessions, where they could meet Face 2 Face. She wasn't ready for that, either. She entered her credit card information to start the session.

Dr. Manngo: What's your issue, my friend?

Lunie: There are so many. I don't know where to begin. SEND

Dr. Manngo: So, start with what kind of day you had.

Lunie: Bad. The police stopped me and I had to wear a sunflower seed walk-about suit and my brother won't have a talk with me. Scooter is missing. Agnes takes things. Rhoda won't leave. SEND

Dr. Manngo: Whoa. Slow down. The police made you wear a suit and walk? Your brother what?

Lunie: The police were investigating the illegal miniature animals and potato guns across the street. Later they stopped me for erratic driving. SEND

Dr. Manngo: Whoa. You were erratically driving in a sunsuit with little animals?

Lunie: Not exactly. It's very complicated and hard to explain. SEND

Dr. Manngo: I have the time. Special deal tonight for extra minutes.

Lunie: I feel like crying. SEND

Dr. Manngo: Emotion is good to have. I have virtual tissues. Cheap. Tell me more about driving.

Lunie: I was mad at my brother and cut off a truck. SEND

Dr. Manngo: I get really mad at Sissy. I use the hate word sometimes. Are you sorry?

Lunie: Sorry, Dr. Manngo. SEND

Dr. Manngo: No. Did you say you were sorry to the truck driver? It's healthy to make amends.

Lunie typed thanks. Once again, Dr. Manngo gave her a new perspective. Emotion was important. It was okay to be mad at Dayton, but she needed to accept responsibility for her behavior and say she was sorry. She wasn't sure she could find the truck driver, but perhaps it was enough to think it.

Phil pressed against her leg. "Okay, food it is," she said.

Twenty

Dayton and Rhoda did not join Lunie for supper. She made macaroni and cheese from a box she found in one of the bags left by "friends" on the back porch. Rhoda appeared when the pizza delivery guy rang the back doorbell. She accepted the large box and went back upstairs.

Lunie didn't know if she had the energy to work on her novel. She wondered if other contestants would turn in fragments, or drop out so that they could spend a year knitting the pieces together. They'd have to pretend they were starting from scratch the following year, but then they'd be able to turn in a completed 50,000-word novel by the end of the thirty days.

She should be writing out her plan for what absolutely had to be done: cleaning out Mother's house; giving Dayton and Rhoda a deadline for leaving hers; dealing with code enforcement issues; letting Larry know she wanted to come back to work, but Sue seemed to need her. Lunie opened the book folder on her computer and typed: Chapter 19.

> Sue was now forty. Her birthday party had been fun, but it was just the girls—her fellow teachers. They took Sue out for drinks and lutefisk tapas at the new Norwegian-Spanish Grill. They sipped chokecherry margaritas and later split a large kringle for dessert. The waiters said, "Uff dah!" or "Ole!" depending on what was ordered, to complete the ambiance. Sue was feeling especially lonely. Ralph Pfizer, her

husband of many years after she had parted from Rolex, had fallen over a cliff during a camping trip, leaving Sue widowed with three young children. Sue missed Ralph, but not that much, because he lacked a spirit of true adventure. Ralph's idea of fun was to chaperone church camping trips. Adult church camping trips. After the third one she had gone on with him, Sue was tired of singing "I've been working on the railroad" with the lyrics adapted for whatever group was there. She was also tired of singing "You are my sunshine" in harmony as a little duet with Ralph. He always stood up at the campfire, and waving his marshmallow stick in the air, would say, "I want y'all to meet my own little sunshine." He'd point the stick, with an overcooked marshmallow precariously dangling, at Sue and motion for her to stand up. "Don't blush," he'd say, and everyone would chuckle, then he'd let the campers know that he had a treat for them and he'd pull out a pitch pipe and expect her to sing. She did, vowing never to go camping with him again. And so she wasn't with him when, after climbing up the mountainside, he was sweating. His last words to his fellow hikers were, "It's awfully hot today. Very hot. Hotter than usual. I think I'll fill my canteen at that waterfall."

Lunie smiled. Another three hundred words. Now Sue would be legally free to have fun, go on a cruise. Move to another state, away from the lutefisk that she detested, along with all Minnesotans who ate it only because it was expected. Lunie had tried it once when a friend of her mother's had sent a case of it along with a case of fruitcake baked by a mysterious order of Lutheran monks in the suburb of Hibbing. Or so Dolce said. Lunie never knew what was true.

She heard a door slam above her and heavy footsteps on the stairs. Dayton rushed into the kitchen and slipped into his shoes he had left by the back door. Rhoda raced behind him carrying their jackets.

"What's happening?" asked Lunie, almost afraid to ask.

"Clive has something he wants to show us at Ma's," said Rhoda.

"How did he get in?" said Lunie. "I had the locks changed."

"I gave him my key and he made more for my friends," said Dayton, letting the door snap closed behind them.

How dare he? fumed Lunie. *How dare he!* She put on her jogging pants and sweatshirt jacket and hurried down the street. *This has gone too far. I'll get the keys back and tell Clive and all the rest they are out of there.*

Clive's battered vehicle and Agnes's Lucky Maids van were in the driveway. The downstairs lights were on and through the sheets covering the windows, Lunie could see shadowy shapes climbing over things as they moved from room to room.

She could also hear a faint yipping sound.

"Over here," said Agnes.

"No, he went that way," said Rhoda.

"What's going on?" Lunie asked Clive.

"It's a good thing Dayton gave me a key. When I came in I discovered a dog no bigger than a demitasse cup, like the ones they sell at Kissy's, running through the kitchen. At first I thought it was a rat, but Agnes said it was the dog that was missing from across your street."

"Here, Scooter," called Dayton. "Where dat good wittle boy?"

"Musta snuck in the house last night after he ran away from his evil owners," said Rhoda.

"The police want that dog when you catch it," said Lunie.

"Well, they can't have him," said Rhoda. "Finders keepers." She dropped to her knees and pushed old newspapers aside.

"You can't keep a dog that doesn't belong to you," said Lunie.

"Scooter's so small they'll never know we have him." Rhoda toppled a stack of empty cereal boxes. "This floor sure needs mopping, Lunie," she said. "My hands feel icky."

"Got him," said Dayton from the living room. "He was in a box of animal crackers."

Dayton

One

DAYTON STRETCHED HIS long feet out over the edges of the navy futon mattress covered with white cat fur, and leaned back against a large cushion with tangled fringe. The futon frame was broken and Dayton remembered exactly when it happened. He and his mother sat on it one afternoon and a leg cracked. "I guess the Kidz Gloo didn't hold," she said. "Ya never can tell what's likely to happen when you find a treasure at the curb."

Fortunately it wasn't his favorite sleeping bed—a twin. So he had used the crumpled futon as a sitting corner until it became covered with electronics he planned to fix, and empty pizza boxes that he stacked. "My leaning tower of pizza," he joked with Dolce. Her laugh had turned into a grunt.

When he and Rhoda had explored the upstairs at Mother's, he mentioned that he was fond of the futon and the big cushion. "Well, then," said Rhoda. "Let's get them."

It took forty-five minutes to unearth both. Working together they folded, then rolled, the thick pad until they were able to shove it out the bedroom window. Clive was waiting below to help them carry the mattress and pillow up the street to Dayton's office.

"There are a lot of stains," said Dayton, apologetically.

"Oh, well," said Rhoda, when they set the futon in the office room. "They are part of your past. What stories they might tell."

"That's why you're my best friend," he said. "You understand everything."

Rhoda sat on the floor near him with her yellow pad. "Are you ready to start?"

Dayton patted the top of the head sticking out of his denim-shirt pocket. "Go to sleep, Scooter," he said. "You're okay now."

Rhoda tapped her pen against her cheek. "Where do you want to begin? Your first memory? Or do you want to talk about, say, all your pets and hobbies? Or do you want to talk about your mom?"

"What's the title of my book?" asked Dayton scratching the little dog's nose.

"It's sort of early to decide," said Rhoda.

"How about, *My Life, by Dayton Pitts, as written by his best friend Rhoda*?" Dayton smiled when he saw Rhoda blush. "Do you think it's going to be a best seller?"

"Not until we get it written. Let's start with your earliest memory," suggested Rhoda.

Dayton closed his eyes and thought for such a long time Rhoda wondered if he had fallen asleep.

"My earliest memory is of nothing."

"Nothing?"

"Nothing. Then, I began having memories," he said.

"Of what?" Rhoda pressed.

"Oh, I dunno. My crib. Lunie. Mother. Cleebo."

"Who was Cleebo?" asked Rhoda, scribbling faster.

"Cleebo, my windup giraffe. Lunie would wind it up for me when I was really little and its neck would stretch and it said, 'Cleebo. Cleebo.'"

"What does Cleebo mean?" asked Rhoda.

"Just giraffe baby talk," said Dayton. "I liked Cleebo a lot, and then it broke. Did you bring any cookies with you?"

Rhoda passed a package of crumbling cream-filled chocolate sandwich cookies that she had found in Mother's pantry. Dayton shook one off and popped it in his mouth.

"So, were you sad when you had to throw away your favorite toy?" she asked.

He opened his eyes wide, "Heck no. I never got rid of it. Cleebo's still in my closet. So are Dubdub, and Quark. I've kept them a secret. I'll show you when we go over next time."

"You are so sentimental," said Rhoda, smiling.

"So was Mother, I mean Ma," said Dayton. "She remembered exactly who gave her what, and treasured everything. I remember when I was in first grade, Wilma brought a box of picture frames to Ma. She said she was cleaning her attic and thought our school pictures might fit in them. Ma still has them. They always reminded her of Wilma and what a good friend she was."

"That's so sweet," said Rhoda.

"Now the picture frames, when we find them, will remind me of Ma. You see why I don't want to part with them?"

"Your mom must of loved you," ventured Rhoda.

"Actually, I don't think so," said Dayton. His smile collapsed and his head tilted until his beard touched the little dog's face. His lips rolled tightly between his teeth to keep further words from escaping.

Rhoda's hand paused above the second page of the yellow pad and said, "Your mom didn't love you?"

Dayton straightened up. "Look, everything from here on out is off the record."

"How can I write about your life if it's off-the-record?" asked Rhoda.

"It's just that way," he said.

"Including Gleebo?"

"Especially Cleebo. Cleebo."

Rhoda put her pen down. "Dayton, if you're telling the story of your life, then you have to tell it. You have to remember that your life is an open book."

"My life is an empty book," he said, beads of sweat glistening on his forehead. He lowered his head so that Scooter could lick his nose.

Rhoda stood up, did four knee bends, touched her toes six times, did ten push-ups, then ten jumping jacks. "There. I feel refreshed. Where were we? Let's talk about your sister."

"You mean Lunie?"

"Did you have any other brothers and sisters?" asked Rhoda.

"Just Lunie, I think," said Dayton. "She was my best friend and took care of me. Brought me food and wound up Cleebo. She helped me get dressed and walked me to school. She didn't like my room though."

"How come?"

"She said it was too messy, and she wouldn't let Mother or me go in her room. That made us mad." Rhoda smiled knowingly to encourage him to continue.

"What didja like to collect?"

"Everything. Mother got me started so I could be an accumulator like her. Trading cards, bubble gum wrappers, fortune cookie sayings, the sports section of the paper, comics, postcards from the national parks, stamps, travel brochures. I had boxes under my bed. Usually I just looked at one collection, but then I'd see how the gum wrappers mixed with the fortunes or travel folders. If my fortune had to do with travel, I'd close my eyes and pick a travel brochure or a postcard."

"That's so cool," said Rhoda. "My aunt Primrose only collected chipmunks. Everything chipmunk. Covered nut dishes with chipmunks on top. Ceramic chipmunks. Once I found a chipmunk flag for her garden. It wasn't always easy to find chipmunk collectibles, you know, especially when cats became popular." She glanced at Dayton. He didn't seem to be listening. She cleared her throat to get his attention. When his eyes met hers, he looked surprised, as if he hadn't expected to see anyone else in the room.

"That's all for today," Dayton said abruptly. "I'll hook up Ma's computer over there and you can write up what you've got so far." He patted Scooter while he stood up. The little dog snuggled in his shirt pocket.

"Sounds like a deal." Rhoda said, puzzled by his unexpected ending of the book session. "I'll help."

They lifted the monitor onto Dayton's makeshift desk, and attached the keyboard and the computer. Dayton pushed over an office chair that was only missing one wheel and sat down carefully. "Will you look at that," he said when the screen lit up. "Ma was writing something. Don't delete anything. It might be important." He slipped on his shoes, tied them, then picked up Scooter. "I'm going to Ma's to get some things. Be back soon."

Rhoda didn't answer.

Dayton whistled as he skipped steps on the stairway, tapped the moose's right ear, and slipped his arms through his windbreaker, the one with the faded Yellowstone Park logo on it. He adjusted it so that Scooter had plenty of air.

"I'll be back soon," he said to Lunie, who was huddled over her laptop at the kitchen table. He was not expecting a response and didn't get one.

The crime scene tape still encircled the Sanders' yard. When Dayton saw that there were no cars in the vicinity, he walked purposely across the street and tore off a long piece hanging down by the mailbox. He crossed again and decided to do a zigzag walk like he and Lunie had done as children—back and forth across the street instead of staying on just one side. Mrs. Wolenski warned them it was dangerous and threatened to tell their mother, until they promised they would never do it again, so they only zigzagged on the next block, where she couldn't see them. He wasn't sure he could talk Lunie into doing anything fun now. She didn't smile much.

Scooter whined from the depths of Dayton's shirt pocket.

"Does Scootie-bootie want to get down and run or go potty?" he asked the tiny animal, in a voice that Dolce would have described scornfully as babytalk. *Don't suck your thumb. Don't talk babytalk.*

Dayton was about to place Scooter on the grass when he realized the dog might run again. Fast. Then he remembered the crime scene tape. He stretched it as far as he could, made a loop at one end for a collar, and a loop at the other for his hand. He had to stoop over, but the leash kept Scooter within five feet of him. Only once did the dog try to slip out of the miniature noose, but Dayton gently pulled him back.

"Scootie, I'll have to get you a real collar and leash," he said, then realized he'd probably have to order it online in case the police were watching transactions at Lassie's Pet Shop just west of the downtown. They had probably already alerted the owner to let them know if anyone was buying supplies for a teacup greyhound. Teenie sweaters, small bowls, extra small kibble. No, he'd have to be careful. Scooter needed a normal life—not racing other teacup greyhounds around a little track while people placed bets. Maybe he could make a little temporary leash out of a necklace or yarn at Mother's.

Dayton watched Scooter do his business, and realized he should have carried a small plastic bag with him. He looked around to make sure no one was watching, but just in case, pretended to pick up the pea-sized turd. Then he quickly wrapped Scooter in his jacket and hurried up Mother's driveway.

He used the new key that Lunie gave him, then placed it under the faded, straw welcome mat so he wouldn't lose it. He remembered when his mother had brought the mat home. She had found it in the trash of a couple who had gotten divorced, along with wedding presents that had their names stitched or painted. He had helped her carry a few boxes containing painful reminders of their happy days into Dolce's bedroom—the first bedroom Mother claimed in the house.

Dayton barely remembered moving into 4073 Bilgewater when he was a small child, or the circumstances. He and Lunie ran from empty room to empty room and up and down the stairs. Dolce had allowed them to pick their bedrooms and Lunie didn't mind that Dayton wanted the larger one. Their mother told them the house was a new start and they would be getting furniture soon. He didn't mind sleeping on the stained avocado shag carpet in the meantime. Their mother was doing the best she could and she frequently told them so. Mrs. Wolenski, one of those nice people who comes by to welcome new neighbors, brought a casserole to the family the second night they were in the house.

"You poor dears," she told Dolce. "Your furniture hasn't arrived yet?"

"That's because we don't have any," said Dolce, who motioned for Lunie and Dayton to leave the room. They made stamping noises like they were climbing the stairs, but hid around the corner to listen to their first visitor.

The women were talking softly, however, and Dayton only heard fragments—something about a divorce, their father's name a couple of times, a few words that his mother later washed his mouth out for repeating, and then Mrs. Wolenski saying, "Here's what we'll do." The next day they went shopping at secondhand and consignment stores and soon beds, tables, chairs, lamps and dishes arrived.

"A house isn't a home without the little things. When my paycheck allows," Dolce told Lunie and Dayton, "we need pictures, books, and bric-a-brac. Knickknacks." That's when she began looking for free treasures everywhere. Lunie didn't like touching objects that she saw by the curb on trash day, but Dayton's curiosity matched Dolce's. While his sister hung back on the sidewalk, or a lawn, he and his mother rummaged and filled his little wagon, an early find, with *objects d'art,* as Dolce called them. Dayton especially liked the discarded action toys he found. One was a giant batttleship that was missing just a couple of cannons. With new batteries it traveled around the kitchen floor and shot rice in every direction. He liked the windup cars (even if a wheel was missing), the toy boats that sank, and especially Cleebo. There was nothing wrong with Cleebo except someone had gotten chewing gum all over his neck. Dayton worked for days to get the gum out, but finally gave up and wrapped a wide ribbon around it to hide the sticky residue.

He remembered that Lunie was disgusted by Cleebo's thready gummy neck. Cleebo was one of the reasons he was back at Mother's this night. Cleebo was in his closet on the top shelf. He would find him to show Rhoda.

"I'm not going to put you down, Scootie," he said, stroking the dog. "You'll get lost again. Wait till we get to my room."

Dayton picked his way carefully from the kitchen, down the hall until he reached the stairs. The house was similar in design to Lunie's, perhaps built by the same builder, but larger. Dayton slipped on decade-old newspaper ads on the first steps, and moved a feather boa and two raincoats on his way up. He was momentarily challenged by a series of shopping bags and a hair dryer, but finally reached the top.

Lunie's former bedroom was to the left, beyond a series of cartons and bins, one containing swimming trophies earned by someone in the next town, and a canoe paddle. A bookcase and broken wing-back chair blocked the doorway.

His room was to the right. He knew that Dolce meant to have it ready for him when he returned from out west. She would have moved things, like the bookcase so he could get to his room. She might even have put sheets on his bed. Dayton's eyes burned with unspent tears.

Dayton shoved at the bookcase. It tipped backwards over a rocking horse, spilling a coffee can of rusty nails.

"See, Scootie, you might hurt your paws if I put you down."

Dayton turned the knob, but the door didn't open. He shoved harder and heard a crash. It sounded like his lamp or maybe a mirror, although he didn't remember having a mirror. He managed to push the door open far enough that he could reach in and flip the light switch. Only one bulb in the overhead fixture flickered on.

His light-blue fiberboard dresser that he had decorated with markers as a child was still in the center of the room, surrounded by a pile of stereo components. He inched in and opened the top drawer, and smiled that it was still stuffed with lumpy dark socks covered over by a red faded sweatshirt. He fingered one and was satisfied with its contents. He ran his hand over two others and knew Mother had added to them. The second drawer was crammed with shirts, several that he didn't recognize and two that he remembered outgrowing in ninth grade. He gazed around the room. Some shadowy objects were unfamiliar. Mother must have piled on things he didn't know about in the few weeks after he left. Before her accident.

Rhoda would love to see the room harboring his science projects from school and his almost-successful attempt to make a functioning robot. He would tell her how he took the two-foot-high robot to school for show-and-tell and, even though its arms fell off when he turned on the switch, his teacher told him to keep trying. That's what he thought the teacher said. That's what he told his mother and Lunie after school, adding that the class had liked his contribution best that day. His mother beamed and said, *"Très si bon!"* She would keep her eyes out for objects that he could use for his mechanical creations and told him that he was welcome to dismantle any of the *objects méchanique* that she acquired so that he could learn more about how they worked. Dayton was confident that Tobor the Robot was still under his bed.

He closed the drawers and stumbled through the room, bruising his shin on a tool chest before he reached his closet. He reached his hand to the top shelf and felt around for Cleebo. Nothing. He could only identify a metal flour canister, a three-quart crockpot, high-heel shoes (one of Mother's favorite collectibles) and jewel cases for compact discs. The cases slid when disturbed, pelting Dayton's chest and the concealed Scooter. The little dog yelped louder than Dayton imagined he could. "Scootie, I'm so sorry." Dayton held the pup to his face and seeing no blood, cuddled him to his beard. "There, there."

With Scooter secure in his pocket again, Dayton continued to search, with no luck, for Cleebo, whom he hadn't seen in several years. He decided to return in daylight, with a flashlight to find his favorite toy. Mother never would have thrown out Cleebo. Nobody would.

He kicked a few boxes out of his way to reach his second bureau and opened the top drawer, surprised to see it stuffed with yarn, patterns and glue. He couldn't blame his mother for filling it in his absence. The second drawer contained his flannel winter shirts and surprisingly, his diary from elementary school. He tucked it in his jacket pocket.

"Time to go, Scootie." Dayton hoped Clive and Agnes would be in the living room. They needed to have a talk.

Two

BY THE TIME DAYTON FOUND his way back downstairs, Scooter was whining. Dayton wasn't sure if the dog wanted something to eat or simply to roam for a bit. He reached in his pocket for pieces of cat kibble he had purloined from Phil's bowl, and Scooter eagerly crunched them. He was still wiggly, so Dayton placed him on the floor, with the admonishment that he come when he was called.

The little greyhound zipped down the hall in the direction of the living room. He seemed to be able to negotiate the maze of objects like a well-trained rat.

"Here, little guy," said Clive. "Where's your master?"

"Coming," said Dayton. He was careful not to get trapped between the artificial Christmas trees. Clive was lounging in his usual place on the sofa, and Agnes had made room at his feet so that she could sit.

"So, you've been upstairs," she said, pushing her curls behind a McConklin-plaid head scarf. "To your room?"

"Where else?" said Dayton as he reached their clearing. Scooter leaped off Clive's lap and bounded into Dayton's outstretched hands. "It will take a little work before I can stay there, and I'll need to find space for Rhoda. Meanwhile, we've got great digs at Lunie's."

"Lunie doesn't seem happy about that," said Clive. "Before she passed out after guzzling my apricot brandy, she told me she wants you both to go. I can't believe you would put up with that."

"Yeah, she wants us all to go," said Agnes. "I'm really surprised by her attitude. You'd think she'd be happy to have company and help to break up the monotony of living alone. Her attitude is almost, well, selfish."

"That's not nice," said Dayton.

"Not nice, but perhaps true, and you need to stop being so defensive. So protective," Agnes continued.

"Not nice and not fair," said Dayton, frowning. "My sister may tell me to leave, but she doesn't mean it. She's even letting me use an empty room for my office. And we had a party at the house."

Agnes knew from experience with Dayton when to change the subject. "Guess what I brought you?"

"A new blender? A camera? Books?"

Agnes shook her head and reached for a brown paper shopping bag. She peeked in and closed the top. "Guess again."

"I can't," said Dayton. Scooter climbed on his shoulder and snuggled next to his beard.

Agnes held out the bag. "Take a look. It's from the Pomphreys' on the next block."

Clive intercepted the sack as she held it out for Dayton. "Sheesh, it looks like a baby Egyptian mummy that belongs in a glass case! It's probably valuable—from their travels," said Clive.

"Exactly right. Duncan Pomphrey smuggled it in from Egypt," said Agnes beaming. "In exchange, I left a ratty old toy I found in Dayton's room. It will be so funny when they see what's in the glass case now." She popped open a bag of pretzels she removed from behind a box of curtains.

Dayton rose in alarm. "You took what from my room? You're not supposed to go in my room, just Mother's."

"It was just a broken animal. Something with a long neck. Way back in the closet," said Agnes, biting into a large chunk.

Dayton's face showed an unaccustomed mix of fear and rage. He gritted his teeth and said, "Agnes, go get it back. Trade it back immediately. You took Cleebo. You had no right!"

Agnes said, "Calm down, Dayton. I had no idea that thing was important. It was stuffed way back on a closet shelf. You know I can't go back for another week when it's the Pomphreys' scheduled cleaning day."

"You've got to go back tonight," said Dayton. "Right now. This minute." He rocked on his feet. Beads of sweat freckled his nose.

Agnes leaned back and studied his increasing anxiety. Dayton was swaying. He looked ready to lunge at her.

"I thought you'd like the mummy," Agnes said, searching for another large salty piece in the bag.

"That's not the point," said Dayton. "Swap it back now."

"I can't go there tonight," she said. "They'll have the security alarm set. It'll have to be sometime tomorrow after I finish at Wilma's."

"Then I'm going in," said Dayton, "and you'll take me there."

Clive stretched and stood. "Dayton's right. You can't leave his Gleebo there. If it's as ratty as you say, they might throw it out."

"Cleebo. Now, hurry," said Dayton.

Agnes didn't hurry. She didn't even stand up. "You don't know what you're asking. I could lose my job with Lucky Maids. I could go to jail."

"Then tell me how to get in and where the mummy case is and I'll do it," said Dayton.

Agnes considered his offer, brushed sea salt off her sweater and stood up. "All right, but don't implicate me if you get caught. I have to take care of my mother, you know."

Dayton went back to his room and returned with a miner's headlamp, then slid into a navy windbreaker. He slipped a pair of extra large dark socks into his pocket, telling Clive he would cover his white tennies just before he went inside.

Clive said, "I'll take care of Scooter for you." Dayton handed him the little dog and went out the door with Agnes, who carried the mummy in the sack.

"You're acting crazy, Dayt," whispered Agnes. "They wouldn't notice my swap in the middle of the night—maybe not even for days."

Dayton didn't answer. He hunched forward and walked purposefully, his teeth grinding.

"I had no idea that that monkey was so important."

"Cleebo's a giraffe."

"I meant giraffe."

They rounded the block and came to Beauregard Lane. The Pomphreys' lights were out, except for one in an upstairs bathroom.

"That's not a good sign," said Dayton, studying the light in a small window on the second floor.

"No big deal," said Agnes. "They read somewhere that if you have a bathroom light on, burglars will think someone's awake and will leave your house alone."

"That's what I'm thinking," said Dayton. "Someone's awake."

"Here's all you have to do. I'll punch in the code so you don't set off the alarm. Then we'll open the door, and you go in. When you get inside, take your first right—that's the library. Go to the far end and there's an octagon table on the left. The glass case is on the table on the right. Do not go to the left. Right?"

"Right."

Agnes, turned the key, then punched in the security code: 4 3 2 1, whispering to Dayton that the Pomphreys really needed to come up with a code more unique than the one preset in the alarm system. She tried the handle and the door opened. Dayton took a deep breath and stepped inside, turned to the left, and bumped into Coreen Pomphrey.

"Exactly what are you doing in my parents' house?" Coreen asked, flipping on the light switch.

"Shhh," said Dayton.

"I don't have to shhhh," she said louder. "I don't have to shhh or shush or whisper."

"I really wish you'd be quiet," said Dayton. "At least quieter."

"I asked you a question, and the only reason I haven't pushed this alarm button right over here is because I know who you are from elementary school. You are the boy who brought the broken robot to show-and-tell," Coreen said. "You look the same, except for the beard."

Dayton couldn't tell if that was a good memory of him or a bad one, but he was relieved slightly. He wondered why she was wearing a hip-length shiny red overcoat, matching beret, and tan above-the-knee boots. She looked like a cherry lollypop, his favorite.

"What's in the bag?"

"Something that belongs in your house. And you have something of mine."

"It's very unlikely that we would have anything of yours. My family collects antiquities," Coreen said.

"Cleebo is an antiquity, too, and somehow he got mixed up with your father's mummy," said Dayton, hoping his answer would satisfy her.

"That explains nothing," said Coreen. "My father's rare mummy is in a glass case in the library, and if it's not, someone's in big trouble." She stared hard at him, then walked across the hall where she could turn on the library's light.

Dayton was astonished by the sight of spears standing in the corners, a marble statue by Michelangelo, a slab of hieroglyphics removed from a tomb, papyrus scrolls encased in glass and hanging on the walls, framed illuminated manuscripts, large leather-bound volumes in the bookcases, and a lamp, the shape and height of a cancan dancer's leg, from high heels to red-gartered thigh, that was topped by a ruffled, beaded black shade. *Mother would love that,* he thought.

Coreen led him to the octagon table, looked in the glass case and shrieked. "I'm calling security! What's this grotesque thing?" She held up the giraffe. "This is disgusting."

"Please don't hurt Cleebo," said Dayton. "Please. The mummy is here. It's safe. Let's just trade."

Coreen seemed to be considering the idea, then a naughty smile played on her lips. "Have a seat," said Coreen, without unbuttoning her coat. She gestured at a Victorian love seat—magenta brocade—covered with protective plastic. Dayton reluctantly obliged and she took a seat on a matching highback armchair. He clutched the bag with the mummy, fearful that Coreen would will it across the room and he would have nothing to trade.

"Cigarette?" She pointed at a flat silver case on a Hepplewhite side table.

"I don't smoke." Dayton cleared his throat. His suddenly hoarse voice made him think of Phil's recent hairball.

"I don't either," said Coreen. "Gave it up in sixth grade after I got caught at Poshville."

"Poshville?"

"That's what we called the private girls' school where I was sent. Don't you remember? In your class one year, and gone for good the next. They wanted to make a lady out of me."

Dayton was having trouble remembering Coreen at all, except the name, perhaps. There had been a Carine, Karina and someone the kids called "Chlorine." Maybe that had been Coreen. Chlorine was a little pudgy, like him, and refused to sit with her knees together in band. He thought she had played the flute. Yes, that must have been Coreen. Here she was sitting across from him, smiling a very sweet and untrustworthy smile, and postured just like the girl in band. Dayton looked away, just as he had done in fourth grade.

"Now, Dayton, tell me how you happened to replace my father's valuable treasure with this." She dangled Cleebo by a fragile ear and waved the giraffe slightly. Dayton panicked.

"I can't tell you," he said, thinking of Agnes and her potential loss of employment.

"Let me guess," said Coreen. "You're protecting Agnes."

Dayton's blue eyes widened. "See, I knew it," said Coreen. "I took a course in body language. I can read all the signs."

"Why did you guess Agnes?" Dayton asked, clearing his throat. He hoped his question was not an admission of guilt.

"Everybody knows about Agnes," said Coreen. "She's been swapping objects, usually art, among her customers for years. She thinks nobody notices that after every cleaning something is missing and something is new. We all have a good laugh, and eventually everything is returned to its rightful owner. My mother, may she rest in peace across the great river of antiquities, said we were very fortunate to have a cleaning person— she couldn't bring herself to call Agnes a 'dust-and-mop technician,' which is on her brochure—who understood the value of artifacts and treasures, and also had a sense of humor." Coreen paused to let Dayton digest her revelation. "You didn't know that we knew, did you?"

Dayton shook his head.

"Well, dear Agnes doesn't know that we're on to her either, so let's just keep it that way," said Coreen, studying Cleebo. "She would die of embarrassment, and perhaps she'd move to another neighborhood or go back to Ireland. You see, we treasure our Agnes."

Dayton's eyes were hypnotically fixed on the swaying Cleebo. "She's waiting outside," he murmured.

"I thought so," said Coreen. "Despite your mechanical abilities, which I admired in grade school, I didn't think you could figure out how to get in this house." She sprawled in the chair, her knees widening dangerously.

"Now may I have Cleebo?" asked Dayton, his eyes locked on the faded yellow creature.

"Hmm," said Coreen. "This is a challenging moment for me. I'm really becoming attached to Clabber."

"Cleebo."

"Cleebo. I can't tell you how sick I am of all the poshiness of this house. The paperwork that details where my parents found or acquired something. Its value for insurance purposes. You have no idea what it's like living in a museum. Did you notice the wrought-iron grillwork covering the windows, the surveillance cameras? There was no way I could have fun as a teenager. No way I could slip out of my bedroom window or sneak friends in during vacations when I was home. My parents were always traveling to countries that have changed their names so many times my light-up globe itself is an antiquity. Do you know the earlier names for Jamahiriya or Djibouti? I do. I was a prisoner in a home museum."

The change in her voice from braggadocio to embarrassing self-pity caused Dayton to take a quick look at her face. Red lipstick that matched her coat; heavy mascara; a hint of tears welling in her pale blue eyes. She sniffled.

"I had no idea," said Dayton.

"No, no one did. I was forgotten Coreen. The girl they called Chlorine. A girl with everything and yet nothing. Do you have any idea how many times I would have traded my gold Mayan earrings for this Geebloo?"

"Cleebo. Cleebo. May I have him back now, please?" Dayton was suddenly alarmed. Coreen stopped dangling Cleebo, studied Dayton's little friend, ran her finger down his long neck, and then cradled Cleebo in her arms. The fabric of her red coat crinkled as she clutched the giraffe.

Dayton tried not to look too concerned. He wished he had his computer handy so that he could e-mail Rhoda for help, or have a quick session with his social counselor, who would know exactly what to say. "Deal with Cleebo, deal with life." His counselor would feel his pain, but pain wasn't what he needed to share at the moment. He needed to figure out how to get Cleebo and get out. Rhoda would just walk over, hand Coreen the mummy and grab Cleebo. Dolce would have laughed and told him to ask Coreen for a date because she came from money. Lunie, well, he wasn't sure what Lunie would do, and Agnes— deep down he felt she was the key to resolving the hostage situation.

Dayton's hands folded and unfolded and he tried to keep from sliding off the love seat. Finally, he said, "Coreen, I have lots of special things in Mother's house. You could have your pick of anything you want. I have a monkey that used to swallow real banana, and a mechanical octopus that I can make work again. You can play with it in the, uh, tub."

Coreen looked up with interest, but shook her head. She stroked Cleebo lovingly.

Dayton had no recourse. "Do you want me to get Agnes?"

"Good heavens, no!" Coreen's thighs snapped closed and her boots hit the floor. She tossed Cleebo to Dayton. "Give me the mummy and get out. But, I expect a trade in return."

Dayton quickly tucked Cleebo against his chest and zipped his windbreaker. When he reached the hall, he heard the lid of the glass case close. Coreen called after him, "I'll be there tomorrow at four to see what you've got, Robo Boy."

"Deal, Chlorine," he called back. He heard the snap of a cigarette lighter, and detected a whiff of smoke before he pulled the heavy mahogany door open and stepped outside.

Three

DAYTON WASN'T SURPRISED that Agnes wasn't waiting for him outside. Clive was, though, on Mother's front porch. He handed over Scooter.

"Mission successful?" Clive asked, sniffing.

"Yep," said Dayton, tucking Scooter in his jacket next to Cleebo.

"Coming back in?"

"Nope."

"Don'cha want to tell Agnes?"

"Nope." Dayton rezipped his jacket, and turned for home.

Lunie was at the kitchen table engrossed in her laptop, an empty bowl, red with the remnants of canned spaghetti, next to her. Not thinking she was watching, Dayton grabbed a handful of kibble from Phil's bowl.

"Cat food makes dogs fart," said Lunie, without looking up.

"Rhoda still upstairs?" he asked, wondering if he should put the dry food back and make a run to the store. He decided that one night of Phil's kibble wouldn't hurt.

"Guess so," said Lunie.

Dayton placed Scooter on the floor, and whistled for him to follow him, but Scooter had other ideas. He squeaked out a barking noise and chased his tail under the table until Dayton got down on his hands and knees and grabbed him.

"C'mon wiggler. We're going upstairs."

Rhoda was still in the office. "I was getting worried," she said. "You were gone for hours."

"I have something to show you. I just couldn't find it right away."

He handed Rhoda the giraffe, wondering if perhaps he should have cleaned up Cleebo first. Cleebo had The Smell. The Smell had permeated Dayton and Lunie's clothes when they were children. It was in their hair. It seeped into the furniture and the rugs, just as the refrigerator's contents had The Taste. Lunie had tried to scrub The Smell out of what they wore to school, and once sprayed both of them with cologne that she found in Dolce's record cabinet. She could smell The Smell, but Dayton said he couldn't, until he went out West for the first time and came home. Unlike the clean, pine-scented mountains, the air in Mother's was musty, more like a never-emptied litter box, or a thrift store where clothing had not been fully cleaned before it was hung by color on racks. At first it surprised him when he returned, then he didn't notice. It was familiar. Home.

If Rhoda noticed The Smell, she didn't wrinkle her nose. She studied Cleebo, top to bottom and the windup key, placed him against an orange pillow, then aimed her camera and took the giraffe's picture.

"Perfect," she said, checking the image. "This could be on the cover of your autobiography."

"Really?" Dayton brightened.

"Now, tell me all about Cleebo. I'm going to type it as you talk."

"I'll tell you, but it's off the record," said Dayton.

Rhoda decided not to argue. She would deal with that later.

Dayton leaned back against the futon and closed his eyes, wondering if this was what it would be like if he actually visited his social counselor's office. He would be told to lie back, get comfortable. Soft music would be playing.

"Hey, Rhoda, do we have any soft music?"

"Sure, Dayt." She found a streaming music station on the Internet. "How old were you when you got Cleebo?"

The Latin music was very relaxing—elevator music with a cha-cha beat. It might not be what his social counselor would have picked, but it would do. His social counselor would probably have a tape recorder running during the session in case he had bad handwriting.

"Rhodie? Do we have a tape recorder handy?"

He heard her sigh. "Not here. Maybe at Ma's. We can look tomorrow."

"Maybe we should wait then," said Dayton. "Bésame Mucho" abruptly ended and he heard Rhoda get out of her chair. "You aren't mad at me, are you?"

"No, Dayton. It's late. I'll see you in the morning."

Dayton knew, without opening his eyes, that Rhoda wasn't pleased, but it would be so much better if the autobiography was recorded, not just typed as he spoke. He settled back, and pulled a blue afghan over his legs. Scooter was snoring, his legs twitching as if he were running.

How *did* he get Cleebo? Lunie said he found it in the discard pile behind Goodwill. Dayton, however, recalled that his mother had given it to him when he was a little boy—maybe for his fourth or fifth birthday. It was inside a large gift-wrapped box covered with shiny paper and lots of ribbon. The amazing giraffe even had a price tag around its neck verifying that it was brand new. Dayton remembered that Cleebo had been covered with soft bright yellow plush with brown spots. When he wound it up, the giraffe's neck stretched as if it was searching for leaves, and it would take three magical stumbling steps before the spring ran down. And, if he listened carefully as he wound it up, he could hear from deep inside what sounded like a little squeaky voice saying *cleeeeebo cleeeeebo*.

Later that special birthday afternoon, after having hot cocoa and watching Dayton wind and rewind his giraffe, Lunie smiled and told him she wished she had one, too. How happy that had made him. He told her that she could play with Cleebo anytime, and he carried Cleebo upstairs to his room, carefully stepping over his mother's pots and cast-iron pans, which had been his turn to wash.

He could tell Rhoda the story of Cleebo tomorrow, now that he remembered it. He would leave out the part about Lunie refusing to enter his room shortly thereafter. That was Lunie's problem. She didn't seem to understand that when you were creating something, like Tobor the Robot, pieces would be everywhere and because you didn't know exactly what you might need for an invention, you'd have to have a lot of extra bits handy.

Rhoda would also want to know about his mother. He decided there really wasn't much he wanted to say. Scooter wiggled in his lap. Dayton stretched out on the floor, placing Cleebo next to his pillow where the little dog soon curled up between the giraffe's stiff legs.

Dayton wished he could fall asleep, but the walk-about costumes on the mannikins cast strange shadows, reminding him of the ghost he believed—no, knew—had inhabited his mother's house when he was young. He would hear footsteps after he turned out the light. The ghost should have been able to walk through things, but this one tripped over them, stumbled and moaned. Once he heard it learning the violin, and another time it dropped a china washbowl and didn't pick up the pieces. He had asked Lunie if she heard it and if she was afraid. She told him not to worry. Ghosts were supposed to be friendly, if there were such things. So Dayton gave the ghost a name—Caliban—but called him "Nabilac" so that no one else would know. Those were the years he liked to spell backwards, and learned to speak Pig Latin, sort of. He called Lunie "Einul," and himself "Notyad," his robot, Tobor. His sister actually laughed when he told her their code names. He wondered if she'd laugh now. He'd try it out in the morning. Rhoda would be "Adohr," and Agnes, "Senga." Clive, "Evilc."

Maybe that's how the autobiography would work. *The True Story of My Life,* by Notyad Sttip, assisted by Adohr. *Perfect,* thought Dayton. He petted Scooter's soft belly.

How does Lunie do it? How does she just sit down and write a novel? *Maybe it's easier to make up a story than to tell your own,* he thought.

Rhoda said Lunie had good ideas about her book, but she was writing in fits and starts. He didn't think it was right that Rhoda was snooping into Lunie's stuff, but as Rhoda told him, Lunie *had* left her laptop on the kitchen table instead of placing it in her room. Rhoda also told him that before she was forced to leave her last dwelling place—that's what she called it—she had been taking a creative writing class online and would gladly help Lunie with her book project. Even though they hadn't known each other very long, Dayton knew he could count on Rhoda for everything. She had willingly donned the acorn suit, and would do it again the next day and the next, if necessary, when they hit the streets again to hype the upcoming Southern Sons of Nutcrackers Festival, which would transition into the Harvest Festival.

Then it hit him, the walk-abouts were supposed to be downtown again tomorrow afternoon and that was when Coreen Pomphrey said she would meet him at Mother's—her condition for releasing Cleebo. He'd lose his job with the tourist bureau if the squirrel was a no-show, but there was no telling what Coreen might do if he didn't keep his end of the bargain. Perhaps he could talk Coreen into meeting him earlier. Yes, he'd call her after breakfast.

Four

THE POMPHREYS' NUMBER WASN'T in the white pages. Agnes might have it in her schedule book, but Dayton didn't have Agnes's cell phone number either. He'd have to go back to the Beauregard Lane house himself, although it was barely light. He showed Scooter where's Phil's kibble dish, water bowl, and the cat box, were located, then bundled up against the brisk air. Scooter whined when Dayton left without him. Dayton rushed down the block and around the corner, pretending he didn't see Wilma looking for her newspaper in the tube—the delivery was late again and she was mumbling. He didn't feel like chatting before he had his coffee.

The Pomphrey house, a mansion compared with most houses in the neighborhood, crowded its lot like an overweight passenger in an airline seat, and blocked two neighbors' views of a duck pond. The county, however, continued to assess the neighbors for a water view, because they could see the pond if they stood on their garage roofs or climbed a tree.

The Pomphreys had purchased their property when Dayton was in second grade. Lunie had to drag him home every afternoon for weeks because he wanted to watch the cranes and bulldozers tear down the original split-level on the lot, and then construct the massive three-story brick mansion with white columns and a slate roof, protected by an eight-foot-high wrought-iron fence. Those who observed the construction from across the street said it would appear that there was an elevator shaft, and a large safe inside. They couldn't understand why the garage doors were extra high and wondered what the Pomphreys would be storing. A private security guard kept neighbors from wandering through during the construction, as they usually did to satisfy their curiosity.

After the fleet of moving trucks, guarded by the armed private security, finished unloading furniture and crates, Dolce made Lunie and Dayton go with her to pick through whatever had been discarded by the curb. Even Lunie admitted that the soft pillows, Roman shades and silky linens were nice finds. Dayton knew she was uncomfortable when he pointed out a little girl about his age watching them from the third-floor window while they sorted through the family's discards and piled them in a baby carriage with a loose wheel and Dayton's little wagon.

It was a year of so before Dayton realized that Coreen was the girl who lived in the mansion. Preoccupied with thoughts of inventing mechanical devices, he hadn't paid much attention to her in class—just during band and then for the wrong reasons. And then she was gone and he hadn't given her much thought until last night.

He rang the bell, half-hoping she wouldn't answer. He'd simply leave a note about the change in plans and run back home. The door opened a crack, and he could see Coreen's face and her diaphanous baby-doll negligee. He sucked in enough air that he could have easily played a three-minute clarinet cadenza.

"Good morning," Coreen said sweetly, opening the door all the way. "Coffee's almost ready."

"I can't stay," Dayton stammered, his face drained of color. "My sister is making waffle-pancakes."

"I am, too," said Coreen. "And I have fresh fruit, powdered sugar and maple syrup for mine."

Dayton focused on her face. He pulled his note out of his pocket and held it out, hoping she would reach up to take it.

"Are you reneging on your offer?" Coreen asked.

"Oh, no. Never. Not at all. It's just that four o'clock isn't the best time today. Could you come to Mother's at one instead?"

Coreen leaned against the door frame, studied her nails, and considered his request. "It isn't as convenient for me, but I'll try to rearrange my schedule."

"Gee, thanks, Coreen," he said, turning quickly and running down her sidewalk. By the time he reached Lunie's, he was sweating profusely and out of breath. Rhoda was pouring cereal into a bowl, and Lunie was checking e-mail.

"Where have you been?" asked Rhoda. "You keep disappearing. Got a girlfriend we don't know about?"

"Good golly, no," said Dayton, unzipping his windbreaker. "I was just out for some exercise before breakfast."

Rhoda handed Dayton the cereal bowl and fixed herself another.

"We do walk-abouts again this afternoon," said Dayton.

"Don't talk with your mouth full," said Lunie.

"We should leave at two to get downtown," he continued. "And someone's coming over to Mother's at one."

"Who now?" asked Lunie. "I hope it will be someone to clean out the house."

"Well, she's going to help with that, in a way. Sort of," he said, hoping Lunie wouldn't ask more questions. "I have to check the costumes." Rhoda placed their bowls in the dishwasher when they were done, and followed him to his office.

"Are you ready to spend more time on your autobio?" Rhoda asked when they reached the upstairs room. "I've been thinking. You don't have to start with something like, my name is Dayton Pitts and I was born on whatever day and my family is . . . Boring. Instead, we could start with your adventures out West, and gradually work in the rest of your life. It's like folding flour into fluffy beaten eggs when you're making a jelly roll."

"I've never made a jelly roll, but I like them," Dayton said, scratching Scooter's head. "Especially with raspberry jam and some whipped cream. Maybe fresh fruit on top." He wondered if Coreen was making a jelly roll at this very moment or if she had a personal chef, the kind you saw on Chef TV, cooking for the rich and famous.

"Are you listening?"

"Yes. Jelly roll."

"So, why did you go out West, and where did you go first?" Rhoda's fingers were poised to type.

"Uh, I went because Mother said I needed to get a summer job, but I don't want you to put that in."

"And so you drove in your camper to the Grand Canyon?"

"No, toward Rapid City, then Grand Rapids."

"Why Grand Rapids?"

"I was lost. I found a GPS at a truck stop in Mitchell but it wasn't working right and the voice told me to turn east when I should have turned west. I still have it, though. I like changing the voices. You can make them sound foreign if you want to." Dayton pocketed Scooter. "One of these days I'm going to take it apart to see how they do that," he said.

"Do what?"

"The GPS. Look inside." Dayton looked at the walk-about costumes and wondered if the squirrel should carry a basket with nuts and candies to hand out to children. But it could be a problem if children had peanut allergies or if chocolate made them hyper. He could carry permission slips, or forget the kids and just eat the nuts and candy himself.

Rhoda had stopped typing. "Dayton, you really seem preoccupied. Why don't I draft your story and then you can tell me if it's correct. I've seen movies about the West and TV shows about the national parks. Would you like that?"

"Sounds good as long as it's all good. When I go to Mother's at one o'clock, I'll wear my walk-about so I can be ready to leave immediately when you come for me," he said.

"Sure," said Rhoda. Her fingers were flying and her chiseled face had a dreamy quality that he hadn't seen before.

Five

DAYTON, HIS BUSHY TAIL TUCKED into a wide belt, arrived at Mother's at 12:25 and was relieved there were no cars in the driveway. Coreen would probably have a limousine deliver her or would drive a Rolls-Royce, powder blue with pink leather seats. He placed his squirrel head and candy basket on top of the freezer in the yard, then noticed that the back door was ajar. He worked his way carefully through the kitchen so as not to catch his fur on something sharp. He didn't know if there was anything sharp sticking out, but there might be. He never knew after things shifted in the night.

What might Coreen like as well as Cleebo? Where would he take her first? Ideas escaped him, except he knew he didn't want to share the contents of his room with her.

"There you are!" she said, crouching behind the living room sofa. "You're late."

"It's not one, yet," said Dayton stumbling over an end table topped with broken ornaments.

"Well, it's one o'clock somewhere," Coreen said. "I've been here for almost an hour. This place is incredible. Absolutely incredible. I've never seen anything like it."

Dayton thought briefly of telling her that she had no right to enter Mother's without him, but thought better of it.

"I haven't found anything as nice as your Glibub, but there are some amazing things here. Have you ever had an appraiser look at the art or some of these objects? They could be valuable. You know, one woman's trash, as the saying goes."

"Lunie and I plan to have an appraisal before the yard sale," he said. "Mother did have incredible taste."

"Did you know your mother had a costume trunk?"

Dayton thought whatever was in the trunk behind the sofa was actually Dolce's clothes, but he wasn't sure.

"Tah-dah!" Coreen popped up from behind the sofa wearing Mother's favorite straw hat and . . . Dayton quickly covered his eyes and turned away.

"Coreen, please," he squeaked, as her laughter reverberated through the room. "Please. Please."

"Please what?" she finally said, barely containing her hilarity.

"You need to wear more than a hat," he said.

"Really!" she said. "You mean, when we sort through a hoarder's prize possessions, we need to be dressed like Heidi, wearing everything we own?"

"More than a hat," he repeated. "Mother always wore more than a hat." He knew that wasn't exactly true, but truth was not necessary at the moment.

"But this is a big hat," Coreen said. "It will protect me when I sunbathe later in your backyard."

Sweat poured down Dayton's neck and trickled into the wrinkles of the squirrel's shaggy neck. "You can't sunbathe in this yard in that hat," Dayton stammered. "You'll, uh, catch a cold. It's chilly out."

"I won't be out there long," she said. "Just long enough."

He heard boxes moving behind him.

"You really need a large full-body hat with a zipper," he said, cringing. "Mother might have one in the trunk." He covered his eyes.

"Dayton, I think we need a truce. I didn't mention how you look in that animal outfit, so I don't think you should talk about the hat. Besides, I might want this hat instead of a Claybu."

"Okay, you can keep the hat, but you really need more than a hat. Really." He heard rustling behind the sofa and the dangerous sound of steps coming toward him. Feet without shoes. A hat walking. With his eyes still covered, he couldn't detect an easy escape route. Then he heard a voice in the hall. Rhoda.

"Dayton, guess what? Dayton? For gawd's sake what is going on in here?"

Dayton didn't dare look.

"Who are you?" asked Coreen.

"Dayton's friend," said Rhoda. "May I ask the same of you?"

"I'm not sure that's your business," said Coreen.

"Dayton, why is a woman, an almost-naked woman, standing in this room?"

"Rhoda, it's a long story, but I want you to meet our neighbor, Coreen Pomphrey," he said.

There was silence as Rhoda digested the information. Then she said, "Coreen Pomphrey? *The* Coreen Pomphrey?"

"You betcha, honey," said Coreen. She touched the brim of her hat with her right hand, and put her left hand on her hip.

"You know her?" Dayton whispered.

"Not personally," said Rhoda, "but from the soaps. Coreen had a leading role on *Days of Tort Lawyers* for a number of years. I used to watch it all the time."

"Two thousand three hundred and twenty-two episodes to be exact, and then they poisoned me with a venomous snake carried past office security by a disgruntled client. I had a great death scene over a six-week period. I even had an affair with a male nurse in intensive care, before I was finally out of work." She studied Rhoda's face. "Then, with Mother dead, and Father going overseas for good, I'm home while I ponder my future."

"Sorry to hear about the show," said Rhoda. "I'm sure something else will come along. You've really got talent."

"I'm at sixes and sevens. Kicksy-wicksy. Restless, at the moment," said Coreen. "Sending out resumés. Hoping for a big break, but if nothing turns up, I may just start my own network."

"Well, then," announced Rhoda, "we have just the opportunity for you, don't we, Dayton? His sister, Lunie, refuses to wear this sunflower seed costume when we go to work as walkabouts this afternoon, and we've got to have three people, according to the contract. I think it'll fit you."

Dayton moaned, his hands still across his eyes.

"Do I have lines? Will the press be there?" Coreen asked.

"You never know," said Rhoda. She tossed the sunflower seed outfit to Coreen.

"And, I shall wear this hat," said Coreen.

Six

EVEN DAYTON HAD TO ADMIT that the walk-abouts had done an excellent job that afternoon. Coreen had gotten into the spirit publicizing the Southern Sons of Nutcrackers, especially when she heard that the past president had a brother in Hollywood. She appeared even happier when two women recognized her and expressed their condolences that her soap character, Veronica Foxx, had been killed off.

"With all the bad things that happen on television these days, you'd think they'd want to keep a sweet character like yours," said one of the tourists.

Coreen figured that her admirer hadn't watched all nine years of the show, or she'd know that Veronica had a sordid past. Veronica had had twenty-three affairs within the firm; had been married five times, including once to a Mormon who had six other wives; she had been jailed on two occasions, once for something she had done, and once when she was falsely accused by the Mormon for trying to lead a wives' revolt across state lines. In the final year that she was on the show, the producer wanted her portrayed as a sweeter, more compassionate character, which wasn't as much fun for her, but then her passing could be mourned.

Coreen knew they'd regret letting her go. She was the only one in the cast who had enough money to supply her own wardrobe. But, she figured her demise was cemented when the

205

producer's wife caught them *indelicado,* as Coreen termed it. She still remembered a bit of French from her boarding school days. Just a phrase or two that had been oft repeated. Her teacher, Monsieur Jacques DuDieu, always said to her: *"Je vous prie de serrez vos genoux, mademoiselle!"* when she was sitting in the front row wearing her plaid jumper with its miniskirt. She would slowly oblige, knowing that he could not have her expelled because her father, Duncan Pomphrey, was a trustee and paid cash for her tuition. When Monsieur DuDieu turned to the board to teach the conjugation of the verbs and their Latin roots, sometimes she'd clap her knees together just to see him jump. French and theater were her favorite subjects even though her grades didn't reflect her future abilities in either.

There would be one more week of promoting the festival before it opened in the town park, then the tourist bureau wanted to make sure that the walk-abouts would be available to help direct visitors to the rides, food booths, and raffle drawings. Coreen said she'd check her calendar, but was positive she could make it. She wondered if there was a more dramatic costume that she could wear, perhaps one less itchy. Dayton said he'd see what he could find. He wondered if he should tell her not to use quite so much makeup.

"It's really better without Lunie," Rhoda said when they were back in his office. "Your sister can be such a downer."

"She has issues," said Dayton, waking Scooter from his afternoon nap. "I'd like to take you out, but you'd better learn to use the cat box during the day instead," he told the dog. He had been alarmed to see the posters with Scooter's picture plastered all over town and in the dog park. Reward for information leading to the return of a valuable dog that was also evidence in a case. Making sure that no one was looking, Dayton had pulled down every poster and shoved them in his squirrel suit. Now that he was home, he'd have to dispose of them properly in Lunie's trash.

Rhoda asked, "So how did you meet Coreen?"

"She went to my elementary school."

"Did she wear a hat?"

"Not that I noticed," he said. "I really don't remember her very well." He wondered if he had mentioned her name in his diary. He hoped not.

"She did a pretty good job for us today, but I don't think you should be alone with her," said Rhoda.

"Are you jealous?" Dayton asked.

"Hah! No way, but someone like that could be trouble."

"She invited us over for dinner tomorrow night," he said, wondering about Rhoda's reaction. "All of us. Lunie, you, me, Agnes. Six o'clock sharp."

"Could be a trap."

"I don't think so. I think she's lonely, rambling around in that gigantic house by herself," said Dayton.

"Agnes says she has people," said Rhoda.

"Her father is always traveling," said Dayton.

"No, I mean people who do things for her. A masseuse, a chef, a yoga teacher, acupuncturist, fitness coach. They all show up when she's in town."

"I'll ask Lunie when I go back downstairs."

Dayton searched briefly in a pile of magazines for his walkabout catalogue, then found it under his desk where Scooter had dragged and chewed the cover and the first ten pages. He was relieved that the section on fall costumes was undamaged; he needed to select a new outfit for Coreen. Paired with the squirrel costumes were various nuts and seeds, autumn leaves from oaks and maples, plus pumpkins, squash and apples that could also be used with the cornucopia for Thanksgiving. He wondered if Coreen would dress as a pumpkin or apple, or would she object because it would make her look even rounder. He turned the page and found farmer costumes. Perhaps that would be more appealing. The farmer page included animal outfits—chickens and ducks, plus several four-legged animals that required two people to be inside a single costume. He tore the horse and cow pages out of the magazine and threw them at the waste basket. He didn't want Coreen to get any ideas about sharing such a suit.

Perhaps Lunie would join them again if she was allowed to select her own outfit.

A few minutes later, when he broached the idea and tried to show her the catalogue, she said emphatically no. And she wasn't the least bit interested in having dinner at Coreen's. "I remember her from your band concerts," Lunie said. "Mother said she needed to keep her *genoux* together. I didn't know what that meant but I could tell Coreen wasn't in band because of her abilities on the flute."

"Coreen doesn't mind that we picked up leftovers from the curb in front of her house. I really think it would be nice if you came along," said Dayton.

"Absolutely not," said Lunie. "I have lots to do here. And we have work to do at Mother's. Have you forgotten?" She typed feverishly.

Dayton pulled out a chair at the kitchen table and faced his sister, the laptop screen between them. He was increasingly worried about her. She was distant, grumpy and friendless. She didn't eat well, even now when the cupboards were full. She didn't care about the value of Mother's collections. Most disturbing, she had thrown away the Grand Canyon coffee mug with the chipped rim. Fortunately, he had rescued it and placed in a safe place in his office. He knew the past few months had been hard for Lunie, but now that he was home, they'd face the world together just like when they were kids. He would help her get through these painful times. She could count on him.

Meanwhile, maybe Lunie should get away—take a cruise. If she felt she couldn't afford such an extravagance right now, Dayton could empty a few of the socks he had found at Mother's and pay for the trip himself. It would be a good way to spend some of Dolce's secret nest egg. But with whom would Lunie travel? Nobody likes to go it alone. He couldn't think of anyone who would travel with someone who would be polishing the ship's brass and dusting her cabin.

Dayton often picked up hitchhikers when he traveled out West. He knew that had its dangers, and realized how lucky he was when one couple, who said they were trying to outrun a family of grizzlies, squeezed into his front seat for about thirty miles before they asked him to drop them off at a bank. They wanted him to wait, but his radiator needed water so he drove to a garage. The fact that the hitchhikers were carrying guns was confirmed on the nightly news when Dayton heard that both were killed in a shoot-out.

Most of the hitchhikers were fine. His favorite rider was an eighty-four-year-old great-grandmother who was headed from Mahwah, New Jersey, to Mendocino, California, to protest a ban on smoking in her bingo hall. She told him the fresh air was killing her and hoped she'd be able to inhale genuine California smog before her trek ended.

Overall, hitchhikers helped him pass the time, and sometimes helped him change a tire or a belt. And they all, Dayton included, swapped lies—who they were and where they were from. He once persuaded a cowboy, who had been thrown off one too many broncos, that he was a flatulence salesman from the break-away republic of East Orangutan. "Really," said the cowboy. "Pleased ta meetcha." Dayton was impressed that he was able to keep a straight face until after he left the cowboy at a rest stop. It was his best story of the season and he grinned for weeks at how he had strung the poor man along for seventy-six miles. In good fun, of course.

Every day, on the road or while working at the parks, he'd use his cell phone to call Dolce. If she didn't answer, he'd leave a message and let her know where he was so she'd know he was all right. She rarely called back. Then he was without cell phone service for a week while he worked on a major roadside cleanup near Hayden Valley at Yellowstone. He called Dolce immediately when he returned to camp. After three days of silence, he left a worried message for Lunie expressing concern that something had happened to their mother. Wilma was the one who phoned him with the dreadful news. His cell phone kept dropping her call and so he only received bits and pieces of what had happened. Lunie. Purge. Cake. Bin. Mother. Dump. A packet from Wilma soon arrived with a copy of the police report, plans for the memorial service and an almost illegible note from Lunie expressing condolences and claiming she remembered nothing. "We can have a private memorial, you and I, when you get back, but everyone said they needed closure now," she explained. "Wilma has written a poem in her memory and I've found someone to officiate." She didn't explain why she hadn't returned his call. Perhaps she was trying to protect him. She was like that as a child, too. Always trying to protect him, and telling him to forget the bad things.

Nonetheless, he had been pissed that Lunie held the memorial without him; without giving him a chance to come home; without letting him have a private viewing to say good-bye. The ranger known as Yellowstone's "Buffalo Belle" sat next to him at a campfire a month after Dolce's passing. As they toasted marshmallows, Belle said, "Your sister must have been trying to shelter you. Your mother would have been pretty well flattened in the Dumpster."

"The fruitcake would have been a buffer," he said, letting his marshmallow catch fire and burn.

"I've seen what happens to tourists in a rock slide," Belle continued, "or worse, when they get out of their cars to take pictures of the bison herd coming down into the valley to cross the road and get to the river. It's not pretty. We can toot our horns, blow our whistles, and tell them to stay back twenty-five yards, but it doesn't always happen. And then, to top it off, I've gotta take time from work to go testify during the coroner's inquest."

"That's what happened with the guy emptying the Dumpster," said Dayton. "It probably cost him a day's work."

"I'm sure he didn't see her inside. It's pretty dark," said Belle. "You must be well aware of that from your position at the parks—checking lost-and-found articles."

"I know. I'm not blaming him. Not his fault. Just doing his job." Dayton shoved another marshmallow on the stick and reached it into the flames.

It really wasn't Lunie's fault either, although he could understand how she could blame herself. Well, some things *had* been her fault, he supposed. It was like dominoes. One little thing spills into another and then your mother is gone forever.

Dayton wished he had spent more evenings talking with Belle, who had a reputation as a bison whisperer. She could maneuver these large shaggy beasts out of parking lots and encourage them to roam back into the fields. Her wildlife skills weren't limited to the bison. Park lore told of her peaceful resolution of an hour-long standoff near Yellowstone Lake between a bull moose and a sixty-five-year-old tourist named Tonda Pease from Dagsboro, Delaware. Dayton admired Belle greatly. Her gravely voice, unexpected guffaws, and occasional coughs reminded him of his mother on her better days. But, just as he was feeling comfortable talking with her about his situation at home, it was time to migrate, as he called it. Dayton didn't stay at just one park all summer. He moved from one to another dealing with lost-and-found emergencies and trouble spots. Within a few weeks of the marshmallow roast, he was on his way to the Tetons, the winter grazing area of the elk. The meadows were devoid of elk during the summer, but that didn't stop tourists from gazing through binoculars for a glimpse. The Jackson tourist bureau, in its handsome center, played up the elk migration and urged Dayton to come back during the winter. He asked to see their lost-and-found as a courtesy visit by a colleague, and soon returned to Jenny Lake, wearing an unclaimed elk T-shirt.

Dayton sighed. He couldn't understand why Lunie wasn't interested in his experiences. She wasn't paying any attention to his presence at the table, so rather than interrupt her typing, Dayton decided to return to his office. Rhoda was in the upstairs front room, her room now. He looked out the office window. The dog catcher's truck was driving slowly down the street, searching between the houses. "I guess they mean business," he told Scooter, "but you're safe with me."

Seven

AGNES WAS LATE, CALLING to say that there had been an un-usually nasty mess at Patsy Tilda's mother-in-law quarters, where her grandchildren had stayed overnight and it had taken several hours to restore the quarters to a presentable condition. She insisted on giving Dayton and Rhoda a ride so that they would all arrive together at the Pomphrey mansion. Dayton had debated whether he should bring Scooter along, but Rhoda persuaded him to leave the dog in the office rather than let anyone else know that they had him. They were surprised that Agnes drove up in the Lucky Maids van rather than her own car. "Hop in the back," she said. "You can sit on the buckets of disinfectant. I hope you didn't get all dressed up. I haven't had time to change."

Dayton was glad that Coreen lived only a couple of blocks away. He could hear the concentrated chemical mix sloshing beneath him and feared that if it spilled it might dissolve his pants.

The truck came to a stop not in front of the house but at the rear, where Agnes was accustomed to entering. She removed her Lucky Maid coveralls that she had worn all day over her long, lavender sequined sweater and black tights.

"Won't she expect us at the front?" asked Rhoda.

"Doesn't matter," said Agnes. She rang the bell. There was no answer but they heard the sound of shouting coming from the kitchen. "That's odd," said Agnes. "It sounds like a fight. I don't recognize the other voice."

"Let me see," said Rhoda, the tallest of the three. She peered in the window and gasped. "This is terrible. We've got to do something."

"What? What?" said Dayton.

"They're going to kill each other," said Rhoda.

"Someone's going to kill Coreen?" asked Agnes.

Rhoda stood on her tiptoes. "Or, she might be trying to kill a guy in a white coat."

"Lift me up," said Agnes. Dayton tried but lost his balance.

"They both have knives," said Rhoda. "And blindfolds. We've got to rescue Coreen."

Agnes grabbed her coveralls and slipped back into them. "This could be messy," she said. "A Lucky Maid must always be prepared. It's our oath and we say it while moving our right hand as if we're wiping the glass door of medicine cabinet." She removed a penlight from her pocket and illuminated the security key pad: 4 3 2 1. She pushed the door open and stepped back. There was no mistaking the shouts and screams and clatter of knives. "You go first," she said to Dayton.

He hesitated.

"Cowards," said Rhoda. "We've got to distract the attackers. I'll yell something, and you run past me and grab Coreen."

"I think it would be better if I yell, and you and Dayton make the rush," said Agnes. "I wouldn't want my cleaning arm to be injured. It's insured, but I'd be out of work and I have my mother to think of, bless her soul."

Rhoda glared. "We're wasting precious time." She shoved the door so that it crashed into the wall, then jumped like a kangaroo into the kitchen yelling, "Moose pee-pee." She later told them it was the only thing she had been able to think of in the heat of the moment.

The clattering and yelling stopped. Agnes and Dayton, deciding it was safe to enter, ran into the room toward Coreen.

She raised her blindfold and said, "What the hell do you think you're doing?"

"Saving you," said Agnes.

"From what?"

"Your attacker," said Dayton. He turned to look at the man in the white coat, who had removed his blindfold.

"Just put down the knives," said Rhoda, "and I'll mediate this conflict so that we don't have to call the police."

Coreen handed Rhoda the butcher knife, blade-end first, and nodded at the man to do the same. He turned over a boning knife, paring knife, and serrated bread knife.

"Anything in your pockets or in your boots?" she asked.

The man extracted a grapefruit knife, an egg slicer, wooden spoon, spatula, and a wire whisk.

"How about you?" she asked Coreen.

Coreen responded by whipping open her silky red bathrobe and removed salad tongs from her hot-pink bra. "Are you quite finished?" their hostess asked icily, noting that Dayton had immediately turned his back to her.

Rhoda nodded, wishing Coreen would show more gratitude for her rescue. The man in white still had not said a word.

"Well, my buttinski friends," said Coreen, dropping her robe to the floor. "I want you to meet Iron Chef Basil Basil. He will be cooking for us tonight, if you get out of his kitchen."

"Basil Basil? The real Basil Basil?" Rhoda was astonished. "I didn't recognize him with the blindfold. I've watched his fusion organic-lobster show many times. He's all the rage on the Reality Cooking TV network."

Coreen's tone changed when she realized that Rhoda was awestruck. "He was showing me how they train teppanyaki chefs at his cooking school by juggling blindfolded," she said with a sugary tone. "And Basil Basil will take reality TV fusion-cooking to a new level. Thanks to my costumes and makeup talents, he will have many guises. When he's on as Chef Ciao Maine, he'll be doing Italian-New England fusion. When he's demonstrating Mexican-Middle Eastern fare, he'll appear as Chef Tequilla Ganoush. Or, on Irish-pasta night, he'll appear as Mac O'Roonie." She waited expectantly for someone to laugh, but Dayton shuffled and said nothing. Rhoda tried to think of an intelligent question.

Chef Basil Basil wiped the knife on his apron, then presented it to Coreen. "For you, my culinary kitten," he said, with an impressive British accent.

"Thanks, Sweetie PI," Coreen responded while further loosening her robe. "The PI, my friends, stands for politically incorrect. That's my approach to the show. My versatile chef, Sweetie PI, and I, plan to offend everyone and grab top ratings. Stereotypes will abound. We'll be the talk of the talk shows. Rude America will love us. I might call it Rude Food. Maybe even encourage food fights. Haven't figured everything out yet."

"Well, I guess we made a mistake trying to save you," said Dayton, studying his feet. "Should we go around to the front door?"

"Please do," said Coreen, "and please return the cooking implements to Sweetie PI. He was about to prepare Peking squab in confit, with Parmesan truffles stuffed with lobster crostini, mussels alfredo, and coddled brussels sprouts—one of my favorite dishes. And, for dessert, torte with strawberries and whipped crème de la crème."

"I'd love to watch," said Rhoda, wistfully.

"Out!" said Coreen, pointing at the back door. Dayton led the way, desperately hoping that Coreen would find something opaque to wear for dinner.

"Guess we muffed that one," muttered Rhoda. Disappointment penned new lines on her long face.

"Quite an outfit she's wearing," said Agnes. "I wonder if it's a bikini?"

"I recognized the bottom from one of her early shows. Veronica was supposed to bring a brief to a meeting of the tort lawyers, but she misunderstood and wore one instead. It was very scandalous at the time," said Rhoda.

It didn't take them long to walk down the drive and around the house to reach the front door. Agnes rang; they waited. She rang again. No answer.

"It's chilly out here," said Rhoda.

"Maybe she's really mad at us," said Dayton, fidgeting, "and she wants us to leave."

"Nah," said Agnes, shoving her hands in her jacket pockets. "She'll come around. She always does."

"I'll give her one more jingle," said Rhoda, "and then we can all go out for pizza."

Agnes waited another minute, then pushed the bell again. This time the door swung open, and Chef Basil Basil, a butler's jacket over his white coat, opened the door and bid them enter. He led them to the parlor and motioned to chairs, before leaving the room. Rhoda and Dayton sat next to each other on a forest-green leather sofa and studied the tapestries and old masters on the walls. Agnes inspected the coffee table for dust and quickly used her sleeve to remove what accumulated since her last visit.

Chef Basil Basil returned with an hors d'oeuvres tray and party napkins imprinted with Coreen's image and gold stars. Dayton limited himself to what looked like deviled eggs while Agnes and Rhoda were more venturesome, sampling pastry puffs stuffed with a gray matter seasoned with *ao nori*—his signature seaweed dish. A Wedgwood nut dish displayed rare chufa nuts. Chef Basil Basil popped one in his mouth and motioned to Dayton to do the same. Dayton pretended to taste one, but slipped it behind the sofa cushions, like he used to do at Mother's house when he didn't want to eat something.

"There you are! Don't get up." Coreen breezed into the room. Her black fishnet stockings clung to her legs and followed her thighs under a metallic gold skirt the size of a dime novel. Her shimmering, low-cut white blouse reminded Dayton of the shade in his bedroom that was in constant danger of falling. He focused on her bright pink lipstick that matched her heels, and her blond wig, and avoided looking at her knees.

"You wore that outfit—" Rhoda began, trying to remember the precise scene.

"Yes, episode 1,467," said Coreen. "I was simply stunning. I nabbed my second show-husband with this one."

"That's right. I remember now. Nate somebody."

Coreen beamed. "Nate Gneiss. He wasn't nice though." She waited for a laugh, and getting none, said, "Dinner should be ready in about five. We could have music and dance in the meantime."

"I love to dance," said Agnes. "We all clogged when I was little and my sister is a professional step dancer."

"How about you, Dayton?" asked Coreen, pushing the PLAY button.

He was picking lint off his sock. "I don't dance. Not me. My mother did when she still had the space, but not me. Lunie doesn't dance either."

"Well, Agnes and I will show you how." Coreen held out her hands and Agnes hopped to her feet. "It's not easy to cha-cha on this oriental carpet." Before they had a chance to move their feet, a gong alerted them to dinner.

Coreen and Agnes led the way chanting, "Step, step, cha-cha-cha." Rhoda tried awkwardly to imitate them. Dayton dragged behind, wishing he were home with Scooter. He wasn't looking forward to eating funny-sounding food. If you like to eat Italian, why not just order a pizza? He couldn't wait for dinner to be over.

Later, in his office, Dayton tried to reconstruct the meal. The hovering camera crew had been disconcerting. He was even more uncomfortable grading the various dishes, for flavor, originality and presentation, especially because Chef Basil Basil had a sabre strapped to his waist. Rhoda had carefully printed her comments about each dish, but Dayton turned in a blank sheet. He wasn't sure what "presentation" meant and he couldn't identify any individual flavors except perhaps the strawberries, but they didn't look like strawberries he had ever seen at Mosby's Market. They were dark, little, and crunchy.

"This is just a pilot for the show," Coreen had explained, handing them all release forms for appearing as they took their seats at the grand banquet table.

"I wish I had dressed for the occasion," said Rhoda, blinking at the bright lights.

"We just wanted you to look like the ordinary people that you are. Agnes, stop inspecting the silver for smudges!"

Coreen had made sure their crystal wine glasses were constantly filled to an appropriate level, and wiped her pink lipstick off the rim when the camera zoomed in on her hands and glass.

Then, after pouring lichi liqueur into dainty cranberry-colored glasses, Coreen raised hers for a toast. "To my friends and the series' success. I give you playdays, heydays, and paydays!"

"Oh, my gosh," said Agnes. "That's what my Irish mother always says. I will gladly drink to that."

Dayton knew Agnes was thinking about the payday part. He wanted no part of any of it, but Coreen immediately had a hook. "And for our second show," she said grandly, "We'll introduce the walk-abouts as our special judges. That will be lots of good publicity for you, Dayt." His mind was fuzzy from the alcohol, but he later distinctly remembered two things. Agreeing to do it, followed the sound of knees clapping from under the banquet table.

And worse yet, Coreen said, pouring herself another lichi liqueur, "I want that little dog on the show."

Dayton panicked. "What little dog?"

"The one you are harboring," Coreen said, with a knowing smile in the direction of Agnes.

Eight

S o, I KNOW YOU'RE UPSET," said Rhoda. "Okay, Agnes is a blabbermouth, but what's done is done." She wrapped Dayton's blue flannel shirt around her thin chest, and sipped her coffee out of the chipped North Rim mug.

"If Scooter's on TV, then they'll come and get him and he'll have to live in a cage until the trial and his little feet will probably fall right through the mesh. Besides, I'll get arrested. It's all Agnes' fault."

"Perhaps you could pretend that you just found the dog, and that you'd like to adopt him," suggested Rhoda.

"Agnes would blab."

"Probably."

"Why not give Scooter to Coreen? She could make him into a star and then no one would dare take him to a shelter."

Although Dayton knew that might be a solution, he was more alarmed by his vision of Chef Basil Basil juggling knives, then serving something small with long legs sticking up, perhaps with a Ping-Pong ball in its mouth, and giving it a fancy name, such as *poularde à chien.*

"How about Agnes, then?" said Rhoda. "She could trade Scooter to a good home—sort of an underground for runaway dogs. A rescue group."

"I'm not talking to Agnes anymore," said Dayton, with an uncharacteristic sullenness.

"I could post a hypothetical on Facebook," said Rhoda. "There's got to be help for you out there."

"I'll think about it," said Dayton. He was startled by a knock on the door.

"Office hours aren't until later this morning," called Rhoda.

"I want to talk to my brother," said Lunie.

"He's in a conference right now," said Rhoda.

"Tell him there's another notice from the building department. I will meet him at Mother's at ten sharp."

"Thank you. I'll check his schedule and see what I can do," said Rhoda.

"You could have told her I'm tied up all day," said Dayton.

"Let's see what she has in mind," said Rhoda. "We could always do the minimum to get the county off your backs."

"I'm really quite peeved, Rhoda. Peeved. I don't know what the rush is. Mother's house was and is cozy. It was the way she liked it and it's the way I like it. My fence is art." Dayton looked out the window. A squad car drifted down the street. The driver's window was open and it looked like he was dangling a dog bone on a string. Dayton feared that it was only a matter of time before they'd want to have a warrant to search both Mother's and Lunie's to hunt for the dog. His sister had been so self-absorbed recently that he wasn't sure what she remembered about Scooter's hideaway, but both Coreen and Agnes knew about the dog and were not to be trusted, and Dayton didn't know if Clive might crack under pressure from the police.

Dayton sat on the floor and leaned back against the futon. He kicked an apple core under the desk where Rhoda tapped on the computer keyboard. He spotted his childhood diary near a stack of paperbacks from Mother's sewing room. There were also a dozen library books that were two years overdue. Mother had never been in an hurry to return them, saying that her taxes helped fund the library.

He stretched his arm and pulled the diary to his lap. The cover had fingerprints all over it, probably from when he was working on Tobor and the grease can spilled. He noted that his adult handwriting wasn't much better than it was in elementary school, some letters slanting to the left and others to the right often in the same word. He smiled when he remembered finding a box of colorful pens in Mother's sewing room. He tested them and brought the ones that worked to his bedroom. He used a different color ink for each month of his diary. Each page contained five days, so there wasn't much room to elaborate on events, but that was okay, because he didn't have much to say.

Lunie had given the diary to him for a Christmas present one year, and even though it was dated for the year prior, she told him it really didn't matter. Back then, she also had a diary—carefully hidden in her room.

Dayton leafed through the pages from long ago. He had written that he had smashed a spider during the second week of January, and then had drawn with red ink around its legs. To his amazement, the spider carcass was still there, although three legs had detached. On February 12 he had scrawled that a girl had given him a Valentine and had asked him to her house for a party. The Valentine showed two naked Cupids kissing and was signed C.P.

A chill went through him as he remembered turning down Coreen. She was anything but cherubic when she knocked him to the floor one day before health class, then stood over him, and chanted, "Can you see London, can you see France, can you see my—" Dayton had closed his eyes and was grateful to be rescued by his teacher. He crumpled Coreen's Valentine and aimed it at the apple core.

On the way home from school that day he had found a broken piñata and took it home to Mother as a present. She pointed to a spot where he could leave it and went back to work on her crafts, fashioning Valentines to sell at the Book and Bridle. It was her last year of leaving cards on consignment there, even those she laminated so they wouldn't get shopworn. "Be a lovey," she said, "and get me my color pens." Dayton located the box and handed them to her. "None of these write," she said after trying each one. She sighed and tossed the box in the corner. Dayton had thought of getting the good ink pens from his room, but didn't. He simply wandered out, shoving the piñata under a rocking chair covered with towels.

He continued flipping pages, many of which were filled with doodles and ideas for mechanical inventions.

His April 22 entry mentioned a disaster on his worm farm. The farm had failed when a bird—he didn't know what kind— had flown in his window and feasted on the little guys. His drawing showed a little worm cemetery and RIP on a cross above it. He had meant to dig up more earthworms, but never got around to it. The large green box that housed the farm was probably still in his closet.

On May 5 there was a reference to Lunie's diary. He had found it wrapped in a sweater in her dresser when he went into her room looking for tape, and decided to read a few pages. She mentioned a fantastic show-and-tell at school when a boy named Fink brought in an X-ray machine for your feet. Lunie had drawn little hearts on the page. Dayton was impressed that Lunie was signaling how much she liked the foot machine. Maybe she'd remember that day now and provide more details about it. But at the time she had been so annoyed that he had been in her off-limits room and had read her diary that she refused to tell him how to find Fink or even point him out in school.

His own diary entry from the next day depicted what he thought that X-ray machine would look like; he had vowed to build it eventually.

By September that year he was out of bright colors and had to use brown. He studied one entry that showed his mother being eaten by a bear. He couldn't remember why he had sketched that or why the stick figure of himself was smiling. His drawing of Lunie showed someone with only eyes. He was about to page through November when Rhoda said loudly, "Dayton, for the third time, don't you want to hear what your mother was writing about?"

He closed the diary and slid it back toward the library books. "Huh?"

"I told you Ma had been writing something, and I've been going through it. Listen to this. Ma was planning to write about her life, but she only got as far as an outline." Rhoda handed Dayton a printout.

Dolce had listed the following: Born. Raised. Married. Divorced. Crafts. Children (two, girl and boy). Cats. Wilma. Food. Ants. Fruitcake order?

"This is it? She didn't fill in the details?"

"Nope. I guess she planned to do it later."

"The fruitcake order with a question mark. Do you suppose it was a premonition?" asked Dayton. He placed the paper in his lap and rubbed his temples.

"Could be," said Rhoda. "People often have visions of how life will end. It actually can shape their life. They may have a dream about an airplane crash and so they won't fly and then *bam!* a plane falls out of the sky into their house. Stuff like that."

"I see what you mean," said Dayton. He didn't really see at all, but he was too tired to discuss it further. He had bigger issues to deal with, such as protecting his little friend. Scooter rolled over and eyed him for a belly-rub. "I'll figure something out," he said to the little dog.

Mother's

One

FOR THE THIRD TIME THAT morning Lunie mopped her kitchen floor, determined to restore it to its pre-Dayton condition. She had vacuumed the living room and hall twice, not caring if the noise at 5:30 AM woke her brother and Rhoda. Inspiration or lack of it had kept her awake most of the night as she tried to figure out how Sue would stay at the community orchestra rehearsal when she had been propositioned by the second chair French horn player. But when Lunie reluctantly got up at five and flipped on the light, she had been horrified at the dust, crumbs, and clutter. She made coffee and plans.

As soon as she finished the first pass around the house, she discovered more dirt lurking, and that warranted a second cleaning, then a third. She scrubbed the counters, emptied the trash, cleaned the cat box, which had odd-looking solids in it, and refilled Phil's bowl, mildly puzzled that he seemed to be eating more than usual lately.

This would be the day that she ridded her pantry of supplies she didn't need or want, and by afternoon, she would tackle the upstairs. She would issue Dayton a new ultimatum, and tape it to the Empty Room's door, if necessary. It was seven, and the downstairs, except for the omnipresent moose, was almost back to normal. She had plans for the moose, too. She had located a discount moving company online that specialized in large objects, such as grand pianos on third floors of walk-up apartment buildings. She would call for an estimate. Dayton wouldn't be pleased but, if he really wanted to keep the mechanical beast, it could be moved to Mother's shed, at least until Mother's was cleaned and sold. With her own home reclaimed, Lunie would be prepared to tackle Mother's. To show Dayton that she meant business, she'd call the newspaper and place an ad for a yard sale. *I've gotten a grip,* Lunie thought proudly. *I've taken charge of my life.*

The chilly dawn beckoned a sunny day, so she decided to take an early walk. She could continue with her plans, and perhaps receive a special blessing from the writing muse to solve Sue's latest predicament. In the last forty-eight hours Lunie had managed to type another sixteen pages, even though they were scattered throughout the book, which she had decided would be at least 160 pages. A short novel.

Lunie glanced back at her front porch and smiled when she realized that Mountain Movers would have to take down Dayton's doors surrounding the moose in order to extricate it. At this point she wasn't concerned about what they might charge. Whatever it took to make things happen would be fine with her.

The yellow-and-black police tape surrounding the property across the street fluttered in the breeze. Tacked on the trees in the yard were new pictures of the missing dog, the one she had seen dash down the street the night the Sanders were arrested, and that she later saw with her brother. It was too early for Agnes to show up for work at Professor Finbarr's, and Wilma hadn't been out to collect her paper yet. Mother's house had an alarming number of plastic bins on the front porch, and a toilet in the side yard where someone had crammed orange and yellow artificial flowers in the bowl. Mother's was definitely on her to-do list for the day.

Lunie broke into a jog when she reached the bottom of the hill, rounded the corner then turned left on Beauregard. She wondered briefly about the television station truck with a large satellite dish on top that was parked out front of the mansion, but jogged on by.

By the time Lunie returned to her block, the sun was above the increasingly barren trees. She walked up the hill to let her pulse and breathing return to normal before she reached her house.

Phil, waiting on the back porch, sped in ahead of her and sat by his empty dish in the back hall. She was about to chide him for eating so much when she smelled and saw smoke. Lunie grabbed the flaming frying pan from the stove and hurled it at the driveway. She filled a mop bucket, and doused the flames that had consumed an unknown concoction. She was horrified when she returned to the kitchen. Cracked egg shells dripped down the sides of the counter. Milk pooled on the floor around a pepper grinder that had fallen or been dropped. She turned on the vent to the stove just as the smoke alarms went off, triggering the moose's recording mechanism and selecting its mating call.

"Dayton," Lunie yelled. "Daa-y-ton!"

"What's up?" He appeared from her library carrying a bowl of cereal.

"Look at this mess!"

"What mess, Loonie-fumey? I was just making breakfast for all of us. What happened to the eggs and bacon?"

"Didn't you see the fire? Don't you hear the smoke alarms?"

"I was watching the cartoons, just like we did when we were kids. Some of the same ones are still on, in rerun. Remember *Mr. Weasel's Trolley*? It was hard to hear it with all the commotion."

"You could have burned down my house. If you want scorched eggs, try the driveway. And, while you're at it, begin packing. You and Rhoda need to be out of here by the end of the day."

"That was very wasteful, Lunie. You shouldn't throw out good food and a good pan. You shouldn't let yourself get so upset. By the way, the episode I was watching was about when

Mr. Weasel decided to build a robot and send it to the moon. Remember my robot, Tobor?"

"Dayton, please listen to me," said Lunie, relieved that the smoke alarms had stopped bleating. The moose was now chattering about tourists and cameras, but it sounded like its battery might be dying. "I cleaned my house this morning, and the kitchen is already a mess. I have no idea what you've done to my upstairs. I've asked you and your friends to leave and you ignore me. I can't take it. I really can't take it anymore."

Still holding his bowl, Dayton walked over to her. Before she could object, he gave her a big hug, a few drops of milk slipping down her back. She stiffened when she noticed that the clothes he was wearing, the ones he had brought from his closet, had The Smell. It was faint, but discernible. It was nothing she wanted to spread into her house the way it had taken over Mother's.

"Lunie, I'm doing my best. Rhoda and I will see what we can do today about moving into Mother's. It's just hard. So many memories. I thought you could understand that. Besides, I thought you were glad for the company. You're my only family. This is the place I can go when I have nowhere else to go. And now I have nowhere else to go but down the block to Mother's house where there is no room. Can't we have a little more time? The walk-abouts have a gig this afternoon."

When Lunie didn't answer, Dayton said, "*Mr. Weasel* is followed by your favorite, *Explorer Daisy's Neighborhood.* Remember her pith helmet and her frog buddy, what was his name?"

"Felsworth," said Lunie. She wondered if Dr. Manngo was online before eight. It probably depended on his time zone. She took her laptop, went into her bedroom and slammed the door.

RHODA WAS THE FIRST TO SPEAK after Dayton went upstairs to his office. "Your sister has anger-management issues and she's becoming more uncivil. I know I shouldn't say anything, but you try so hard to be nice and then this. She wants to kick you out again. Make her only brother homeless."

"I'm beginning to agree with you," said Dayton, "but she always comes around. I saw a box of chocolates at Mother's that we could give to her as a peace offering. What's on the schedule today?"

"Walk-abouts at four, then we have a run-through at Coreen's for the next cooking show episode. She said the chef would prepare a six-course meal made out of Chinese cabbage, tofu, almonds, mahi-mahi in a prune reduction, Bavarian cream and citron," said Rhoda.

"Lunie hates citron."

"Lunie doesn't want to be a judge," said Rhoda.

Dayton tossed a pink pencil eraser for Scooter to catch. The dog sped toward it, but instead of bringing it back to Dayton, he growled, laid down, and chewed it into tiny pieces.

"Maybe what we should do," said Rhoda, watching the eraser crumble into slobbery fragments, "is to go through things at Ma's this morning. Get Lunie off your back."

"That's a lot of work," said Dayton.

"I'll help in a minute," said Rhoda.

"Oh, my gosh," said Dayton, when they reached Mother's an hour later. They could hear someone inside and the sound of objects landing in boxes.

"I'm glad you're here," said Lunie. "I've placed the ad and a sign goes up in the yard later today."

Dayton looked in horror at the contents of the cartons. "That's Mother's favorite rolling pin."

"How can you tell? There are six of them, and two are missing handles."

"And, her blue curtains. You can't sell them. She was going to hang them in my room."

Rhoda touched Dayton on the shoulder and motioned for him to go outside. "Look," she said, "if it makes her feel better, let her have her yard sale."

Dayton looked crushed. "Whose side are you on? You have no idea what these things mean to me and how long we've had them."

"Just a few things. One or two. Maybe some broken stuff."

"Broken stuff can be fixed," said Dayton. "Mother had lots of glue."

"I'll bet we could find a couple of things to sell and that would make your sister happy."

"All right," Dayton said reluctantly.

"Where do you want to start?" asked Rhoda, steering him toward the door.

"Ma's craft room," said Dayton in a resigned tone.

Rhoda grabbed a brown shopping bag as they passed Lunie in the kitchen without saying a word.

They threaded their way carefully down the hall to Mother's living room, then Dayton pushed open the door to the craft area. It was unchanged since the last time he had seen his mother in there—"disarray befitting a creative person" as Dolce so often said. "Artistes can't work in a sterile environment," Dolce added. "And there's serendipity in the hunt. If you knew exactly where your scissors were, you'd miss the inspiration of a potential collage of construction paper scraps that spilled on the floor. You wouldn't have thought to use a blue marker on a card instead of red."

Lunie never understood her thinking, but Dayton, the inventor of mechanical things, did. If all the parts were organized, you might not have thought to use glue instead of string, or a bolt instead of a stick.

"This is an amazing place," said Rhoda. "I never imagined she had so much—"

"Stuff," said Dayton. "Good craft stuff. You can't make things if you have to run to the store all the time to buy materials. You'd never get anything done."

"Did she make that piñata?"

Dayton flushed. "I gave it to her."

"You must have inherited her talent, then," said Rhoda. Dayton decided not to explain. He was filled with unexpected sadness.

"Well, what do you want to sell?" asked Rhoda, picking up dried-out tubes of acrylics.

"I don't know. I'll have to look around," said Dayton. He could imagine his mother painting her cards and fashioning reindeer out of paint sticks, and snowmen out of paint rollers. She showed him how to make stamps by carving potato halves, and he knew where he could find the one he made, then hid under her chair when she told him that she couldn't tell if it was a cat or a dog. He was too embarrassed to tell her it was really a swan.

"How about these?" asked Rhoda. She held up three crocheted pot-holders. Stained. Charred. Orange.

"Oh, no," said Dayton. "Let's take them to Lunie's." He stuffed them in his pocket, and studied the room.

"What about these turkey garlands?"

"They'd be great as part of the walk-about costume," he said. He wrapped the garlands around his neck.

Rhoda looked at her watch. "Hey, we've got to get going. Coreen's going to pick us up at three and we have to finish the additions to her costume."

Lunie wasn't in Mother's kitchen when they walked through and they didn't see her outside. "Will you look what she's done!" said Dayton. He grabbed the box Lunie had filled with two toasters, a split garden hose, frying pan, mismatched place mats, and cookbooks without covers. "This is from my half. It's not for sale." He pointed to another box. "That one isn't either." At his frantic motioning, Rhoda picked it up and they hurried back to Lunie's.

Two

LUNIE WAS ON THE PHONE in the living room when Rhoda and Dayton tiptoed through her kitchen and up the stairs with the boxes.

"Yes, start the ad tomorrow," Lunie told the man in classifieds, "and we'll run it for a week. Put in it that there will be new items every day."

She left a message for Mountain Movers providing the specifics of the moving project.

With great satisfaction, Lunie finished lettering the yard sale signs, tacked them on stakes, and went back to Mother's, where she pounded them in the front yard.

Raiders Dixie Bistro agreed to rent her six tables they used for catering, and Clive said he would deliver them during his lunch break. Lunie had decided that she wouldn't try to price each item, but rather have everything on each table marked as the same price—fifty cents or a dollar. Priced cheaply enough, items would sell quickly. She'd also have a pile marked "free."

Feeling generous, she would let Dayton use three of the tables for his sale items. When he had money jangling in his pocket, she hoped he would get into the spirit of things.

Lunie dragged large leaf bags that she had filled from the kitchen counters to the front porch where they would be near the tables. Once the movers arrived, she'd have them bring the moose over as a featured item.

She had almost reached Mother's stove, an early goal, but there were still so many things that were broken or dirty that Lunie knew there was no way to sell or give them away. She started a junk section between the shed and the freezer and within minutes the heap was knee-deep: cracked plastic laundry baskets, torn lamp shades, rusty tin-can art, stuffed animals without eyes or ears, and a smashed piñata.

"What are you doing?" yelled Dayton, charging down the street with Rhoda loping behind. "You can't have a yard sale without me!"

"I'm not," said Lunie, with her hands on her hips. "We're doing this together. Tomorrow, and until the house is empty. I ordered tables for both of us."

"Oh, man!" said Dayton, covering his face with his hands. "I can't believe you're doing this. I thought I could trust you, my sister."

"Well, I am," said Lunie. She was surprised at how calm she sounded, and how uncalm Dayton was.

Rhoda tugged on Dayton's sleeve and motioned for them to walk over to the shed. "Look," she whispered, "your sister has gone completely off her rocker. I really meant it when I said we need to play along with her until we can figure out the next step."

Dayton thought for a moment, then nodded. "Okay. A few things." Then he looked at the growing junk pile. "I can't let her get away with this." He ran over and grabbed the piñata. "This is something very special. I gave it to Mother. She loved it." With that he hurried back up the hill.

Rhoda watched Lunie carrying boxes from the house to her triage area for the yard sale. "Hey, Lunie, Dayton has agreed to have a table. Satisfied?"

Lunie kept sorting. "I'd be more satisfied if he would fill up the three tables I've allocated for him, but it's a start."

Clive showed up earlier from work than expected and Rhoda helped him unload the tables and set them up. Lunie immediately placed items on the dollar table, with full boxes beneath it for easy restocking. Rhoda sat on the edge of Dayton's table and awaited his return. She was about to look for him when he ran into the yard, his face red. He put his hands on his knees and leaned over to catch his breath.

"You owe me big-time, Lunie-catchatoony!" Dayton panted.

"What for?" she said, surveying the neatly arranged items on the five dollar table.

"There were big guys at the house trying to knock down the entryway and steal the moose. In broad daylight! Can you believe how brazen that is. Fortunately, the cops came by again looking for Scooter, and I called them over and the big guys left. Turns out they didn't have a license for anything. They all got tickets."

"You stopped my movers?" asked Lunie.

"Your movers?" said Dayton. "You were trying to get rid of the moose? Well, you know what I think, Lunette Pitts? I think you don't deserve something as magnificent as the talking, butt safe moose. I'll take it back."

"Good. Take it back."

"Good. I now have taken it back."

"Now, get rid of it."

"You can't tell me what to do with my moose!" said Dayton.

"Figure it out," said Lunie. She covered her tables with frayed orange bed sheets. "I'm going home. To my house." When she reached the street, she saw a car that looked like Coreen's turn the corner and drive slowly toward Mother's. Lunie kept on going.

Coreen pulled to a stop in front of Dolce's house. She got out, walked around to the passenger's side, leaned against the door and took a small white pad and pen from her pocket. Her short, emerald green wool coat drifted open. Dayton turned his face. "Go see what she wants," he begged Rhoda.

Rhoda returned. "She's thinking."

Dayton asked, "About what?"

"All she said was she has grand ideas and she'll see us at three." Rhoda waited for Dayton's response, and when there was none, she said, "Let's go inside and see if we can find anything for your table."

LUNIE IMMEDIATELY CALLED Mountain Movers and left another message, apologizing for her brother's behavior and any problems that he may have created for them with the police. She begged the movers to return. There would be no trouble this time, she insisted.

Lunie would drive to the bank later to make sure she had enough change for the yard sale, but first, while Dayton and Rhoda were at Mother's, she'd take a few minutes to check in with Sue. Where had she left off? Chapter 19 would relate what happened after the tragic death of Sue's husband Ralph Pfizer.

> Sue had genuine tears for Ralph at the calling hours and funeral, and even asked the children's choir to sing "You are my Sunshine" a Capella. But, nobody, not even her best friend, Wendi Larsen, knew that Sue was not unhappy to have the children call her Ms. Coley again, even in the middle of the year, instead of Mrs. Pfizer, which was hard to say and even harder to spell. Besides, it didn't sound very Minnesotan, which is perhaps why the Pfizers had never been invited to join the Norse and Hest Riding Club. Ralph blew off the social slight, saying it was probably because they didn't own a horse, but Sue believed that it was really their last name that stood in the way of admission. She wouldn't be eligible now, as a widow lady, but at least the reason for exclusion was more clear.
>
> In the months that followed her birthday dinner, Sue's dedication to motherhood was the talk of the town of Starbuck. She was devoted, packing elegant lunches with embarrassing daily notes of encouragement, such as, "Eat your carrot sticks and you'll get an A on your math quiz," or, "Remember that Mommy loves you even when you get caught chewing the gum you stole from my purse yesterday." Or, "Please see if you can

find out if your science teacher is single and tell him I need to talk with him about something." She hadn't meant to put that one in Ralph Jr.'s insulated lunch bag, but it had gotten mixed in with his turkey baloney sandwich made with healthy grain bread.

She was waiting for Ralphie to come out of school, when his handsome science teacher, with his photo ID badge hanging from his neck, rushed over to her car. He held the note out and said, "Ms. Coley, your son said you wanted to talk with me about his grades. I have a better idea, let's go to happy hour at the Norse and Hest—on Fridays they have wonderful *edamerost* and *kardemommeboller* fresh from the oven, I can guarantee you they are hot, hot, hot!"

Lunie grimaced. She still wasn't happy with Sue's flings and constant need for male attention. It was a bit surprising to her that Sue had stayed married to dull Ralph as long as she did. Lunie hoped she had been true to her man despite his roving eyes. They were such a perfect couple in public. No, they had to be perfect at home, too. She was his little sunshine, after all. But every little sunshine has a passing cloud, and perhaps there were secret communications from Rolex, who had married, and was elected to high public office. He would want to meet Sue in private—a hotel not far from the Capitol, where doormen were well-tipped not to recognize the Harley-riding governor. He assured her that no one would know, but after her third midnight tour of the city's art museum (that's what she told Ralph), the tabloids had pictures, the governor was disgraced for a couple of days, and Sue, disguised as a maid, narrowly escaped through the service entrance. She continued to vote for Rolex, who won again by a landslide. And she thought of him often when she taught the children about modes of transportation. Motorcycles were at the top of her list of spelling words.

Lunie wasn't sure that Rolex should end up as governor. He was handsome enough, and Sue was among the female campaign workers who carried placards proclaiming "Rolex is hot, but he won't keep the state in hot water." Perhaps the nod to current governmental affairs wasn't a good one. She'd have to think about what other career he might have had.

Lunie's prewriting was interrupted by the phone. *Great, the movers are coming back*, she thought. It wasn't Mountain Movers, however, but Coreen, speaking in her most theatrical voice.

"Lunie, dah-ling, I want to invite you to dinner tonight."

"No, thank you, I'm busy."

"I don't think you are busy at all, dah-ling, and I think you need to put on your fetching little sunflower seed suit and be one of the judges."

"Nope. Not going to do it."

"I think you will when you hear my proposition, dah-ling."

Lunie listened, asked Coreen to repeat her proposition, then said, "I guess I could change my plans. Just have Dayton bring the suit home after you're done with the walk-abouts."

"Ta-ta," said Coreen.

Coreen's proposal was irresistible, but Lunie would have to get Dayton to buy in, and that was not going to be easy. Perhaps Coreen would know how to convince him. Meanwhile, all Lunie had to do was wear that dreadful suit one more time and judge some cook's dinner.

Dayton and Rhoda bustled into the kitchen, each carrying a bulging cardboard box.

"Glad you're coming with us tonight, Lunie. Coreen's dinners are something," her brother said.

"Where are you going with that stuff?" said Lunie, in alarm. "You were supposed to be taking things out—moving out—remember?"

"Not in the cards for today," said Rhoda. "We're getting ready for the yard sale. Isn't that a priority with you?" She hurried up the stairs to change into her acorn suit.

Finally, thought Lunie. *Progress.* She would have a few hours to write before she had to don the sunflower seed suit. A double knock on the back door startled her. A uniformed officer was outside holding an envelope. She opened the door slightly, enough to talk but without inviting the man wearing a badge inside.

"Are you Lunette Pitts?" he asked. "I have a subpoena for a Miss Lunette Pitts at this address."

"For what?" asked Lunie.

"Has to do with the dog incident across the street. I have to deliver these things rather than rely on the mail," the cop said with a rueful smile. "Are you Miss Pitts?"

"I'll give it to her," said Lunie, not sure of what to say.

"I have to hand it to her in person, ma'am."

"Just a minute, then."

Lunie closed the door and hurried to the front hall. "Rhoda, you've got to come downstairs now!" There was no answer from upstairs. "Rhoda!"

Dayton opened the office door. "She's very busy now. Did you have an appointment?"

"Listen, there's a cop at the back door with a subpoena for her—for when she was using my name when we went over to the Sanders'."

"So the subpoena is for a Lunie, not a Rhoda?" said a voice from within. "I think you should deal with it, Lunie."

"Not fair, Rhoda," said Lunie. "I could have you charged with identity theft."

"That isn't a nice thing to say to our guest," said Dayton. "I'm closing this door now. We have to dress or we'll be late."

The tic returned to Lunie's eye. She waited outside the Empty Room's door, hoping that the squirrel and acorn would appear and she could escort Rhoda to the back door. She heard talking, then silence.

Eye twitching, Lunie returned slowly to the kitchen, wondering what she could tell the cop. If she tried to explain would he believe her? Or should she just accept the subpoena and deal with Rhoda later?

The officer was still standing on the back porch, but he was looking at the roof and talking to a radio strapped to his sleeve.

"Ma'am, I've called for backup. Burglars dressed in the weirdest outfits I've every seen just ran across your roof. Good thing I was here." He handed her the envelope and a pen. "Sign here, Miss Pitts. I've run your name through records and see you were stopped for reckless driving the other day."

Lunie heard sirens coming from around the block, and car doors slamming. She nodded to the officer and closed the door.

Three

THERE WOULD BE NO MORE WRITING that afternoon. Lunie's eye lid was so busy fluttering that she could barely see. She placed the subpoena on the counter without opening it. She was afraid the words would leap out, like a spring snake in a can. Manngo. She needed Dr. Manngo.

She quickly located his bookmarked site, typed in Lunie and her credit card number. She was relieved that he immediately responded.

> Dr. Manngo: Lunie, what's today's issue?
>
> Lunie: Rhoda took my name and said she was me when the police came about the little dog that belonged to the people across the street who raise teacup greyhounds and now the police think I'm Lunie. SEND
>
> Dr. Manngo: You signed in as Lunie. You're not Lunie?
>
> Lunie: Yes, I'm Lunie, but I'm not that Lunie. Rhoda was that Lunie. SEND
>
> Dr. Manngo: Hmm. I'll talk with Rhoda, Lunie.
>
> Lunie: Rhoda is in her acorn suit. She's a walk-about. SEND
>
> Dr. Manngo: Hmm. I don't understand.
>
> Lunie: She dresses up as Alice Acorn and walks around with my brother, a squirrel. SEND
>
> Dr. Manngo: Do what?

Lunie: They talk to tourists. SEND

Dr. Manngo: Hmm. I want to help you, but I need thinking time. There's no charge today for thinking time.
Just a charge for the answer.

Lunie: I'll wait. SEND

And wait she did, until she had to awake the screen saver
four times. She fed Phil, sipped a cup of tea, and frequently
checked for a response. Finally, Dr. Manngo replied:

My sister just called— she'd—Never mind. Come back
tomorrow when I don't feel so— Never mind. I'll have
an answer tomorrow when I'm less uncalm.

Even though the good doctor hadn't provided specifics,
Lunie was comforted to know that he was working on her case.
Yes, it was complicated. He would probably have a staff meeting of his colleagues. He would be consulting his books, and
perhaps someone in legal. She could wait because he cared.

She logged out just as Wilma breezed in without knocking.

"I hope you're all right, poor dear," she said, looking around
the room. "The officers said your house was being burglarized
and they are looking for a pair of oddly dressed outlaws. This
neighborhood just isn't safe anymore. And I worry especially
about you." She bent down to see what might be hiding under
the kitchen table, then continued her search of the downstairs.

"What on earth is that?" said Wilma.

"A moose," said Lunie.

"I can see that, but what is it doing here?"

Lunie thought about answering, but didn't feel like it.

"Well, that explains why you had that illegal entry built,"
said Wilma.

"It's all going to be taken care of," said Lunie.

"I hope so," said Wilma. "Not to change the subject but
I see you're having a yard sale. One of my best neighborhood free verses is about a yard sale. Like to hear it?"

Lunie wanted to say no, but didn't. Wilma took silence as
affirmation.

Ode to Yard Sales

When I can't regift my presents
And clothes no longer fit
And the teacups match no more
I spread them out on tables
and stick on little prices
then sell them to people
looking for a bargain
Then I fritter the money I make
at other people's yard sales.

"Your mother thought that was really cute," said Wilma. "She especially liked the ending because it's so true. If you need help tomorrow, let me know. Buyers always come early."

"Thanks, Wilma," said Lunie, wishing she would just go away. Wilma pulled out a chair, sat down, and prattled on. "Have you thought of writing poetry, Lunie? It is such a release. And it doesn't have to rhyme. I know, I know, there are people that write in complicated meters and rhymes, but a little bit of free verse is liberating and most people don't understand the complicated poems anyway. They understand "Roses are Red," but not

"And then there are the dances; there's the Nini
With more than one profession gains by all;
Then there's that laughing slut the Pelegrini
She, too, was fortunate last carnival,
And made at least five hundred good zecchini
But spends so fast, she has not now a paul."

Wilma smiled. "See? Well, I can tell from your face you don't get it. You know, I still remember Lord Bryon's *Don Juan* that I memorized in high school. Now, don't get me wrong, I write sonnets as well as Shakespeare, but who talks that way now? And what's a zecchini? A squash?" She didn't wait for Lunie to answer. "Just put your thoughts down in short lines. You could write about the ordinary. A favorite chair. Your cat. I must tell you that I do love my poetry group. They tear, no, shred, my writing to pieces, and then we put it back together, and I feel so cleansed, like I've had a day at the spa and ordered the facial mud mask as well as the massage. The poetry group is the subject of one of my new poems, too. I called it 'Rip Me up and Tear Me Down.' They also liked my Carl Sandburg imitation of 'Fog Comes in on Little Cat Feet.' I called mine, 'Clutter comes in on little kitty feet.' You know that's how clutter turns into hoarding. A piece of paper here, and few pillows there, Christmas cards that aren't discarded. It just builds."

Lunie leaned against the refrigerator.

Wilma checked the clock. "Lunie, dear, this has been almost as much fun as my chats with your mother. I almost had her talked into writing when—oh, so sorry to mention it." She looked at the clock again. "Well, I hoped the police would return with news that they had apprehended the perps, but I guess not," said Wilma. "I told them I would keep you safe in the meantime, but I must now away to make supper."

"That's very kind," said Lunie. "I'm plenty safe. Don't worry about me."

"What's that squeaking noise coming from upstairs?" asked Wilma. "It sounds like a small animal in distress."

Oh, no, that dog's still in the house. Lunie thought quickly. "It's just the moose. It talks and can even throw its voice. Amazing ventriloquist feature." She wasn't sure that Wilma believed her so she rushed to the moose, flipped its switch, and the moose brayed like a mule.

"Oh, my," said Wilma. "That is quite an invention."

"It has a large range of sounds," said Lunie. "It squeaks, barks, talks like tourists—I'd love to demonstrate all of them, but I have to get ready to go out for dinner. Bye."

The phone rang. Lunie waited to answer it until Wilma was out the door.

"Lunie, you're my one phone call," said Dayton. "We need bail."

I'll pay you back at dinner," Coreen told Lunie when they were outside the single-story brick building that housed the sheriff's office, city police, small holding cells, and fire department. The rest of the official offices, including the county court, supervisors' offices, school board, clerk, and records were in a three-story glass-front building across the street. Lunie knew both well. The building department was on the third floor and she knew that her former co-workers would be watching the walkabouts leave the holding cells. They would see that she was with them. They would notice that she was trying to shield her face from the cameras and that Coreen was making sure that the striped sunflower seed was photographed from all sides. Coreen was giving statements to the press.

"It was a huge misunderstanding," said Coreen, waving her arm dramatically as cameras snapped. "My friends, the squirrel, and the acorn, were simply cleaning the gutters on Lunie's roof when someone—and I'm not naming names, but they will hear about this tomorrow from my lawyer—thought they were burglarizing the squirrel's house where he lives with the acorn. And they have responsible jobs with the tourist bureau, just as I do."

"Miss, miss," interjected a recent graduate from journalism school, "can you spell your name?"

"Of course I can spell my name. Next question."

"What *is* your name?" asked a reporter from Channel 5.

"Coreen Pomphrey."

"Can you spell that?" asked the J-school grad, preparing to scribble furiously and hoping that she could read her handwriting by the time she returned to the newsroom.

"Yes," said Coreen, without looking at the eager woman.

The TV reporter texted his station, then said, "Wow! *The* Coreen Pomphrey! We air the Torts at three."

"Veronica Foxx died, you know," said Coreen, brushing lint off her shoulder.

"How do you spell Veronica?"

"Miss Pomphrey, how do you explain your involvement with the acorn and the squirrel?"

"I don't. Now, if you excuse us, we have an important engagement." She motioned for Dayton and Rhoda to get in Lunie's car. "See you at dinner." She headed for the parking lot, answering an occasional question from the cluster of reporters trailing her.

Lunie slowly eased her car from the curb and drove away. After they rounded the block and turned onto the highway she said, "I'm waiting."

"For what?" said Dayton, in a voice tipping toward uncontrollable giggling.

"An explanation," said Lunie.

Rhoda was quickly convulsed with hilarity.

"C'mon, you guys," said Lunie. "Get serious." The corner of her eye twitched furiously.

SCOOTER WHINED, WAGGED, AND raced around Dayton's office. "Good, Scootie-snootie," said Dayton. "Come to Papa." He fetched three puppy kibble bones from his pocket and broke off small pieces for Scooter. "Papa got them for you at the drive-through window at the bank," he said.

"We don't have much time. Coreen's expecting us," said Rhoda, adjusting her acorn hat in the mirror.

"Be a good doggy," said Dayton. "We won't be very late." He gave Scooter another biscuit before they went downstairs.

Lunie was waiting in the kitchen. "You each owe me $225 for the bail," she said.

"Coreen's waiting," said Rhoda.

"So am I," said Lunie.

"So, here's an IOU," said Dayton, pretending to write on a piece of paper. "You'll get your money. Let's go. You still have to change when we get over to Coreen's."

If Coreen's deal hadn't sounded like a solution to some of her problems, Lunie would have turned her back on Dayton and stayed home. She might have checked in with Dr. Manngo. She might have worked on her book after the bile slipped back down her throat. She might have had one of the cans of beer left behind. Maybe two, even though she rarely drank. Instead, she sighed, grabbed her purse, and followed Dayton and Rhoda out to her car.

Not only was the cable TV crew still in front of Coreen's house, several of the reporters and photographers, who had interviewed her outside the jail, were waiting with cameras in her front yard. Lunie drove right on by.

"You've passed her house," said Dayton.

"I know," said Lunie.

"There's a parking place," said Rhoda.

Lunie kept driving.

"You've got to go back," said Dayton. "She's expecting us."

"I don't want to have my picture in the paper," said Lunie. "You've caused me enough trouble."

"Then go around the block again, drop us off, and walk back. You can always go in the servants' entrance instead of the front door," said Dayton.

"Yeah, sure, like they won't notice me."

"Probably not if they are looking for the walk-abouts. You can always tell them you're Agnes," said Rhoda.

Lunie circled the block, let her passengers out and they were quickly surrounded. She did as Rhoda suggested, and in the twilight, no one noticed her slipping past them and darting to the back entrance. She could see Chef Basil Basil chopping a cylindrical vegetable she didn't recognize while a video camera zoomed in on his red-stained hands.

She hesitated, then knocked. The knife flew at the door, and the tip came through, narrowly missing Lunie's hand, which was poised to knock again. Chef Basil Basil yanked the door open, shouting words that Lunie didn't understand. She wondered if the words were names of items on the menu, but his demeanor told her otherwise.

"Take three," said the cameraman.

The chef motioned for Lunie to leave the kitchen, and she was happy to oblige. She saw the sunflower seed suit draped on a chair in the hall. A note pinned on it directed Lunie to the downstairs "powder room," where she could change. Lunie figured from the commotion outside that Coreen was granting interviews.

The powder room was as large as Lunie's living room, and filled with more artifacts—particularly statues of nudes, and paintings by the old masters of nymphs bathing. Large gold-framed mirrors were on three walls above the marble sink with gold-plated fixtures. The nearby Victorian-era dresser was topped with more makeup than the cosmetic counter at Dell's Department Store, Lunie observed.

The sunflower seed costume no longer smelled factory fresh from the box. It was infused with whatever scent Coreen had been wearing downtown. Lunie wished she could air it out before dressing, but she could hear voices in the hall. The mirrors told her what she had feared: She looked ridiculous in a shiny black elongated outfit that went from her neck to her knees. Black stockings covered her shoes and rose about the kneecaps and fastened with garters. Her pointed hat looked like something a fishing guide might wear on a intensely sunny day. Coreen had additional instructions: Put stripes on your face with the body paint in jars #3-5 on the right side of the dresser.

Lunie's only comfort was that no one would recognize her. She opened the door and stepped into a throng of reporters.

"Hey, are you Lunie?" asked the cameraman, swinging his camera into her face. "Didn't you break up that dog ring?"

"Can you spell Lunie?" asked the J-grad.

Lunie panicked and was about to hide in the powder room when she heard Coreen tell the media to leave her alone. "You're nothing but small petunia paparazzi," Coreen scolded. "If you want to watch the filming, it's on my terms."

"There was a hush in the hallway, and the reporters and cameramen made a path for Lunie. She walked with as much dignity as she could muster in the direction of Coreen's voice, and found the hastily remodeled dining room.

Dayton and Rhoda were seated at a special table designated for the judges. The new wall between the dining room and the kitchen had been folded into several sections so that Chef Basil Basil's culinary artistry would be visible to the judges and whatever studio audience Coreen intended. Dayton motioned for Lunie to take her seat next to him. "Isn't this incredible?" he whispered. "Did you ever dream that we would be on a cooking show?"

Coreen made a spectacular entrance moments before the taping was to begin. Her red feather boa draped around her neck and trailed just below the plunging neckline of her transparent lace silver camisole. It barely reached her sequin-covered red chiffon eighteen-inch skirt, with black lace stockings and knee-high silver boots. Dayton turned away, but every mirror in the dining room showcased Coreen. Rhoda said in an awestruck whisper, "Episode 1,975 in her soap opera."

"Ta-dah!" Coreen said, twirling her boa. "Are we ready, boys?" she called out to her camera crew.

"One minute," said Jack. "My contract calls for starting to film at 4:00."

"Don't be silly. Put away that union card. You're working for me, or I'll get that nice man from Channel 5 to take over."

"Take one," said Jack.

That was the cue for Chef Basil Basil to juggle six knives of while wearing his *toque blanche* over his eyes.

"Notice the cooking awards embroidered in his chef's hat," whispered Rhoda. "This special toque was presented to him at the award ceremony when he placed first, second, and third in every contest."

After the wild applause from Coreen and the reporters, Chef Basil Basil took a deep bow, lifted his pleated white toque above his bushy eyebrows, and bowed again to the judges.

Coreen immediately explained to the camera the premise of her new reality cooking show. Each week Chef Basil Basil would have a guest challenger. The panel of judges would not only render a verdict on the quality of the dishes, they would also each suggest an ingredient by secret ballot. "This being the new pilot," said Coreen, "we've selected the famed Chef Argyle to be the challenger." A white-suited figure wearing a shorter, simpler toque, stepped into the room and bowed to Chef Basil Basil, Coreen, and the judges.

"That's Agnes," gasped Dayton. "I didn't know she could cook." Coreen gave him a silencing-look.

"It's time for the judges to write their secret ingredients that they want worked into the meal." Coreen handed each of them a piece of paper the size of a fortune cookie message, and a pen.

Lunie's mind went blank. She couldn't think of an ingredient in anything. She couldn't even think of a food.

The squirrel paused only momentarily, then wrote his suggestion, and so did the acorn. They folded their papers and handed them to Coreen.

Jack looked at his watch.

Coreen said, "Lunie, just jot down anything. We need to get going."

"Speak, O, little sunflower seed," pleaded Coreen.

Lunie's eye twitched. Not a word could she summon.

"Anything. Just say anything," Coreen hissed, her cami heaving.

"Fruitcake," mumbled Lunie.

"Not fair," said the squirrel. "She said it out loud, and besides fruitcake isn't an ingredient. It's already something."

Chef Basil Basil shouted something unintelligible and lunged with his sabre in the direction of the judges. The piercing sound of a whistle stopped him. "Hand me that!"

ordered Coreen, disarming him. He pulled a dart out of his apron pocket and hurled it above Lunie's head and it landed squarely in the nostril of a mounted rhino.

"Enough," said Coreen. "There will be no fruitcake. Think of another ingredient, Lunie, and make it quick."

"Moose," mumbled the sunflower seed.

"There she goes again. She didn't follow directions," complained Dayton. "Shouldn't you disqualify her for speaking rather than writing it?"

"I'll take her suggestion, but just this one time," said Coreen. She flicked one end of the boa, then turned to Chef Basil Basil and Chef Argyle and opened up the little papers after a dramatic pause. "Your special ingredients proposed by the judges are moose, grits, and bubble gum. To your stations. You have sixty minutes."

"I can do mousse, but bubyam?" Chef Basil Basil was stumped, to Agnes' ill-contained delight. The chefs scurried around the kitchen, opening cupboards, drawers, the two large refrigerator freezers, and the pantry. Coreen gave a breathless narrative of their moves, but it was mumbly to Lunie's ears.

She covered her face with her hands, forgetting that it was striped with body paint. Why had she mentioned fruitcake? She closed her eyes. Her mind had gone as blank as a schoolroom slate. She shuddered. Someone seemed to be scribbling in scritchy chalk on the slate: *You are responsible!* To her horror, Lunie realized that the words were in her mother's handwriting. Mother was repeating words from the police incident report, words that Lunie barely remembered reading. If she had read them, they didn't make sense at the time. Suddenly, more of what had happened became clear. Lunie remembered the white box truck, with Van's Delivery painted in blocky letters on the side, stopping in front of Mother's just when Lunie was headed home from a walk.

"What are you unloading?" she had asked the driver.

"Four hundred and forty-five blocks of fruitcake," Van said, opening the back of the truck. "They're only three years old."

"Mother doesn't want them anymore," Lunie now remembered saying, hoping the driver would believe her. There was no more room in Mother's for one of these bricks, even if she had a craft project in mind. "She said to tell you just to drop them in that Dumpster," continued Lunie, pointing at the rusty metal box on Mother's property line.

"Okay, just sign here," said Van. He then backed his truck next to the Dumpster and with Lunie's help, tossed all the fruitcake on top of the neighbors' construction debris.

"Thanks," said Lunie. She found a $20 bill in her pocket, handed it to Van, and continued on her walk, unaware that Dolce was watching from her living room window. Lunie hadn't realized that Mother made a desperate dash for the Dumpster, scaled it like a mountain climber, and hurled fifteen fruitcakes onto her lawn before she slipped deeply among the rest. According to the autopsy, Dolce, though trapped, had gnawed her way through several packages.

If Mother had heard the trash hauler coming, she evidently didn't yell for help or couldn't be heard over the clanking of the lift picking up the bin and depositing its contents. Wilma had seen it all. "Don't blame yourself," she had told Lunie before the memorial service. "An accident."

But you're responsible, Dolce continued to scribble.

Eyes still covered, Lunie's voice returned. Loudly. "Nooooooo! I didn't mean it."

"Why are you screaming, Sunflower? You haven't even tasted the first appetizer," said Coreen. "If you're going to continue to cause scenes, I'll replace you with someone who has self-control."

"Sorry," whispered Lunie. "It won't happen again." She opened her eyes, and studied the appetizer created by Chef Argyle in front of her. Rhoda and Dayton were already sampling theirs. They tasted small bites, looked at the ceiling, smiled at each other and made notes on their score cards.

Lunie stared at the purple blobs dropped on saltless rice crackers, surrounded by garden weeds drizzled with pink squiggly lines, which she hoped was frosting.

"Judge No. 3, please commence tasting," ordered Coreen.

With the camera hovering, Lunie's fork approached a blob, and halted. Her mother was frantically scribbling. *Eat it. Eat all of it or— Remember the starving— You will sit at the table until you finish!*

Lunie's fork moved tentatively toward her plate. She inserted the tines into the purple matter, tempted for a moment to make a fork pattern on the top, like peanut butter cookies.

"Okay, open wide. Here comes the airplane." Coreen snatched the fork and brought it to Lunie's pursed lips. "Lunie, this is your last chance," she snarled, "or my offer is off the table and you are out the door."

Lunie's mouth opened and her tongue tried to toss the sample down her throat before she had to taste the purple blob. Too late. Her taste buds were in disagreement. How could she make a decision? She picked up a cracker and popped it in her mouth. And then another.

"That's better," said Coreen, with a stage smile to the camera. "Write down your thoughts, please."

Lunie picked up her pencil and marked her card, which had a range of numbers and a place for comments.

Coreen collected the judges' cards. "Judge No. 1, the acorn, said the freddo bubble gum on rice crackers, with a drizzle of framboise, had a clean, spring-like essence, and gave it a 4. She felt it could have used more imaginative vegetables—something with crunch. Very expressive," said Coreen and beamed in Rhoda's direction.

"Judge No. 2 describes the dish as a happy pairing of wild and tame, with the addition of bubble gum reminding him of a carefree childhood. He gives this dish a 5. Nicely done," said

Coreen. Dayton nodded in pleasure, and winked at Agnes, whose toque could no longer confine her curls.

Coreen scowled at Lunie. "Judge No. 3 just wrote, 'Nummy, num, num,' and forgot to circle her numerical rating."

"Next appetizer, please," Coreen said. Chef Basil Basil entered with three small plates on a bamboo tray. A trail of almonds circled a Napa cabbage leaf that was stapled at either end to shape it like a boat. He had carved miniature Statues of Liberty out of carrots, and whittled angels to row the boat out of Dakon radishes. The angels were perched on a mound of blue and white sauteed grits.

"This is a tribute to my birthplace in New Joisey where I could see the statue, even through the smog," said the chef.

"What happened to his British accent?" asked Rhoda.

"It depends what he's cooking," said Coreen. "You should hear Sweetie PI when he prepares Hungarian goulash or french fries. I selected him for his versatility. Now, prepare yourselves for the entree."

Lunie froze when Chef Argyle's main course of tofu moose, brussel sprout reduction and hash brown grits appeared in front of her. It reminded her of the mud pies she made in Mother's backyard.

"Seed, you look positively kicksy-wicksy. This just won't do for my TV show. I had my doubts, but Rhoda and Dayton convinced me to give you a try," said Coreen. "I'm replacing you with your understudy. You may go. Leave."

Lunie sagged with a mixture of gloom and relief. She left without a look back at the other judges, chefs or Coreen, and mumbled an apology to the cameraman for tripping over the power cord as thick as a well-fed black snake. She heard Coreen call for her understudy to have a seat, and to introduce herself. An eager-to-please voice said, "Wilma Wolenski. I'm a published poet and I'm writing a cookbook."

Lunie gathered her clothes and slipped out the front door.

Four

DAYTON'S THEATER-STRENGTH COLD CREAM removed most of the pale yellow and gray stripes on her face by the third try. Lunie applied more cold cream with a paper towel, but left it on to soak in, giving her raccoon-like features. She hung the seed costume on the moose's antler where Dayton could find it.

She wanted to go to bed, but it was only 7:12. She opened her dictionary. Kicksy-wicksy. That was exactly how she felt. Restless. Anxious. Who wouldn't be? Coreen must have seen it in her face, or the way Lunie tapped her fork on the plate rather than insert it into the food. She looked up the only person she could be sure understood her.

> Dr. Manngo: Hey, how's it going, Lunie?
>
> Lunie: My life is spinning out of control. SEND
>
> Dr. Manngo: What do you mean by spin? How does that make you feel?
>
> Lunie: Dizzy. It was the menu. I was a judge for a new reality TV cooking show. SEND
>
> Dr. Manngo: Sounds like fun.
>
> Lunie: I was thrown out for being kicksy-wicksy. SEND
>
> Dr. Manngo: That sounds like fun. I'm glad you're having more fun.
>
> Lunie: Not fun. I had to eat awful food. SEND
>
> Dr. Manngo: What kind of food?

Lunie: Grits. Purple things. SEND

Dr. Manngo: You don't like purple?

Lunie: It was okay, I guess, after I tried it. SEND

Dr. Manngo: Trying new foods is good. Part of the healing process. I like rugalach. You can get it online. Also groats and grunion. Very tasty.

Lunie: I felt silly dressed as a sunflower seed. I didn't want to wear the costume on TV. SEND

Dr. Manngo: You wanted to judge nude? Naughty girl. Just kidding. Be yourself. Deal with kicksy-wicksy and you'll deal with life.

Lunie knew she was blushing under the cold cream. She'd given the poor doctor the wrong impression once again. She was not one of *those* women. Lunie knew he was right about trying new foods and dealing with her anxieties, which were in more abundance than the items on the yard sale table.

The yard sale. I've got to be up early, she thought. She hoped Dayton and Rhoda would be quiet when they came in. She left a note on the kitchen table reminding them about the yard sale and to please tiptoe and whisper.

If they saw the note at 2:30 AM, they didn't try to be quiet, nor did they wake up when Lunie knocked on their doors at six AM. At 6:32, she pounded. Scooter was silent, also. At 7:01, she left the house with her mug of coffee. Early shoppers were already at Mother's, and had removed the blotchy sheets covering her tables.

By 8:00, when the sale was advertised to begin, Lunie had made $35, and had to restock from boxes under the table. Wilma dropped over at 8:19 when she picked up her paper.

"I'd be happy to help you, dear."

Lunie said, "I'm doing okay so far."

"Sorry you didn't feel well last night. We had a wonderful time. Do you want to know the outcome?"

Lunie wanted to say, "Not really," but that wasn't what Wilma wanted to hear, so she nodded yes.

"It was a tie," she said. "Everyone was quite surprised that Agnes could cook that well. Of course, we all knew Argyle was Agnes in disguise. As you might suspect, Chef Basil Basil didn't take it very well. He's demanding a throwdown tonight. Coreen has called the press. She's getting wonderful publicity for her new show. It's a whole new career and she can work from home."

"That's nice," said Lunie, trying to make change for a $20 bill for a customer who was purchasing a 75 cent porcupine candlestick with a slot on the side for toothpicks.

"And, she's leaving you in last night's episode when it airs. Your departure is part of the reality, Coreen says. I'm so inspired I could write poems all day today, but I think I'll whip up rhyming recipes for my own cookbook. If the show's a success, I can promote it."

Lunie forced a smile. She hoped no one would recognize her wearing the sunflower seed costume, especially anyone from work.

Wilma surveyed the items on Lunie's tables. "Not that I would want this back, but this snail-and-shell platter is something I gave your late mother. And so is that cauliflower teapot with the cracked spout. She adored the design that the tea stain made."

"Please take them, Wilma," said Lunie.

"Absolutely not. It's just that they meant so much to Dolce because of our friendship."

"Please, I'm sure she'd want you to have them back."

"No, Lunie, she would want you or Dayton to treasure them, just as she did," said Wilma.

Lunie quickly slipped them under the table, out of view of customers.

"And, oh my! I can't believe you're selling her 78 records? We listened to them for hours years ago. This was her favorite: 'Gus Lumbardi's Small Latin Band with Big Band sound.' Not that I want to influence your decisions about what to get rid of, dear."

Lunie placed the records with the teapot and platter and covered them with a newspaper she had planned to use for wrapping breakables. She was relieved when Wilma wandered back across the street. By 11:30 Dayton still hadn't appeared. Lunie decided to uncover his table and sell things for him. There were only six items for sale: a book about manners, a cell phone with a dead battery, an empty box of cereal, a pair of scissors; a pink eraser, and a chipped faux Fiesta Ware saucer. She sold the eraser to a five-year-old boy for a penny just before Dayton wandered down.

"How's it going, Lunie-money?"

"Steady stream of business. It's amazing what people will buy," she said, unpacking another sack from the house.

"Rhoda will be here in a minute. We've got walk-abouts from three to five, then Coreen has scheduled another taping tonight. Her challenge for the chefs involves what you'd fix if you were stranded on a desert island without a grocery store, but we expect a throwdown from Basil. Pretty cool, huh? Wilma's the third judge and Omar Billings is the understudy."

A maroon van slowed and stopped. Lunie said, "Can you run things for a moment while I go inside?"

"Sure," said Dayton. "No problemo."

Two middle-aged women poked through the items on Lunie's tables, studying the maker's marks, and looking for chips and cracks.

The brunette held up orange pillow cases and said, "Have you got the rest of this set?"

"We have lots of bedding, but it's not for sale," Dayton said.

"How about furniture?"

"Not for sale," said Dayton. He busied himself by moving his merchandise into different positions.

"The ad in the paper said you had antiques and craft items."

"We have some, but not for sale."

"Can we look inside the house?"

"No, this is it," he said.

"What about this snail platter?" asked the blond, who had lifted the table skirt and bent down to see what she could find.

"Absolutely not," Dayton said. "Give me that."

"I'd like to buy it."

"It's mine. It got out here by mistake," said Dayton, panicking.

"Then catch," said the woman, tossing the platter to Dayton. "Let's go," she said to her friend.

Lunie returned with another sack. "Did they buy anything?"

"I can't believe you were going to sell the snail-and-shell platter," complained Dayton, clutching it to his chest. "I have so many happy memories."

"Of snails? We never ate snails. Mother never even used this platter. What are you doing?"

"I'm packing up. I'm done with this sale. You can't just sell off stuff without my permission. It's not right, Lunie. Just not right." Dayton ran over to the yard sale sign, ripped it out of the ground and hurled it at her tables, knocking over a peacock lamp. Beheaded, the peacock fluttered, staggered then self-destructed into a cloud of dusty feathers.

"See what you made me do?" yelled Dayton. "Mother loved that lamp. I loved that lamp. It's over!" He swept the five remaining items off his table, stuffed them in his pockets and ran back up the street, still clutching the platter.

Lunie picked up the teapot, wrote $5 on a sticker and placed it with twelve slotted serving spoons on her table. It sold within the hour for $1.65 to a man who asked, "Didn't I see you on the nightly news, bailing out that squirrel and his friends?"

"It was my twin, Sue," said Lunie. "She's from Minnesota and rides a motorcycle."

"Remarkable resemblance," said the man, studying her face, "but your eyes seem different."

"That's sisternal twins for you," said Lunie. "Identical except for the eyes. Would you like everything else that's on this table for a dollar?"

"Nah. The wife collects teapots. Got anymore?"

"Sure, if you watch the table for a minute, I'll get some," she said, tucking her money in her pocket. She knew that at least three teapots—one shaped like a mushroom, another like a house, and the third like a drunken flowerpot—were in the stairwell to the basement, and there were probably dozens more scattered throughout the house. When she returned, the man was gone, and so were five of the slotted spoons, and a tape recorder without a cord. *Good,* thought Lunie. She shook dried-out tea bags out of the pots, wondering if she could sell them, too.

With a break in customer traffic, Lunie brought more boxes from the house and priced the larger pieces. She moved all the little items to a single table and made a sign that indicated that everything was two for a quarter. She taped the yard sale sign back together as best she could and added peacock feathers for color, and pounded it back in the ground near the street.

Fifteen minutes before the advertised closing time, two cars parked and disgorged small children who ran to the tables. Their mothers, carrying diaper bags and infants, yelled at their kids to not touch anything. Lunie smiled hopefully and thought, *If they break anything, it's yours.* She removed the two-for-a quarter sign and quickly wrote another one that announced that everything on that table was free. "Free," she whispered to three little boys, sticky with a red substance, and to two girls, who looked like they had recently been crying.

"Really?"

"Here are bags. Fill them with anything on this table you want." As she hoped, they wanted it all.

"Put that stuff back," yelled one mother.

"The lady gave it to us."

"Put it all back. Now."

"Hurry," whispered Lunie. "Pretend this is a race. I'm going to count to three and then you run as fast as you can to your car. The winner gets feathers." The children dodged and ran, threw their bulging plastic bags into their cars and quickly returned for feathers.

"You some kind of pervert?" asked the lanky woman, with a drooling baby on her hip. "You shouldn't give things to children you don't know. Whaddya trying do? Get them to come over when we're not around? Are you a mole-est-er?"

"Oh, no," said Lunie, hoping the women would not notice her suddenly twitching eyelid. The larger of the women dialed 9-1-1 on her cell phone.

"Just stay there," she said to Lunie. "We need a background check on you."

"For what? This is just a yard sale. You came to it. I didn't invite you."

Sirens screamed in the distance.

"What do you call this?" said the woman, holding up the classified ad from the paper. "And that." She pointed an accusatory finger at the sign. "These are invitations to your house. Creep."

The same officer in charge of the Sanders' dog ring screeched to a halt, the lights on his car flashing.

The women barely let him get out of his car before they surrounded him, protectively gathering their children.

Lunie was transfixed. Both eyelids were twitching. She saw Wilma step out on her porch, then cross the street, and take the officer aside for a few words in private. They both glanced in Lunie's direction. The officer then wrote down information about how to reach the women, and they ordered their wailing children to hand over the plastic bags as evidence. Lunie heard the officer's partner call headquarters for a photographer.

Wilma took Lunie's arm as gently as a retriever carries a bird. "Just tell the officer your name. Everything will be all right, dear."

"Lunette. Lunette Pitts," she said. Her voice quavered. "Everyone calls me Lunie. That's spelled L-U-N-I-E."

"Address, please," said the officer.

"It's 4027 Bilgewater," said Lunie.

"But this is 4073," he said, looking at the house numbers.

"It's my mother's house. I mean was. She died."

"She was my best friend," said Wilma.

"Name, please."

"Lunette. Lunette Pitts," said Lunie.

"No, your mother's."

"Dolce." The officer looked puzzled. Wilma spelled it for him.

"Never would have guessed," he said. "Just a moment." He went back to his car and used his laptop to contact headquarters. When he returned, he said, "Miss Pitts. Your name is in our files. I see you were stopped for a traffic violation the other day, but then you helped solve a crime, and then there was something involving fruitcake and your mother, Dolsy."

"Dol-chey," said Wilma.

"And, I also see that there is suspicion—I know I shouldn't tell you this—that you may be harboring a stolen dog, or at least have information to its whereabouts. And now this. Miss Pitts, do you have any idea how serious these allegations are?" asked the officer.

"I just gave them—"

"Lunie, you have the right to remain silent," said Wilma, clapping her hand over Lunie's mouth. "Don't confess to anything without talking to a lawyer."

"But—"

"You can release her to my custody," said Wilma. "She's been under a lot of stress lately. I'm sure we can clear all of this up over a little cup of tea. As a matter of fact, I just came back to get a teapot she promised me."

Lunie blinked hard.

Wilma walked over to the table and looked under the skirt.

"Where's the cauliflower teapot, Lunie?" she asked.

Lunie, who had prided herself on honesty, was quickly slipping into a morass of what? Of white lies? Bald-faced lies?

Taradiddles? Confabulations? What harm could one more bring?

"Dayton took it!" She closed her eyes, trying to create a mental picture of him clutching the snail-and-seashell platter *and* the teapot as he ran away.

"I'm so relieved," said Wilma. "We'll make tea at your house in a bit."

Lunie heard the officer talking into his shoulder speaker. "Yeah, she lawyered up, even before I could tell her that I thought those women were lying. I've seen them around town."

He listed to the crackling voice from headquarters.

"I guess we have no choice," he said.

"Miss Pitts, I have to open a formal investigation. We may need a psychological evaluation. Are you seeing a counselor?"

Lunie thought for a moment. "Do you mean 'see' see?"

The officer's brows furrowed. "See-see?"

"I mean, see someone in their office," said Lunie.

"Oh, that kind of see-see. Yes."

"No," said Lunie. If she had to explain her answer later to a judge, so be it. It was a technicality, but she could truthfully say that she had never seen Dr. Manngo. She wished she could see him now. Perhaps that wasn't the answer the officer wanted to hear, but Lunie was afraid that if she admitted that she had a counselor of any sort, she would be admitting that she had issues, even though as she and Dayton had agreed, everyone has issues.

The officer handed her a card. "Call me if you think of anything relevant to the investigation," he said. "If you remember any details. And you might want to see-see someone."

Lunie nodded and tucked the card in her pocket.

"I'll help you close up everything," said Wilma. "By the way, one of my poetry friends is an attorney. He's not very good. Tends to write epic poems about his legal experiences. 'Ode to Juvenile Justice' and things like that. Most of us don't have the heart to tell him that his material is boring, especially after he won a prize in the state Judicial Poetry Slam—they all call it the 'slammer'—or his 'Constitutional Iliad.' "

"Why would I need an attorney?" asked Lunie, more worried about explaining the sale of the cauliflower teapot than the episode with the yard sale shoppers.

"Lunie, dear, those women, even if they are scam artists they could make big trouble for you," said Wilma. "Accusations are the rage these days. Everybody's doing it. They probably want money and think you'll settle." Wilma fluffed the sheets and let them fall over the yard sale merchandise. "Ready for tea?"

"I'll be okay," said Lunie. "No tea today, thank you."

"Then I'll just walk with you to make sure you get home."

"Wilma, I'm really all right." Lunie tried to out pace her, but the poet's feet gathered speed and kept a metered pace.

"Dayton will be there with you, right?" asked Wilma.

"As far as I know."

"Good. I'll check on you in the morning. I'll even let my Bunco group know that something has come up and I'll help you out tomorrow."

"I'm really okay."

"See you tomorrow, then," said Wilma. She turned back toward her house, her lips forming unspoken rhymes.

Five

HOW DOES THIS LOOK?" Dayton twirled in his Christmas tree walk-about. "I know it's jumping the season, but what the hey. I think it will make a statement at tonight's taping."

Rhoda smiled with approval and went back to studying his childhood diary entries. "I'll suit up in a minute," she said.

"Wait till you see what Wilma plans to wear. I'm not telling, though," said Dayton. "She's such a good sport."

Rhoda didn't answer. Her chiseled face was thoughtful, almost tender. "Do you remember what happened on May 25th when you were in fourth grade?"

Dayton said quickly, "Nope. Not a clue." He tossed little pieces of bone-shaped kibble to Scooter. "An early gift from Santa, baby boy."

"Well, it says here, if I'm reading your handwriting correctly, that on May 25th you went into Lunie's room and—"

"Did not," said Dayton.

"Then, why did you say you took it?"

"Made it up."

"Did you ever give it back?"

"Of course. Well, actually she came in my room and found it. It was just a stupid piece of paper. I mean, why would she keep a note from somebody who liked her feet?"

"Was she mad?"

"Don't remember."

"This finally gives me something to go on," said Rhoda. "Something for your autobiography."

"You can't write about the foot note," said Dayton. "It will wreck things. Lunie and I are trying to have a sensible adult relationship."

"Don't worry," said Rhoda. "I'm making up your life story so I'll just change everything. It just gets my creative juices flowing to have something concrete for inspiration."

"Suit up, Rhoda. We don't want to keep Coreen waiting." Dayton tossed another biscuit to Scooter and handed Rhoda's extra-tall elf suit to her. "Do ya like the bells on your sleeves and slippers?"

Rhoda said, " I hope they don't interfere with sampling food."

"Ready?"

"Coreen wanted me to bring a laptop so I could take notes. She's going to have her cameraman post a clip from the show on You Tube. It will be viral in no time. This is so big for us, Dayton. Big. But I don't have a laptop."

"Borrow Lunie's. She's busy with the yard sale. Consumed by it. Life is passing her by," he said, placing Scooter on the futon. "Daddy will be back soon. Maybe tomorrow you can go with us, Scootie-cutie."

"Lunie won't like it if she finds out."

"Leave her a note."

While Rhoda scribbled a few words and tucked the laptop under her arm, Dayton located Lunie's car keys in her purse and motioned to Rhoda to hurry. "We'll need to drive the other way around the block so we don't pass Lunie at the sale. If we had time to walk, I would, but these tree boots aren't made for walking." Dayton laughed a ho ho ho, and looked at his elf to see if she caught his humor. She didn't.

He parked just beyond the TV trucks, then the Christmas tree and elf slipped as unobtrusively as possible past them so they could enter Coreen's by the back door. Through the kitchen window they could see Chef Basil Basil juggling a mixing bowl, a brown egg, and a live flounder.

"He's promised to give us lessons," said Dayton. "The judges, chefs, Coreen, and the audience will all juggle on the season's finale." He rang the bell. Clive answered. "Do you have tickets?"

"We're the judges, Clive," said Dayton. "Let us in."

"Coreen says everyone has to have tickets to the show. It's already very popular."

"Clive, *we are the show*. Let us in."

"All right, this time, but make sure you have tickets from now on." He sniffed.

"Watch out!" Rhoda shoved the Christmas tree's tinseled top toward the door. A flounder narrowly missed Dayton as it whizzed by and flopped in the stainless steel triple sink. Chef Basil Basil grinned and took a bow. "So, vat you doing in my kisshen?"

"Just passing through," said Dayton. "It's a good thing we're only judging you on your food and not your accents."

Clive quickly stepped between Chef Basil Basil and the walk-about tree, keeping the man in the chef's toque from decorating Dayton's face with the egg.

"There you are, my dears," said Coreen.

Her sheer blouse failed to conceal—oh, it was too embarrassing for Dayton to contemplate. And her gold lamé wraparound skirt was more like a tea towel or hankie. Dayton turned his face and wished he had worn opaque sunglasses. He would then judge food only by taste, not presentation. For tomorrow's taping he'd wear a blindfold. Perhaps Chef Basil Basil had an extra one.

"Dayton, you really need to apply green paint to your face. Red is not the color of a treetop," Coreen said with a throaty laugh. "Our studio audience has been seated, and as soon as Wilma gets here, the judges will make their grand entrance." She noted that Rhoda had a laptop and nodded her approval.

She handed her digital camera to Clive and said, "You take pictures and then the elf will send them out. It will be like a visual appetizer for our reality show."

"Where's Wilma?" Dayton asked Rhoda. He had no idea who Coreen would have as an understudy if Wilma didn't show.

"She's here," said Clive.

Coreen had a final word with the cameraman, and then waved grandly to the audience. A stagehand appeared with two signs, one for applause and the other for laughter, which he explained to the audience.

Dayton studied the crowd, a melange of neighbors—Cora Newton, plus the Billings—and nine women in red T-shirts that read: BRING BACK VERONICA FOXX. He later learned that they were officers in a national group boycotting the Tort soap after Coreen had left the show. Four handpicked members of Wilma's poetry group were also seated, each with a pen and paper in case they suddenly became inspired by an exotic vegetable or a cooking term. Since taping the pilot, Coreen had brought in a construction crew to expand the mansion's dining room. The heavy European and Middle-Eastern furniture and artifacts were in storage. Studio lighting had been installed, and so had comfortable seating for the very select audience. Dayton was a bit concerned when he saw one of the police officers assigned to Scooter's case sitting in the back row.

The lights dimmed, the audience was signaled to clap and cheer. Coreen appeared in a spotlight that swept the floor and changed colors. Her skirt positively glowed.

"Welcome. Welcome. Thank you," she said, bowing dangerously. "Our resident celebrity chef, is our own Chef Basil Basil, and tonight he is challenged by the queen of Irish potatoes, Contessa Sheila." Into the spotlight stepped Agnes, wearing a tall white toque decorated with shamrocks.

Coreen waited for the sign-stimulated applause to die down, then introduced the famed walk-abouts and their newest addition to the judge's panel. From behind green and silver curtains stepped Wilma dressed in white as an Emily Dickinson walk-about. Her wig, parted in the middle, featured straight black hair pulled around to a bun.

"Fantastic," murmured Rhoda. "So authentic."

"She'll be great when the writer's conference comes to town next month. I've already ordered costumes for us," whispered Dayton. "Mark Twain for me and you'll be Scarlett O'Hara. You can wear it for New Year's Eve, too."

"You want me to stay that long?" asked Rhoda.

"I friended you, remember?" said the tree. "Friending is forever."

Wilma took a seat next to them, adjusted her wig and gave a discrete wave to her poet friends.

"Tonight's menu for our chefs was inspired by members of our first audience: potatoes, leeks, mutton, mint beef kidneys—"

Agnes beamed. Chef Basil Basil glared, his eyes crazed.

"And, to make things fun, tonight's bread will be inedible. It will be made into decorative shapes of the chef's choosing." Coreen waited for the applause card to drop, and said, "Let the cooking begin!" That simple phrase became a trademark for the show's weekly introduction.

Coreen commanded the stage, prancing over to where Agnes aka Sheila deftly assembled mutton and mint rolls for her appetizer, while Chef Basil Basil took a leek, threw it to the floor and stomped on it.

"Fame is a fickle food," Emily Dickinson said, wagging her finger at the chef.

Agnes set her sautéed rolls aside on a warming tray, glanced at the clock, and began working on her kidney-potato-parsnip and goat cheese pizza as her entree. Coreen breathlessly described her every chop and dice for the studio audience, occasionally muttering warnings to Chef Basil Basil to show his culinary skills rather than his temper. At her direction, he washed the crushed leek and tossed it in a blender along with mango, cucumber, and seltzer for a chilled soup.

Coreen danced behind the judges, reminding them and the audience, to note the chefs' styles of cooking. "It's part of the presentation," she said.

Dayton glanced at Wilma's pad, which they each had found next to their scoring sheets. Wilma had written "Cloves drift in on little spice feet."

He was tickled that the cameras not only focused on the chefs' activities, but also on the judges and a small sign that he had made with Mother's markers that advertised his walk-about business and a phone number to call. It was Lunie's home number, but he'd get his own in a few days.

Chef Basil Basil seemed to have regained his stride and was down to work, thinly slicing five pounds of multicolored potatoes and dropping them in a pan of hot olive oil for a quick sear. They would then be placed in a parchment paper pouch, under mutton, a gob of butter, porcine mushrooms and Irish mint from the hills of Kilkarney. Cooking *en papier* was one of his signature dishes, but he preferred using fish to mutton.

Just as Chef Sheila was garnishing her lemoncelli tapioca meringue, photographed by Clive, there was a loud knocking on the front door. When no one answered it, the doorbell rang and rang. Coreen motioned to the camera crew to continue taping. The racket stopped, then continued at a side door before the kitchen door burst open. It was Lunie. She looked around, ignored the chefs, pushed past Coreen and made her way to the judge's table. "Give me that!" she said. She grabbed her laptop. "You have no right."

Lunie turned to the stunned audience. "She had no right to take my laptop. She just moved into my house. Actually, he moved into my house then and invited her to stay. They are slobs and won't help me clean Mother's."

"Out of here, Lunie," warned Coreen. When Lunie didn't budge, Coreen said, "Stop the taping." The camera crew stopped, but not Clive, who was determined to document every-thing.

"Come with me," said Coreen, steering Lunie toward the hall. Lunie looked back at the studio audience. The women in the red T-shirts pointed at her and chanted, "Show wrecker," but at least one poet looked sympathetic. The neighbors were huddled in a whispered discussion, and averted her gaze.

"I'm shocked," said Dayton. "She hasn't been herself."

"We'll resume in five," called Coreen. "Meanwhile, wine for everyone, including the judges."

Out of sight of all involved, Coreen pinned Lunie to a brocade-covered wall. "Look it. I don't know what your problem is—why you're trying to ruin me. I have never been happier in my life. I'm finally my own woman. I have my own show. My own friends. No longer poor little rich girl, Coreen. No longer dependent on the networks.

"Lunette, I offered you a piece of the action. I had a deal with you to buy your share of your mother's house and half her stuff. Then working with Dayton, I would use the Mother's as the first venue for my new reality show called *Hoarding for Dollars*. After that episode, I would set the house up as a place for your brother and his friends to live. Maybe I'd even have an office in the front for when I'd get bored here in the mansion. I envision a costume room for all my hats.

"But you, Lunette, you couldn't handle solving your problems. You appear to enjoy misery and making life miserable for those around you. Now, take your precious laptop (I would have bought you six more if you had just waited until the end of the show) and get out. Out."

The deputy from the back row materialized and said, "I'll see her home, Miss Pomphrey."

He took Lunie's arm and gently steered her toward the front door. When they reached the squad car, Lunie said, "I'd rather go to Mother's."

"Whatever," said the deputy. "But, if you know what's good for you, ma'am, don't go back to Miss Pomphrey's."

"Thanks," said Lunie.

Six

L UNIE STOOD IN MOTHER'S DRIVEWAY, waiting for the officer to drive off. He didn't. The shrouded yard sale tables loomed in the shadows. Lunie wasn't sure why she wanted to visit her former room, but the urge had been growing since she discovered that her laptop had been unplugged and removed from the kitchen, and Rhoda's note had been left in its place.

She could still hear the officer's radio crackling, and then mercifully, he had a call to an accident. His blue lights illuminated the tables for a second as he sped up the street.

Of course, the back door was wide open. Lunie's thoughts had become spidery since she had left Coreen's, darting and wanting to grab something substantial; hoping to get a grip. Her room had been a haven. She knew Dayton and her mother didn't respect the DO NOT ENTER sign she had taped to her door in third grade, but at least their stuff never made it beyond the hall outside her room.

She would have the house all to herself for a little while; everyone was at Coreen's. The kitchen and hall lights were on, as was a cat lamp in the living room. Dolce liked it because when the lamp warmed up, the cat's eyes moved from side to side and it bared its teeth. "Cute," Dolce had purred when Dayton brought it home as a gift, ignoring its missing ears.

Lunie squeezed down the front hall, making a note of what she'd add to the yard sale in the morning. She found the stairs and kicked the boxes, clothes, and pans out of the way. At the top, she pushed to the left. She knew Dayton's room would be exactly as it had always been. A mess. She had heard on TV that hoarders were clutter-blind. She doubted it. She knew that Dayton and their mother knew exactly what their house was like. Maybe they didn't notice The Smell and The Taste, but they had to see the mess. They just liked it, the way she liked CLEAN. And her room had always been spotless. Rebellious, she had never saved anything, except her diaries, Fink's note, and her favorite pair of Buster Brown brogans that had come from Fink's Family Footware. Kissy's later moved into that location when the town's only shoe store closed after the discount mall opened.

Lunie pushed a set of broken wicker patio furniture out of the way, and placed a box of balled socks on top of the ottoman. The box was heavy. Lunie was puzzled and picked up one. It clanked. She opened it and was astonished to see coins and bills of every denomination. She opened another, then another. The contents of each was the same. Did Dayton know about the money? Is that what he was squirreling away in the chest freezer? She had been so quick to dismiss his "you'll never guess what I found" comment.

But where had the money come from? As her mother's executor she thought she had uncovered all that there was of value—namely a small life insurance policy, two bank accounts, and several thousand dollars in the credit union. Her mother couldn't have. No, she wouldn't have. She wouldn't have risked her position as a senior teller. . . . But some people just didn't trust banks. That had to be it. And who would know better than someone who worked in the bank. Lunie vaguely remembered her mother regaling Dayton with stories about how easy it was for tellers to help themselves to just a little— not that she would ever do that. While young Dayton played with his Cleebo, Dolce described a teller she called Juanda who was deft with cash and coins. She always took the customer's cash deposit to a workstation out of view, and when she returned, she'd smile and say, "You're short five dollars." Or it might have been three dollars, or perhaps fifty cents in coins. What could the unsuspecting customer do but adjust the deposit ticket, mumbling, "But I counted and recounted before I left home." Juanda would then count the deposit in front of the customer and, of course, it would be short. "So easy," said Dolce. "Not that I would ever try it. Honesty is a virtue."

No, whatever her mother's issues, Lunie did not think grand theft or even petty theft was one of them. It was wrong to even think that of the deceased.

Lunie could see the sign on her door through the boxes, bags, and wicker furniture. Someone had crossed out her name, but the warning to keep out was still visible, although the smiley face next to it was clearly an addition from Dayton.

She pushed open the door, not sure if there was anything left of hers there and flipped on the overhead light, still a 40 watt bulb. Dim, but bright enough to illuminate the small space she had occupied for almost fifteen years. She grimaced. Why would she expect the room to remain as she left it? Her mother had crammed storage bins filled with who knows what into the area where Lunie had sat at her desk, done her homework, and occasionally penned her diary. She had been increasingly careful not to say anything that she didn't want Mother or Dayton to know about, even though she hid the diary under her mattress or in her closet.

She moved cartons and bins onto a pile of things where her bed had been located so that she could set her laptop on her desk. The desk was there, but not its companion, the scuffed wooden straight-backed chair. Dolce had more comfortable ones stashed throughout the house but this one would help improve posture, she had told Lunie.

Lunie pried her way to her closet. It was filled with Mother's hats—many red—from a club that wore purple, but had disbanded when they decided to take up Colonial dancing, which required outfits from a different period. Wide neckties that had come and gone in fashion were coiled across the hats, like a nest of silken snakes. Lunie hesitantly reached behind them. Her fingers didn't recognize most of the items—lotions and perfume samples—until they touched familiar leather. For the first time in days, her lips turned up at the corners without twitching. She gently pulled them out so as not to cause a cascade of barely balanced objects.

Her shoes. Her Buster Browns from elementary school. Worn until they pinched. Mr. Fink had given them to her. Every time she had walked passed Fink's Family Footware, she had spent several minutes admiring the shoes on display in the two glass windows on either side of the doorway. While Mr. Fink greeted customers and sized their feet with large metal plates, Mrs. Fink trotted to the back of the shop, returning with the boxes filled with tissue paper and shoes of every style and size. Mrs. Fink, and sometimes Little Fink, changed the window displays, waving to Lunie as she studied the new styles. Once her brother opened the door to the shop before she could stop him, and pretended he was there to buy shoes. Mr. Fink sized his feet and let him try on several pairs, sliding store socks over his grimy feet. Lunie simply watched, enjoying the fragrance of leather and polish.

A few months later, when she was alone and admiring the window display, Mr. Fink, with his thick glasses and slicked back hair, joined her. "So, what do you think of my shoes?"

"They're beautiful," Lunie responded, hoping he didn't notice her navy tennis shoes with holes in the toes.

"I have a pair I can't sell," he said, clearing his throat. "My wife and I wonder if they would fit you."

"Can't sell?" asked Lunie, her heart beating.

"Can't sell."

"I don't know if my mother would let me," said Lunie.

"If I put them by the curb—" He pointed to a spot where merchants stacked their garbage bags and trash for pickup.

Lunie beamed. That was how she "found" her beautiful brogans. Sturdy. New shoe smell. Laces that weren't frayed. She could still read the size inside. And, for once Mother was pleased. "That's what I've been trying to tell you, Lunie. Never buy anything new when you can find it at the curb or at a yard sale. We are a country of waste, I tell you."

For two days Lunie was so overcome with the shoes' beauty that she refused to wear them, and then she realized that Little Fink had been looking at her feet, puzzled that she wasn't sporting her gift. She wrote a thank you note to the Finks and drew a picture of herself, smiling, and pointing at her shoes. She immediately wished she hadn't drawn herself in pen, or at all. But she was late for school, and it was a day she had to drag her flower-painted bass through the streets for music class. She had a solo in the orchestra's arrangement of Old MacDonald, which the group was going to play at an assembly. "Old MacDonald had a donkey," the children were to sing, and Lunie had to recreate the braying sound on her instrument.

Embarrassed that she had the bass tethered to her after school, she simply handed her note to a customer with twin girls, who was going in the shoe store. She asked the woman to please give the note to Mr. Fink.

After she had outgrown the brogans, and even though they were not worn out, Lunie couldn't part with them, although in later life she feared they might be the start of an inherited tendency toward excessive collection.

How small her feet. How big the kindness. Lunie's eyes were hot and wet. She decided to rescue the shoes and take them home into fresh air—something she should have done long ago. She pushed back down the hall and emptied a large shopping bag so that she could fill it with as many heavy, bulging, money-filled socks as would fit. Lunie had seen all she need to see. Now that Coreen had backed out of the deal, she was even more committed to emptying Mother's house.

Seven

LUNIE DECIDED TO AIR OUT the brogans on the back porch. The leather needed a rest from The Smell, as did the clothes she had worn inside Mother's. After a refreshing shower and change into clean sweatshirt and sweatpants, Lunie's glumness had moderated. Dayton and Rhoda would be out for the rest of the evening. She could work on her novel or visit with Dr. Manngo. The problems of the day had been troubling and she hadn't had time to sort them out. An objective outsider might be able to set her on a constructive course. She logged in as herself and noticed he was offering new online services on his Web site: spa day; virtual massage; facials; acupuncture without needles; hot rocks; peddies 4 good feet. She was again amazed at Dr. Manngo's entrepreneurial abilities and was glad that he was keeping his prices reasonable—under $20 for five or ten minutes.

> Dr. Manngo: Hey u. What's happening?
>
> Lunie: What do you mean u? SEND
>
> Dr. Manngo. Lern txt. Nu. u txt?
>
> Lunie: No. SEND
>
> Dr. Manngo: Txt fn. Twt nxt. LOL

Lunie wished she had a text dictionary. Larry, her supervisor, texted people all the time, and so did a woman in accounting. Her thumbs never stopped moving over a tiny keyboard on her phone. She tried to show Lunie once how easy it was but Lunie's thumbs covered too many keys and the effort to write a message to someone three tables away, just because she could, seemed absurd. Even after that session, she still wasn't sure what LOL meant. Was it Lots Of Love, Lots Of Laughs, Laugh Or Leave? The only time she could think that texting would be valuable for a person of her age was if she had been kidnapped and thrown in the trunk of a car, and then she would text the police, if she knew how to reach them, and if she had a cell phone with a keyboard that she could see in the dark. Maybe she did need to become more modern. Dr. Manngo was such an example of adapting to technology at whatever age his age was. Yes, after she was done with the business at Mother's, she'd use the contents of some of the black socks to upgrade to a fancy phone like Larry and Chrystal had. Chrystal would probably be flattered to show her how to use hers when Lunie returned to work.

> Dr. Manngo: Okay, back to session. Lunie, tell me your issue, and then I'll tell you mine.

Lunie hesitated. What first? Probably the most serious were the yard sale customers and their false accusations. That would be the best starting place, but her fingers went in another direction.

> Lunie: I think my mother stole money from a bank. SEND
>
> Dr. Manngo: Did she get away? Did she hide the $$$$?
>
> Lunie: I think so. SEND
>
> Dr. Manngo: Did you tell the cops?
>
> Lunie: No. SEND
>
> Dr. Manngo: Good. Don't tell. I'll help you search.

Lunie was relieved. The doctor-patient confidentiality would protect her and the family's reputation. It was right not to tell the police if her mother hadn't been a suspect all these years.

> Lunie: My bigger problem is the people who came to the yard sale and accused me of . . . of SEND
>
> Dr. Manngo: Of hiding $$$$$?
>
> Lunie: I tried to give their children junk, just to get rid of it. SEND
>
> Dr. Manngo: Where did your mother hide $$$$$$$?
>
> Lunie: And then Rhoda took my laptop. SEND
>
> Dr. Manngo: Is Rhoda your mother?
>
> Lunie: No, my mother's dead, remember? SEND
>
> Dr. Manngo: Oh, yes. Where do you live? I'll help you look for the money. No charge. As I always say, deal with $$$ and deal with life.

Lunie considered Dr. Manngo's offer to help, but the power flickered and her computer shut down before she could answer. Perhaps there was a lot more money stashed in the house. Dayton might be right. They should go through everything carefully. But is that how she wanted to spend the rest of her life? Opening smelly socks in Mother's house? Her mother likely would have LOL, seeding some socks with coins, and the rest with absolute junk. That was a distinct possibility. At least Dr. Manngo didn't advise her to contact the police. It would simply complicate her various cases.

Lunie felt extraordinarily tired and she needed to get up extra early to replenish her tables before the first shoppers arrived. She decided, however, to spend just a few minutes with Sue, although it was hard to remember where she had left off in the novel. Lunie need to buy a ream of paper on her next trip to town so that she could print out her book and get an idea of the flow and gaps.

She did know that Bob, the cad, wasn't really Sue's type. Sue would realize that quickly, not necessarily during their day on shore in Aruba, but later that night at the ship's lavish chocolate buffet. Sue was having too much fun on shore and believed Bob that he was planning to leave Deloris when they returned to Ohio. Bob confided in Sue, over chocolate cordials, and with juice from a chocolate-covered strawberry dripping down his chin, that he knew that Deloris had been unfaithful.

"What a fool I've been. How blind. My little Deloris. I never suspected that when she said she was going to knitting classes that she had become entangled. And then there was the mysterious message on the home answering machine. And the new lingerie that arrived in gift boxes. How blind I was to her dalliance." Bob popped another strawberry in his mouth, this one dipped in white chocolate.

Sue was overcome with pity. His passion was now understandable. His need for intelligent conversation, which they hadn't had yet. His need for a fling, which they had.

"Come back to Piketon with me, ViVi," said Bob, aiming his gooey chocolate face precariously close to hers. Sue shuddered. He reminded her of Booger Wayne, her sticky kindergartner, who watched her every move the day Rolex came through the snow for her.

"No, Bob, not now," said Sue, regaining her composure. "Let's go get a hamburger on the Lido Deck."

"But they stopped serving at eight," said Bob, making kissing noises, although his lips were hidden in syrup. He stuck his finger in a fountain of chocolate, and tried to touch her tongue.

My Rolex wouldn't be so crude, thought Sue. I never should have let him go. Woe is me. I was so wrong to let him drift off into the unknown, and then not answer his letters when he became the head of the oil company. We could have had such a glorious life in Texas.

Lunie knew the story had taken a saccharine turn, but if she was going to pitch her novel as a romance, this would probably be credible. She always knew that Sue had a sensible side, even if it had been limited to her sensible shoes—the **brown** leather teacher shoes with gel inserts.

"Go back to Deloris," said Sue. "Wash up and go back."

"But Vivian, I thought we—" pleaded Bob.

She peeled off her Vivian Valencia name tag. "My name is Sue, and I get headaches from chocolate."

There. That's a good stopping place for this chapter. Lunie would begin tomorrow with Sue borrowing a satellite phone from a wealthy British explorer, whom she meets in the casino, and she calls Rolex.

Lunie hit SAVE, and turned off her computer. She decided to conceal it into her room rather than leave it out where Dayton or Rhoda could find it.

THE HOUSE HAD BEEN ODDLY QUIET during the night. If Dayton and Rhoda had come home, they hadn't made noise. The lack of activity kept Lunie awake, fitfully glancing at the clock and moving Phil off her feet.

At five-thirty she slipped into her clothes and padded past the moose—a beret rakishly covering one glass eye—for the kitchen and coffee. She sighed when she discovered that her newly purchased bag of coffee beans now contained only enough to make one pot. While it brewed, she leaned against the windowsill and remembered that she hadn't filled the bird feeders in several days. As the first rays appeared, a frost glistened on the lawn. It would be a chilly day. Lunie would wear extra socks and take gloves.

Lunie realized she had carelessly left the shopping bag with socks on the back porch near the Buster Brown shoes. Before she headed for the yard sale, she moved the sack into her room, emptied the numerous coins and bills into a backpack that she kept in her closet—at least $16,500, by her quick estimate—and tucked clean underwear, a few shirts and jeans around the money so it wouldn't clank if Dayton or one of his friends nosed around. She slipped her laptop into the large outside pocket, and closed the closet door. She dropped the black odoriferous socks into the trash, which she placed by the curb on her way down the street.

As anticipated, yard-salers were in her yard, poking through the boxes and sacks. Lunie rushed down the hill, her breath frosty. The large crowd was a good sign. Her ad that called it an estate sale was probably an enticement. Estate implied antiques and other items of value. She would keep her eye on anything that clanked, rattled or was concealed in socks.

By the time she had finished her first cup of Thermos coffee, Lunie had sold another $45 worth of stuff and had made three trips inside Mother's to drag out more. One crafter had asked about artificial flowers, and Lunie had immediately gotten rid of the entire dusty garden from the living room. The hall Christmas trees were an early sale, as were the sewing machines, and a child's playhouse—dismantled for years in the corner of Dolce's craft room. Mother had intended to set it up for Dayton, but by the time he spotted it, he was a freshman in high school.

Lunie waved each time the deputy drove past during his morning rounds. She briefly wondered why Wilma's paper was still in the tube. When someone was looking for wicker, she tossed a set out the upstairs window. If someone asked about fishing rods, she brought an armful from the back porch. She was making grand progress and her money bag was filling.

After a rush of customers, at least "lookers," before the sale officially started, there had been a lull and suddenly business picked up again. She was happy to oblige, making repeated trips inside and pulling out this and that. If a customer dickered, she took his lowest price, often saying, "Here, take it. I have lots more."

By ten she was sorry that she hadn't packed a peanut butter sandwich. A blanket of clouds kept the ground from warming, although the frost had been silently swallowed by Mother's lawn. She was glad she was wearing her fleece-lined boots.

At 1:35 she was distracted from one such transaction by the sound of a loud and persistent honking. Her car pulled to the curb, with Rhoda waving wildly from the driver's side. Coreen's baby-blue Rolls bleated behind it. Clive hopped out and raced over to Lunie. "I'll watch things here. You've got to go home and help Dayton. It's an emergency." He gave Lunie a push in the direction of the street. Rhoda and Coreen had not waited for her; they had already sped up the road to 4027 Bilgewater. Lunie hesitated for a moment, bewildered. Annoyed. But, whatever was happening to Dayton, it was happening at her house. She had to at least go see.

She jogged up the street, glad to pump some warmth into her chilled legs and arms, and entered her kitchen. Coreen and Rhoda were opening cupboards, pulling out drawers, moving things in her pantry.

"Wait a minute!" yelled Lunie. "What's going on?"

"Don't you have any secret compartments, any hiding places?" asked Coreen, continuing to ravage the kitchen.

"I do not," said Lunie. "I asked what's going on and I deserve an answer."

Rhoda said to Coreen, "Let's check the living room. There's got to be something."

Lunie tried to block their way. "Where's my brother? What have you done with Dayton?"

"Finally, a note of concern from his loving sister," said Coreen, her lips pursed.

"We only have a couple of minutes, if Agnes is correct about the raid," said Rhoda. "Either help or get out of the way."

"Raid? Help with what?" Lunie's eyelid twitched.

"Agnes got a tip from the off-duty deputy hired by Coreen to control the media at the cooking show taping that the cops know that Scooter is here. She gave him all the leftover mousse last night to learn the details. We've got to hide the dog, or we'll all go to jail as accomplices—you especially, Lunie, because this is your house and you have a rap sheet a mile long," said Rhoda.

"I had nothing to do with the dog," said Lunie.

"That's not what the police report says. You were at the neighbors and, as they opened the door when you knocked, the dog got out," said Rhoda.

"That wasn't me," said Lunie.

"It was Lunie," said Rhoda. "Now think. Where can we stash Scooter until the coast is clear? Coreen has a plan for his permanent rescue after the cops leave."

Lunie knew of no secret passages in her house. She had cleaned thoroughly so many times that if a board had been loose in the floor or somewhere in a closet, she would have detected it years ago.

Dayton came down the stairs cuddling Scooter. He looked as distraught as the day in fourth grade when he returned home from school and couldn't find Cleebo. Mother had covered it over with her large acquisition of boxes of broken ribbon candy.

Lunie looked around her house. Coreen and Rhoda were finished tearing the living room apart, even removing cushions from the sofa.

If she let the cops "discover" Scooter, she'd be able to reclaim her house. But what would Dr. Manngo say? He might hate his own sister, but he would certainly not approve of her ratting on her brother and his friends. She glanced at Dayton's desperate face as he neared the moose, which seemed to be observing the chaos.

The moose.

Lunie blinked. "Dayton, the butt safe," she said. "Quick."

Her brother's face brightened with understanding. He slipped the small dog into the secret compartment and begged him to be quiet. "Just for a few minutes, Scootie-tootie, then you and Daddy will play ball." He locked the safe.

Lunie had never seen Dayton's face so filled with gratitude for her. He reached out to hug but pulled back in fear when there was a knock on the makeshift entryway. Scooter yipped. "Shush," whispered Dayton.

Lunie heard voices saying they would surround the house while someone would go around to the kitchen entrance. She heard knocking at the back.

"I'll get it," said Coreen. "Now compose yourselves. Act like everything is okay." She opened the door, and squealed with delight. "Well, lookie who's here. Good morning, Sergeant Sam Dell. May I call you, Buddy, just like I did when we were in band? You played the snares, didn't you? We did a duet one time, remember? You were such a handsome fellow. I believe I had a crush on you."

"Oh, Miss Pomphrey," said the tall uniformed man, taking off his reflective sunglasses, "I wasn't sexpecting, I mean expecting, to see you here." He tried to only look at her face, not at her unbuttoned red shiny coat.

"Well, Buddy, my reality TV company, which I have just formed, takes me to new locations. We're going to film an episode here later today of *House Cleaning*. Teams of professional and nonprofessional cleaners will compete to see who can straighten and sanitize a room most quickly. And, in case you find this mess, alarming, well, we're just setting up for the show. You can't have contestants come into a set that's already cleaned up, now could you?"

"Perhaps in getting your set ready," said the officer, "you've noticed evidence of a small valuable dog—a greyhound that could bed in a teacup, Miss Pomphrey?" The officer shifted nervously, trying to step away from Coreen's advances. Her coat was slipping off her left shoulder.

"My friend, Lunette, who has graciously offered the use of her lovely home for the show, has a cat—an ugly one—and you know that cats and dogs do not get along, officer. Now, what is your badge number, Officer Dell? I will want to be able to give it to my attorney when we chat later this morning."

"That won't be necessary ma'am."

"Refresh my memory. Is that Dell with one E or two?" said Coreen, the coat slipping off her right shoulder as well.

"Actually, one, but there are two Ds in Buddy," he said, handing her his card.

"Buddy, write your home phone number on here, and I'd like to have you work for me when we tape. I always need extras, and a big, good-looking hunk like yourself would be able to keep my fans under control when you're off-duty."

"I can't do that," said the sergeant loudly for the benefit of his squad, who might be listening outside. He wrote his home number on the card and handed it back. "Now, let me have a look."

"Please make it quick," said Coreen. "We have lots to do."

Sergeant Dell stepped inside, and Coreen loosened the sash on her coat.

The officer gazed at the kitchen. Nothing could be hidden there—all the drawers were open and their contents exposed. He glanced around the living room. No need to further disturb the sofa. "I'd like to see the upstairs," he said, heading toward the moose. He stopped and cocked his head. "I hear a scratching noise coming from this thing."

"I can explain it," said Rhoda, giving the silent Lunie a glance. "This moose was a gift from my brother, Dayton. He likes mechanical things and he thought I would too. I love this moose, and it makes incredible sounds. Here, turn this dial and push that button." Rhoda motioned for the sergeant to do as she suggested. He hesitated, then followed her directions. The moose was silent in the front, but whining in the rear.

"It has two sets of batteries," said Dayton. "The ones in the front must be wearing down. I just replaced the ones in the rear yesterday." He kicked the moose in the chest, and it opened its mouth and coughed out a feeble, "Watch out for the cliff, Mabel," followed by the sound of screaming, that faded as the batteries tried their dying best.

Dayton kneed it once again, and the moose brayed its mating call. "See," he said proudly, "I just need to get it adjusted. Front and back. Sides and center."

The sergeant made notes. "I've never seen anything quite like it," he said, shaking his head. "But I still need to look around the rest of the house if you don't mind."

"I'll go with you," said Coreen. "I just love exploring bedrooms."

Shaking her head, Lunie went back to the kitchen. "Got any fresh batteries?" asked Dayton.

"Doubt it," said Lunie. "I don't know what's in my kitchen anymore. What's this?" she picked up a piece of yellow paper on the countertop.

"Oh, we found it taped on the screen door this morning," said Dayton.

"It's another note from the building department," said Lunie, her heart pounding. "It's from Larry. He's concerned that there's been no progress. He says it's a friendly reminder but that my return to work depends on an effort to resolve the violations."

"I can only find AAA batteries," said Dayton, rummaging in a lower drawer. "I know the moose takes a dozen D's."

Lunie read Larry's note a second time and a third. She could hear the officer and Coreen walking from room to room. Rhoda sat on the cushionless sofa and thumbed through a recent issue of *Tidy House* magazine.

There came another knock at the door. "I'll get it," said Rhoda. She returned shortly. "Some guy wants to know if Lunie lives here."

Lunie panicked. It was probably someone from human resources, or perhaps the counselor that the police department wanted her to see about the yard sale customers.

"Lunie?" said an unfamiliar voice from the back porch. She placed Larry's note on the table, and stepped toward the door.

"Lunie?" repeated the stranger. He was holding her childhood brogans. "I can't believe you still have these."

"Fink?" she whispered in disbelief, as she realized that the short man with slicked-back hair and wire-rim glasses could be none other than her schoolmate. "What are you doing here?"

"May I come in?" he asked, glancing briefly at the mess, but focusing his soft brown eyes on hers.

She nodded. "My house isn't always like this."

"I've waited so long for this moment," Fink said. "I so regretted letting you slip away. It was an adolescent thing. I was so overwhelmed by my feelings that day when I wrote of them to you. But look what I've carried in my wallet, all through med school—podiatry, you know—and every hour of my practice." He unfolded the note she had written in Miss Pembroke's science class: "I like your feet, too." He glanced at Lunie's snow boots. "You know, in all my years of removing bunions and corns, dealing with Morton's neuroma, ingrown toenails, and Plantar's warts, I've held your feet in my mind as the standard of perfect, natural beauty."

Fink moved closer, her faded note in his outstretched palm. "I came back to Mosby Gap see if I could find you and make up for all those lost years. Will you come away?"

Lunie was too stunned to speak. She heard Dayton tinkering with the moose. Scooter whining and scratching. Rhoda rustling the magazine. Coreen and the officer upstairs in the Empty Room, the futon thumping. Her grip was lost.

"I know this is sudden," said Fink, "and you obviously have company, but sometimes it pays to seize the moment—try on those glass slippers—as my father, may he rest in peace, used to say." He stared intently at her face, his eyes pleading.

Lunie's voice had run out of battery power; her heart pounded.

"Tell you what," said Fink, "there's a yard sale down the street. If you want to come with me, I'll meet you there in a few minutes. Please, Lunie. I've thought of no one but you all these years."

Then Fink was gone, closing the door quietly after placing the brogans where he had found them.

Lunie didn't move. She wondered if she had been dreaming. *Her* Fink had been in *her* kitchen? Rhoda had let him in, but nobody else had noticed, least of all Dayton, still trying to revive the moose. Had she made him up? Had Fink meant what he had said?

"Lunie, when you go back to Mother's will you get the batteries from her bathroom?" asked her brother. "They're behind the toilet—in a cereal box."

Mother's.

Suddenly Lunie's feet moved toward her bedroom. She opened the closet grabbed her backpack filled with her clothes and the money.

"I'm leaving," said Lunie, pausing next to Dayton's feet, which were protruding from under the moose.

"If you can't find the batteries behind the toilet, they might be upstairs in my closet," said Dayton.

"Listen, Dayton, I'm going. I really mean it," said Lunie.

"He heard you the first time," said Rhoda, from the sofa. "He already told you where the batteries might be." She turned a page without looking up. "By the way, tell Clive that Coreen wants us there at five today."

"Dayton, listen," said Lunie, ignoring Rhoda.

"Lunie, I'm not listening," he said. "I'm really busy. We've got to get the moose working if we're going to save Scooter."

Lunie gave his feet one last look, but didn't answer. She hurried to the kitchen and scribbled a note that said, "Feed Phil." She bolted out the back door, past the officers who where having a smoke, their backs turned. She sucked chilly air as her feet flew down the hill. But where was Fink's car? *I must be too late!* Hot tears filled her eyes. She slowed her pace. Why hadn't she answered him moments earlier instead of standing mutely, stupidly while his eyes pleaded? Why hadn't she shouted, "Yes! Fink, I love you! I've always loved you!"

Then she realized Clive was talking with a short man with glasses, a man holding two motorcycle helmets. Beyond them was a shiny blue Harley parked under a large maple near the neighbors' Dumpster.

When she ran closer, she saw Fink check the time on his large gold wristwatch, then look around anxiously, until he saw her. His face wreathed into a smile and he handed Lunie a metallic blue helmet that matched his bike. She wasted no time strapping it under her chin, then gingerly climbed on the back of the Harley. She hesitated for a second, then wrapped her arms around Fink's waist.

"Hang on. We're going where it's hot," said Fink. "Barefeet time!"

The motorcycle roared to life. Lunie pressed her nose into Fink's leather jacket, savoring the fragrance of the saddle soap cleaner.

Clive chased them down when they reached the stop sign at the corner. "Lunie, what's going on?" he yelled. "What about the yard sale? You can't just leave like this. Lunie!"

"Deal with Mother's, deal with life," she shouted, without looking back.

Readers Guide for *Mother's*

Backstory

I'm often asked about the inspiration for my books. *Mother's* began when the manager of a bookstore asked me to speak to a group of writers who had entered a national contest to pen a novel in thirty days (http://www.nanowrimo.org/). Of course I agreed, but wondered how anyone could successfully complete a good book in that time. (Each of my children's books takes a year to write.) How could anyone with a job find that kind of uninterrupted time? As it turned out, my talk never happened, but a seed was planted. Lunie crept into my mind. She'd been laid off from her job for thirty days. Nothing unusual is on her schedule, or so she thinks. She will enter the novel-writing contest.

Then her brother arrives, infiltrating her neat, orderly life with his presence, messes, and friends. Dayton is lovable but increasingly annoying and inconsiderate. Lunie, a timid sort, feels powerless. The seed sprouted and flourished.

Characters are always a surprise when they arrive and take over. They may remind me of someone or a situation, but they are always themselves. I may hear my mother's voice in Dolce's words, but Lunie's mother not mine. The book is not autobiographical, even if parts, such as the refrigerator Taste, may be a vivid childhood memory.

Although much humor is intended, there are issues to explore in the story: Sibling relationships. Growing up in the same house but having totally different experiences or views of people and events. Boundary issues. Relationships. Clutter and neatness gone amok.

I'm not a hoarder, nor is anyone in my family, though I've known folks who are. Sentimental, I admit to having a problem with saving things, especially paper. I can't part with books, or special cards. I don't know what's important and immediately regret discarding scraps of paper with notes on them. And, don't ask about my closet.

My mother was the same way. When I opened drawers after her death I found, for example, my pigtails with ribbons that she had hacked off when I was about four and unwilling to sit still to have my hair yanked and brushed. There are always surprises in boxes and drawers, and I intend to leave some of mine for my children.

Coreen is outrageous and scary in her unpredictability. An inspiration for part of her behavior came from the futile efforts of our high school orchestra director who constantly reminded the clarinet players to keep their knees together. Of course, Coreen's cooking show is absurd, but it's inspired by TV cooking competitions that often include bizarre elements.

I've also discovered that life imitates imagination. As a cellist, I know that it is difficult to carry a large instrument, and that it is an absolute no-no to paint a wooden one. So, I wrote the episode about Lunie's mother painting a decoration on the cracked stringed bass that Lunie is forced to drag around town. But long after that section of the book was completed, my husband and I were on a cruise and heard the sounds of a lovely string quartet. We stopped to listen. He nudged me. I was amazed. The cellist's instrument had been painted with pink floral designs.

Another inspiration came from a hoarder's yard sale where nothing was for sale. Well, three things. I bought one. *Mother's* took more than thirty days to complete. Thirty days times thirteen, in fact. Sidetracked by events, Lunie's still working on hers.

Book Club Questions

1. People live parallel but different lives, even in the same house. Memories of childhood events may be entirely opposite. How is this true of Lunie and Dayton? Give examples. What role does their mother play in their memories of her and growing up in her house?

2. What options did Lunie have to solve her problems other than Dr. Manngo? Why or why not did his counsel appeal to her?

3. Dayton also sought counsel from Dr. Manngo. Why or why not was Dr. Manngo helpful to him?

4. Therapists have been known to say, "All roads lead to mother." Would Dayton or Lunie's better understanding of their relationship with Mother help them to change? How did their early childhood contribute to his hoarding and her cleanliness fixations, and Dayton's defensiveness of Mother?

5. In Lunie's book, Sue is her alter ego. How does her development of Sue's character lead to Lunie's decisions in the final pages?

6. Why are Rhoda and Dayton attracted to each other? What elements of Rhoda's character most bother Lunie?

7. Wilma, Dolce's friend, seems to want to help Lunie (p. 106), but is concerned about the fence. Does Wilma have ulterior

motives? Is it a surprise that Wilma participates in Coreen's cooking show? Why is she a problem at the yard sale?

8. Dayton accuses Lunie of making assumptions about his friends during the planning of the party and the party itself. Is Dayton prone to making assumptions? Give examples.

9. Clive Turkel and Agnes say they are caretakers of Mother's house in the evenings. Why does this appeal to each of them? What are their ulterior motives? What happens when Lunie changes the locks? Did you think her plan would work?

10. Dayton is writing his autobiography as told by Rhoda. He says his life is "an empty book." Would you agree?

11. When Dolce first divorced she had no things. Wilma Wolenski asks when the moving truck is arriving and Dolce says there will not be one. Is this situation enough to make a person a hoarder? Is hoarding a genetic disorder or does it come from some sort of life situation?

12. Why did Dayton steal Scooter, the teacup greyhound? How does this act fit with his personality?

13. Why, on numerous occasions, does Rhoda pretend to be Lunie?

14. Agnes, the cleaning service lady, takes Cleebo, Dayton's broken childhood giraffe toy. She exchanges it for an Egyptian artifact from the Pomphreys' house, another family for whom she cleans. How does Dayton react? What happens as a result?

15. Owning and borrowing: Which characters have the most difficulty with boundaries—that is, what belongs to whom? Discuss the ramifications of Rhoda taking Lunie's computer, Dayton borrowing Lunie's car, etc. When is it okay to borrow? When is it appropriate to not share? What other intrusions have you observed?

16. What is "The Smell"? What is "The Taste"? Have you experienced either?

17. In the second section we hear Dayton's concerns about Lunie's "hostility" toward him and his idea of a cruise for Lunie. Are you convinced his is as clueless and kind as he seems?

18. What does Dayton's take on hitchhikers tell us about his thought process? (p.209)

19. How did Dayton hear about his mother's death? What did Belle have as an explanation for Lunie's behavior at that time? Do you think her explanation fit the situation?

20. How does Coreen know about the dog Scooter? Why did Agnes blab about the dog?

21. Dayton, Lunie, and Coreen grew up in the same neighborhood and attended school together. What history, memories, baggage do the three of them have from the early years? Do you think the adult versions of Dayton and Lunie are as much of a surprise to Coreen as she is to them?

22. Have you attended a class reunion to discover classmates who, as adults, are nothing like you would have expected?

23. Does Lunie really bear any responsibility for her mother's death? Why does she think it is her fault?

24. Mother's is full of modern-day references to Facebook, cooking chef shows, texting, on line counseling, the "rage" for child abuse accusations. Is the story of hoarding and family dysfunction painted here age-old or a contemporary tale?

25. While the author savors the humor of each situation, hoarding and family dysfunction are serious problems. In what way does humor help us to look at ourselves and at some of the more serious issues people face today?

26. We are all some place on the spectrum of neatnik or hoarder. As exaggerated and outrageous as this tale is, where do you fit in? Do you have Christmas cards saved for the last twenty years or a collection of boxes ready for mailing gifts? Is it hard to part with sentimental items that have no use?

Acknowledgments

I value the support and critical reading that comes from those who admit to laughing out loud, are busy with red pens. Such feedback is invaluable—encouragement, suggestions, and corrections. So, special thanks to my husband, Jim, Abigail Grotke, Denis Malloy, Nancy Miller, Julie Franklin, Barbara Konecky, Dan Russo, Jennifer Nelson, Bert and Barbara Stafford, Dan Labeille, Shanna Hart, Lenn Johns, and Pam Gastineau. And to hoarders, accumulators, collectors and super-neatniks I have known and loved.

The verses quoted on page 244, beginning with "And then the dances," are from Lord Byron's *Don Juan* Canto IV, LXXXIV.

About the Author

 Linda Salisbury is the author of the award-winning Bailey Fish Adventure series, and *Mudd Saves the Earth* for children. Her newest compilation of humorous newspaper columns is titled *But You Don't Look Funny*.

In addition to writing books, Salisbury free-lances for several publications, plays cello and viola, enjoys boating and travel, and lives with her husband, Jim, and several elderly cats at Lake Anna, Virginia.